D0069497

GERMANY IN THE EIGHTEENTH CENTURY: THE SOCIAL BACKGROUND OF THE LITERARY REVIVAL

GERMANY IN THE EIGHTEENTH CENTURY: THE SOCIAL BACKGROUND OF THE LITERARY REVIVAL

by

W. H. BRUFORD

Fellow of St John's College and
Emeritus Professor of German in the
University of Cambridge

D2 30

'Sage man sich daher, dass die schöne Literatur einer Nation nicht erkannt noch empfunden werden kann, ohne dass man den Komplex ihres ganzen Zustandes sich zugleich vergegenwärtigt'

GOETHE, *Ferneres zur Weltliteratur*

CAMBRIDGE
AT THE UNIVERSITY PRESS
1971

Published by the Syndics of the Cambridge University Press
Bentley House, 200 Euston Road, London NW1 2DB
American Branch: 32 East 57th Street, New York, N.Y.10022

ISBN 0 521 09259 0 paperback
ISBN 0 521 04354 9 clothbound

First edition 1935
Reprinted 1939 1952 1959
First paperback edition 1965
Reprinted 1968, 1971

First printed in Great Britain at the University Printing House, Cambridge
Reprinted by offset-litho in the United States of America

LIBRARY
ALMA COLLEGE
ALMA, MICHIGAN

CONTENTS

LIBRARY
ALMA COLLEGE
ALMA, MICHIGAN

PART IV

REACTIONS ON LITERATURE

PREFACE

This book is intended in the first place, as the sub-title indicates, for the English student of German literature and thought. Its main aim is to provide material for a sociological study of eighteenth-century German literature by describing the chief classes of society in that age, and the political and economic conditions under which they lived. In a final chapter some general characteristics of that literature have been discussed, features which seem to have resulted from the reactions of whole groups to political and social conditions, rather than from the fortuitous similarity of individual points of view. To study these social influences in detail in particular works is beyond the scope of the present volume. In the absence of suitable presentations in English of the social history of the period, it seemed desirable to concentrate attention to begin with on the historical facts, especially as the German works on this subject, such as those of Biedermann, Freytag, Lamprecht, Sombart and Steinhausen, being written for different readers and with different ends in view, fail to answer many questions which arise in the mind of the English student. While gratefully making use of these writings, and many monographs on particular phases of the subject, the author has endeavoured not only to select and present the material in a manner better suited to the present purpose, but also to draw more fully on contemporary memoirs, essays and books of travel, especially on those by English travellers. Imaginative literature, on the other hand, has intentionally not been used as a source, because to do so would have interfered with the author's purpose of studying the influence of the world in which the writers of that day lived upon that which they created, but attention is frequently drawn to particular features in literature, to which a knowledge of the social life of the time lends a new significance. The wider conception of Modern Studies which has steadily been gaining ground in this country for the last twenty years, and is paralleled by the growing interest in 'Kulturkunde' in Germany, calls for such attempts at a synthesis of disciplines formerly isolated, in spite of the difficulties and dangers which the specialists in each field affected will necessarily perceive.

To the general reader the present work may be of interest for the light it throws on the evolution of the German national character. It is apparent to any student of eighteenth-century German life that many traits, of which the Englishman only became aware late in the following century, were clearly in evidence in the Germany of the age of Goethe, a land of many other types besides poets and thinkers. It is of some importance to the ordinary citizen to know what this Germany was like, especially at a time when it is the expressed aim of many leading political thinkers in Germany to correct the 'liberal' aberrations of the nineteenth century and undo the work of the French Revolution.

The author gratefully acknowledges his indebtedness to many Cambridge and Zürich teachers and friends, and especially to the late Professor Karl Breul for constant help and encouragement.

W. H. B.

1934

PREFACE TO PAPERBACK EDITION

The motto prefixed to this book is intended to convey its general purpose. It is a sentence from a late essay of Goethe's, where he expresses his confident hope of good results from a process of which he sees the first beginnings around him, the growth of what he calls 'world literature'. By this he means not only a body of great literature of all peoples, readily available in translations, but also living contacts between the nations of his day, brought about through their literature and their literary men. In the passage quoted Goethe reminds his readers that to understand and appreciate a nation's literature, they need to find out and bear in mind all they can about the whole complex of its ever changing life.

After the first World War, many of us engaged in the study of foreign literatures felt strongly that the purely literary approach, though very helpful, was insufficient in itself as a guide to the understanding of a nation's life and thought. What had been called in war-time the 'problem of the two Germanies' arose from the contradiction between our impression of Germany derived from the German classics and our experience of Germany as a threat to our existence. Had Germany ever really been the 'nation of poets and thinkers' which early Victorian England had learned to admire through Carlyle? If we understood the earlier Germany better, might we not be less puzzled by later developments there, and also perhaps better understand the intentions of the classical German writers, and the effect they produced on contemporaries?

In spite of an understandable reaction, in the thirty years which have elapsed since this book was first published, against 'extrinsic' methods of studying poetry and works of art, Goethe's statement would probably be accepted now by the majority of literary scholars. To judge by the published programmes of several of our new universities, there is also widespread agreement that if the study of a modern foreign literature is to be a preparation for life, it ought as far as possible to be combined with that of at least some aspects of the history and culture of the country concerned. Even with our nearest neighbours there is some danger of a failure of communication if, though knowing their language, we are unacquainted with the traditions that lie behind the commonest words, the failure that is so obvious in our dealings with oriental peoples or with Russia.

My immediate aim was to write a social history of Germany in the eighteenth century, in which some outstanding features in the literature and thought of the age would be linked up with everyday life and current traditions, without any attempt at a general account of the higher civilization of the time, in literature and the other arts, or in philosophy and religion. This concentration seemed necessary to make possible within a single volume a fairly full picture of the political, economic and social background of the intellectual and artistic achievements of the age, which have found many historians. The very thorough German work on the social and cultural history of the period by the 1848 liberal, Karl Biedermann, seemed to me to include in its four volumes too many topics better treated by others, and to leave the reader confused. I wished if possible to bring out the enduring patterns in German life, and to illustrate the picture from German memoirs and the impressions of foreign travellers. The sociological study of classical German literature in the last section is a sketch which I have amplified in two later books, *Theatre, Drama and Audience in Goethe's Germany* and *Culture and Society in Classical Weimar*.

W. H. B.

November 1964

PART I

POLITICAL STRUCTURE AND SYSTEM OF GOVERNMENT

Chapter I

'KLEINSTAATEREI'

'Germany is undoubtedly a very fine country', writes David Hume in 1748, 'full of industrious honest people, and were it united, it would be the greatest power that ever was in the world.' Germany was not at this time, like France and England, a single national state, but, in reality though not in name, a loose confederation of states, the boundaries and authority of which were so ill-defined that it is for many purposes misleading to speak of the 'Germany' of that age without explaining what territories the name is intended to cover. From the earliest period of what may properly be called *German* history (the time of the Saxon emperors) the Empire had shown a tendency to disintegrate into the tribal units which had only been brought together by force to make it, and these units themselves soon began to split up into smaller ones, through the lack of a law of primogeniture and the incapacity of their rulers to distinguish between personal ownership and political authority. 'Particularism (Kleinstaaterei) marks German history', says Professor Haller, 'from the very beginning.' The result was that long before the eighteenth century the Empire was a short name for a collection of virtually independent states.

Many general causes have been suggested for the growth of particularism in Germany. The one least in dispute is the geography of the country. The abundance of barriers in the interior and the absence of clearly marked natural boundaries on its borders made the centralisation of authority much more difficult in Germany than it was in either England or France. If the Hundred Years' War was necessary to teach the English kings in their island the lessons of geography, it is not surprising that Germany should have remained for so long politically amorphous and divided against itself. The Franks might succeed in conquering the other five tribes, but only a series of rulers endowed with the genius and vigour of a Charlemagne could have maintained a hold over clans which, although they spoke dialects of the same language, possessed a marked individual character and were widely scattered over a land merging almost imperceptibly, on two of its boundaries at least, into the adjoining territories. The area was too vast to form a single unit, given only medieval communications, and it was constantly open to invasion. Moreover, it was almost inevitable (as Mr McDougall has suggested) that with boundaries so indefinite the growth of national feeling should be long delayed. Then the facts of geography strongly reinforced other causes in bringing about that endless struggle with the Papacy, which deprived the German kings of the only force making for unity in their lands, for a rich Italy so near at hand was an even more tempting prey to the king of an undeveloped Germany than France was to Edward III. It was its geographical position, finally, which more than anything else put Germany at a disadvantage when the routes of world trade became sea-routes in the age of colonial enterprise, the great epoch of national expansion and unification.

We find no parallels in the history of the Holy Roman Empire to the successive steps by which England achieved a greater and greater measure of unity. No German king was able to establish a system of common law. The maintenance of peace and justice had to be left to the territorial princes from the beginning of the thirteenth century. No effective system of taxation made all parts of the country conscious of a common authority or drew representatives of scattered provinces and towns together in one assembly like the English Parliament, for the Reichstag was not really a comparable institution. No industry grew up like the English cloth trade based on national organisation, in spite of the promising start made by the Hanse. No literature was produced comparable with that of even pre-Elizabethan England in continuity of tradition and wideness of appeal, to reflect the life of the whole country in a language understandable by all. It is not surprising then that the same forces which in many other countries fostered a strong unified state—the growth of the money-system and the consequent replacement of feudal organisations by a professional bureaucracy and a standing army, the invention of gunpowder, which left no baron's castle impregnable, the spread of education among the laity and the extended application of reason and experience to secular problems, the Reformation and Counter-reformation with their innumerable political repercussions—all these factors, in Germany, strengthened the hands, not of the emperor, but of the territorial princes.

The history of the separate states that made up the Empire is a subject of baffling complexity, but there are typical features common to most of them which may be described. The oldest princely families can be traced back, it seems, to the counts appointed by the Carolingians to administer justice in their name in the various provinces of their realm, and granted a fief in return for their services. With the extension of feudalism, from the ninth century onwards, the offices became hereditary, being now inseparable from the fiefs, which, owing to testamentary dispositions, marriages, purchases of land and other purely personal transactions, were continually changing in extent. By taking advantage of weak kings, and especially of the strife between Empire and Papacy, Hohenstaufen and Guelph, these hereditary officials and landowners gradually acquired various regal rights, first legally confirmed by the *Statutum in favorem principum* in

1232, when Frederick II, too deeply engaged in Italy to retain much authority at home, gave the princes full rights of jurisdiction in their own lands. From now on they were referred to as 'domini terrae' and definitely supported by the emperor against the towns, the Church and the minor nobility. But their lands were made up of many separate portions and their authority precarious, being founded on a variety of legal titles not necessarily connected with each other. A prince might be landlord here, chief officer of justice there, in a third place he might have a near relative in power and in a fourth he might hold fishing or hunting rights. As his sons had all at first an equally good claim to his rights and estates at his death, it proved very difficult to concentrate power in the hands of the head of the family, but successive generations gradually overcame this difficulty in most states and apart from a temporary set-back round about the fourteenth century the princes continued to increase their power at the expense of the emperor, the lesser nobility and the towns.

The set-back occurred during the transition from the feudal natural economy to the money-system, when the towns, the pioneers of the new system, were at an advantage through the possession of ready money, as well as of skill in organisation and abundance of enterprise. More and more of them secured their independence from their lords, and for a time it seemed that city-states or city-leagues might be able to assert themselves successfully against the princes as in Italy. The princes, to pay for military support and for the services of their new non-feudal officials, had to pledge lands and rights to such an extent that their position was seriously weakened, and their former claims to feudal service made almost worthless. The small revenues they enjoyed were still paid mostly in kind, and it proved almost impossible to impose direct taxation. The lesser nobility took advantage of the situation to make themselves almost as independent of their prince as he was of the emperor. Fortunately for the princes however the knights did not join forces with the towns, as in England, for each estate thought only of its own interests, so that in the leading states the princes soon had them under control again.

The princes survived this crisis by the conversion of more and more payments in kind and manual services into money dues, while credit became easier to obtain owing to the great expansion of the metal currency. Their chief rivals, the towns, declined economically and politically owing to the loss of their privileged position at home and abroad, combined with a decay of civic spirit. Most important of all, the dynastic ambitions of the princes were aroused by the success of their more powerful neighbours abroad.

The fate of any individual territory depended above all on the personal qualities of its ruler. In some districts, particularly in the south and south-west of Germany, a number of small independent authorities, Free Towns and Reichsritterschaften, survived in all their medieval variety until the end of the eighteenth century. In all the larger territories, although no two of them developed in the same way, some form of absolute government was gradually established more and more firmly.

But however powerful the German princes might appear to be in their own domains, in European politics they were almost negligible factors until the world was startled by the achievements of Frederick the Great. Though constantly threatened by powerful neighbours they were too jealous of their dynastic rights to seek strength in unity. Accordingly the Empire, never a solid structure, was even in the fifteenth century nothing but a loose league of princes. Its titular head might still be endowed in theory with the power of a Roman emperor, but in practice, as J. J. Moser said, 'he had not a foot of land or a single subject; no country was governed in his name or was a source of revenue to him'.

The German monarchy had been elective from the beginning, but down to the year 1250 the succession had remained for a century or more at a time in the same family. As the princes had by then come to look upon the emperor not as their lawful overlord but as a dangerous rival, they took care that there should be frequent changes of dynasty. At the same time the right of election came to be restricted to seven princes, the Kurfürsten, the rest being at the time indifferent. The hereditary succession of the Hapsburgs (from the year 1437) became possible only because the Kurfürsten had so whittled away the authority of the emperor at successive elections that they did not fear him any longer. The title was an expensive luxury now that few could afford, for the emperor had no dependable revenue in spite of all attempts to make a general levy. A strong personality might perhaps still have brought the princes to heel, but none was produced. The results of the listless rule of Frederick III (1439–86) were not retrieved even by Maximilian I.

From the fifteenth century onwards the Reichstag made frequent attempts to reform the Empire, but their only result was to make the impotence of the emperor a patent fact. Provision was made for maintaining the peace of the realm by the so-called 'Grundgesetze', the Golden Bull, the measures concerning Landfriede and Religionsfriede, the Exekutionsordnung of 1553 and Charles V's Wahlkapitulation. A serious attempt was made to put the administration of justice in the Empire, its military defence, and its finances in order, and in each of these reforms the essentially federal nature of the Empire was clearly reflected. The emperor was allowed no control over the *Reichskammergericht* or Supreme Court of the Empire which was established in 1495. The court was given a permanent meeting-place, not in Vienna but first at Speyer, then from 1684 at Wetzlar, its members were appointed for life and paid not by the German king but by the electoral princes. It was agreed at the Diet of Cologne in 1505 that the new military forces which were meant to replace the feudal levies of earlier days should be provided and maintained by the German princes, each contributing his due share of men and money according to the importance of his territory. The various Estates of the Realm (Kurfürsten, Fürsten, Reichsstädte, Reichsgrafen) agreed to make a regular contribution towards the cost of the Reichskammergericht, and other moneys could be raised for government purposes, if the Reichstag consented, in the form of the so-called *Römermonate*, levied on the various Estates in a fixed proportion.

In justice, military affairs and finance a certain measure of unity had thus apparently been achieved, on the initiative not of the head of the Reich but of the leading princes. There seemed to be the beginnings of a federal constitution here, but further development in the direction of a confederation was prevented, first by the excessive number and variety of political authorities concerned, and secondly by the nature of many of the existing institutions of the Empire, which were still those of a feudal state.

The confederation would have had to include, in the eighteenth century, kings of European importance like those of Austria and Prussia, the electoral princes, 94 spiritual and lay princes, 103 counts, 40 prelates, 51 Free Towns, in all some 300 separate 'Territories', each jealous of its time-honoured privileges and little affected by any memories of a common inheritance. This multiplicity of interests prevented even the modest beginnings of a federal constitution outlined above from working satisfactorily in practice. The *Reichskammergericht* proved ineffective because the territories, unwilling to lose any of their own authority, tried to have the right of appeal to it denied to their subjects, or if they were unable to obtain this concession, refused to contribute towards its upkeep. In 1769, for instance, the territories were half a million Thalers in arrears with their contributions. Consequently the number of judges had to be reduced from 50, the staff first proposed, to 18 or even at times to 12 or 8. The result was the accumulation of business graphically described by Goethe in *Dichtung und Wahrheit*. In 1772,

61,233 cases still awaited trial. Similarly the imperial military force provided for by the Diet of 1505 was in practice of little real value. The troops remained under the control of the territory that provided them. The prince who paid them appointed their officers and was responsible for the commissariat even when they were acting with other contingents. Uniforms and equipment were of the utmost diversity, discipline was lamentable, funds were always inadequate, and the human material pressed into service in this universally despised force was naturally of the poorest.

The features that had survived from the feudal state were the office of king and emperor and the Reichstag. Backed by no army, no revenues, no state Church (for after the Thirty Years' War religious disunity had had to be accepted as permanent), the emperor was now the not undisputed fount of honour and for the rest little more than an occasionally picturesque anachronism. The emperors strove to maintain their authority. Shortly after the establishment of the *Reichskammergericht* the emperor set up, for instance, a rival institution, the *Reichshofrat* in Vienna, and endless disputes followed as to the limits of their respective competency. No decision was ever reached while the Empire lasted and both courts continued to perform similar functions. The *Reichshofrat* had the reputation of being even more slow and inefficient and certainly more corrupt than the other court of appeal.

The *Reichstag* had lost the authority it had once possessed as a feudal council of the realm, at which the emperor's principal vassals appeared in person to confer with him, when it was made a perpetual assembly in 1663. The change was a natural one given the tendency towards a federation. The result of it was that the Diet became an assembly of envoys, who, not having full powers, had to await instructions before expressing an opinion on any important measure. There was no debate. The envoys dictated their instructions to clerks. This not only caused infinite delay but also made it possible for rulers to dissent in cases where they would not have had the heart to do so if they had been present in person. Their decision announced from a distance had an impersonal quality. Since, moreover, for a measure to become law, some hundreds of authorities had to vote on it, and a majority had to be obtained for it in each of the three chambers of the Diet, as well as the emperor's assent, it was almost impossible to put through any far-reaching measure in the public interest. If any measure was agreed on, it had become usual for the constituent states, the real centres of executive power, either to take no notice of the *Reichsschluss* or to look upon their acceptance of it as an act of grace. Like the coronation of the emperor, the meetings of the Diet were a time-honoured but empty show. The Chamber of Electoral Princes, nine in number during most of the eighteenth century, formed a sort of cabinet and dominated proceedings. It was in practice usually sufficient if they obtained the concurrence of the Chamber of Princes, the third Chamber, that of the Free Towns, being in the eighteenth century negligible. Consequently, hardly any but negative measures were passed, all in the interest of the higher nobility, and most of the time was taken up in endless disputes about trifles, questions of precedence, congratulations on happy events in the emperor's family and the like. For the transaction of this kind of business few states were willing to maintain a separate representative. Usually an envoy represented several states, and not more than some score of envoys were ever present at once.

Das liebe heil'ge röm'sche Reich
Wie hält's nur noch zusammen?

So the boon companions are made to sing in Goethe's *Faust*, and it was a common question. Yet memories of the earlier glories of the Empire were not entirely dead. However much theorists might say in defence of the existing state of things as a guarantee of freedom, the consciousness of belonging to a people that had maintained the Holy Roman Empire saved many Germans from utter dejection and shame in times of political impotence and lent Germany a status among the European nations to which its actual political and economic condition could have given it no claim.[1]

[1] The best account of the constitution of the old Empire is probably still C. T. Perthes, *Das deutsche Staatsleben vor der Revolution*, Hamburg and Gotha, 1845. K. Biedermann, *Deutschland im 18. Jahrhundert*, I, 185 ff. and L. Häusser, *Deutsche Geschichte*, I, Berlin, 1854, contain additional details.

Chapter II

BENEVOLENT DESPOTISM

We have seen that the real political authority in eighteenth-century Germany was not concentrated in the hands of the emperor, but distributed among the rulers of the three hundred or more sovereign states, ranging in extent from Austria to the tiny domains of the Reichsritter in Swabia.[1] It is in fact hard to draw the line between these last-named 'sovereigns' and the multitude of other landowners who, though not 'reichsunmittelbar', enjoyed almost all the powers of independent rulers. Their inclusion would bring the number of authorities nearer to three thousand than to three hundred. It is the use of their power made by these authorities that we must examine if we would understand how Germany was governed in this period, and in the present chapter some features which seem typical for the great majority of states will be singled out, and some few examples cited. Leaving the republican Free Towns for a later chapter, we may attempt to give a concrete first impression of the autocratic system which prevailed in all the remaining states by a method favoured by contemporaries, the description of a typical day in the life of some of their rulers.

The day of Ernst August of Weimar, the grandfather of Karl August, and a sufficiently representative ruler of a small state in the first half of the century, is described by Pöllnitz in 1729 as follows. The duke did not rise before midday, after breakfasting in bed and perhaps amusing himself before rising with his violin, or, if he felt disposed towards business, by receiving reports from his architects, gardeners and ministers. (The order in which they are named is instructive.) His first task on rising was to inspect and drill his guard,

[1] See Appendix II.

consisting of thirty-three men. Then came a walk, and at two or three o'clock the chief meal of the day. Dinner might last anything from three to five hours. Ernst August drank freely and talked a great deal, though usually on topics very little to the taste of the cavalier who leaves us this description. After coffee he would play quadrille with his two ladies-in-waiting and a major of his army, or spend the evening in his room, smoking, fiddling or drawing. A few miles away from him lived the more serious-minded Duke Friedrich II of Gotha, who rose every day at seven and spent an hour in prayer and devotional reading before dressing and giving audiences to his ministers and other callers. At midday he dined with the duchess and his children, and other people of distinction, and after this function, which lasted an hour and a half, he would walk in the gardens or read till five. A visit to the assembly of the nobility in the house of one of their number, where he would play hombre, took up an hour or two, and on his return he supped and retired at nine o'clock.[1]

We have a livelier picture of a still smaller potentate, the Prince of Wallerstein, in Lang's memoirs.

The lever of the Prince took place on our lucky days at eleven o'clock, but more often at two. As soon as the groom of the chamber threw open the folding doors of his bedchamber, all who had been waiting for hours in the ante-room entered, the marshall, the equerry, the physician-in-ordinary, we secretaries, the gamekeepers and any strangers who might be there. The Prince, who was now in the hands of his friseur, talked to people in his usual charming way, and anyone whom he addressed would try to produce some witty or amusing reply. As soon as the Prince got up from his chair and gave his further directions to this one or that, all who were not specially commanded to remain would withdraw. Then the Prince usually joined his family for a while, after which he hurried to mass and gave audiences till dinner, which took place at varying times, sometimes late in the afternoon.

[1] C. L. Baron de Pöllnitz, *Mémoires*. Nouv. éd. corr., Liége, 1734, I, 204 ff.

After dinner a ride to a farm or a hunting-seat was followed by individual audiences or conversations. In the evening he played cards, or gave a reception or concert for the court. Supper, never before midnight, did not occupy long, and the Prince would take one of the guests back to his room with him, unless he contented himself with the secretaries, who were still waiting in his ante-chamber at two or three in the morning. Often he would walk past the poor martyrs pretending not to notice them, and begin to read or sign papers in his study, while they fell asleep on their chairs.[1]

Frederick the Great distributed his time rather differently. In his prime he used to devote ten hours a day in peace time to state affairs, four to study and writing, and two to society and music. He dressed immediately on rising, at four in summer and five in winter, usually in the same old blue coat faced with red, yellow waistcoat and breeches and dark brown high boots. His friseur was given a very short time to arrange and powder his hair, and when his toilet was over, every hour in the day was methodically devoted to some particular piece of business or amusement. Instead of receiving those who had business with him in levers and audiences, with their fuss and waste of time, he required them to communicate with him in writing, and indicated to his secretaries what reply was to be made by means of a note in the margin. By using every moment of his time he was able to keep all important affairs of state under his personal control. He dined, usually with eight or nine of his officers and one or two men of letters, precisely at noon, and often remained with the company till three. At table he tried to put everyone at their ease and delighted in witty conversation. Until his old teacher Quantz died in 1773, Frederick used to fill in the intervals he allowed himself between work, and an hour before supper, by playing the flute, either alone or accompanied by one or two other instruments, and he devoted

[1] K. H. von Lang, *Aus der bösen alten Zeit*, 1842. (Reprint Stuttgart, 1910, p. 129.)

much time to perfecting himself in the art of writing—in French. He retired to bed at nine o'clock.[1]

These brief descriptions already indicate that the methods of government varied from state to state in Germany according to the personality of the prince, though all states resembled each other in being dependent on the whims of an absolute ruler. But no state, however small, was governed by the prince without assistance, though in all he was the ultimate authority. An elaborate machinery had everywhere been contrived for translating what was in theory merely the prince's will into action, machinery that for long periods could be left to run itself. Government in the German states was despotic, and it was exercised through a bureaucracy, organised with varying degrees of efficiency in the different states.

The growing complexity of society, reflected in the rise of distinct classes and occupations based on the division of labour and the increasing use of money, had made a professional and non-hereditary civil service necessary from the thirteenth century onwards over wider and wider areas of the Continent. The princes still based their own rights on the hereditary principle, and great landowners continued to inherit powers of patrimonial jurisdiction with their estates, but the great majority of offices ceased to be hereditary because no longer remunerated in land. France and Burgundy led the way in the rational organisation of the state, followed by Austria and more slowly by other German states, particularly after the Renaissance and the reception of Roman law. By the eighteenth century there was an elaborate bureaucracy in every state. Round about 1500 a further great advance in efficient administration had begun in Germany,

[1] For descriptions of Frederick's day see Dr J. Moore, *A View of Society and Manners in France, Switzerland and Germany*, London, 1779, II; N. W. Wraxall, *Memoirs of the Courts of Berlin, Dresden, Warsaw and Vienna*, London, 1799, I, 114 f., and H. Prutz, *Preussische Geschichte*, Stuttgart, 1901, III, 41.

the institution of central governing bodies or councils. The medieval chancellor and other high officials had been dismissible, but not whole-time state servants with special offices where they could always be found. They were usually ecclesiastics, they moved about with the court, and their organisation was very amateurish. From the sixteenth century the princes found it necessary to have whole-time officials, drawn partly from the nobility, partly from the middle class, and in this case trained in law and without independent means. The leading officials formed the prince's council or 'Hofrat', with definite duties, forms and traditions, and from this council a number of committees, each the nucleus of a later government department, branched off. In all states the local nobility, mistrustful of this process, strove, with varying success, to maintain at least their old right to the chief offices, or 'Indigenatsrecht'. While the smaller states were busy imitating Brandenburg-Prussia and Austria, these states themselves, Prussia leading, extended the power of the ruler further and further at the expense of the towns and the nobility, until a standing army and an efficient and reliable bureaucracy made the central authority almost irresistible within the state. The result of this single-minded pursuit of order and power was in Prussia the well-policed military state, and in other states various approximations to this ideal.

Though the driving power behind this development came mainly from the princes themselves, their desires were reinforced by the general trend of Protestant opinion, for after the Reformation the idea had gained ground that princely rank was a sacred trust from God, involving responsibilities on the part of the prince but calling for unquestioning obedience on the part of the subject. Rulers were taught now to take their office seriously, for a new moral value was attached to work as such, quite apart from its results. They in their wisdom and under God's guidance were answerable for the physical and spiritual welfare of their ignorant subjects, whose main characteristic was always assumed to be their inability of themselves to help themselves. This doctrine, so repugnant to the sense of corporate self-determination of the early Middle Ages, and that of individual self-determination that ripened later, justified any infringement of individual liberty, from regulations concerning food and clothing to the pressgang methods of Prussian and Austrian recruiting sergeants. In the seventeenth and early eighteenth centuries more stress came to be laid on the duty of the subject to obey than on the prince's responsibility for his welfare. Many rulers came to look upon their office less as a trust than as a sinecure, the fortunate holder of which was justified in exploiting it for his own personal advantage. In no case was very much heed paid to the wishes of the great body of subjects; there were usually no organs to express them. Where the despotic ruler, of his own choice (as in Prussia under Frederick the Great), subordinated his interests and those of his house to what he conceived to be his duty to the 'state' we may speak of 'benevolent despotism'.

After this preliminary survey we must look a little more closely at the aims and methods of German absolutism in their local variety. We have noticed already that after the breakdown of the decentralised medieval state, the central governments had gradually extended the scope of their activities. The prince and his privy council were responsible for foreign policy, for defence, for the administration of the prince's private estates and property and, mainly from this source, for the financing of his expenditure, whether for his court or for what would now be looked upon as public services (for no distinction was yet made between his private and public liabilities). The prince was the fount of justice and his council the supreme instance short of the *Reichskammergericht*. In most states an attempt had been made at some time since the spread of Roman law to codify the law of the land, in particular to define the duties of the subject in a *Landesordnung*, but by the eighteenth century most of these codes were very much out of date. There was nothing in any of these functions that had changed in principle since the Middle Ages. But the Reformation had brought the established church in Protestant lands also under the control of the government, a heavy responsibility as well as a source of power. Even in Catholic states it came to be felt necessary to exercise a similar but less far-reaching control over Church affairs. That the young might be brought up in the pure doctrine, schools had to be looked to, and many princes set up state universities, where only the established religion was taught. The government also frequently attempted to control many things in its subjects' life, in addition to religion, that are now felt to be purely private matters.

What was then called 'police' covered every kind of regulation considered necessary for the health, prosperity and moral welfare of the subject. Under this head were included the first sanitary regulations, concerning water-supply, drainage, the removal of rubbish, etc., as well as the provision of qualified apothecaries and midwives. This was no less a 'police' matter than the patrolling of the streets and the prevention and detection of crime. Any control of industry and trade that was attempted (generally in the interests of the prince's treasury), the regulation of prices, of hours and conditions of labour for apprentices, measures to prevent competition, the prohibition of begging, all came under the same head. In these matters the territorial governments took over and applied to a wider area the control that had been exercised in the Middle Ages by town councils and gilds, whose grip was now weakening. There was a similar precedent for sumptuary edicts, still considered necessary to prevent the spread of luxurious habits, lest the time-honoured external distinctions between various classes of society should be obliterated. They were designed to secure for every one the status due to his rank, just as the economic regulations aimed at a decent living for all in the traditional style of their class. In both matters modern individualism refuses to recognise any norm and finds the older practice tyrannical. There is nothing more characteristic of the old régime than edicts such as the one promulgated in Brunswick in 1758, forbidding servant girls to use silk dress-materials, to wear gold or silver ornaments, or shoes made of anything but plain black leather, or the one in Posen instructing the wives of burghers not to wear capes, or to wear their hair down their back. The German papers naturally noted with interest about that time that in Constantinople the Sultan was prohibiting under pain of death the use of silk jackets and muslin-lined turbans. It was well-meant but misplaced zeal, however, that inspired patriarchal guardianship of this kind. A good 'Landesvater' like Karl Friedrich von Baden really considered it to be the duty of his Hofkammer 'to teach his subjects even against their will how to order their domestic affairs', or, as he expressed the ideal again with unconscious humour, 'to make them, whether they liked it or not, into free, opulent and law-abiding citizens'.

The administrative machinery that had been evolved by the eighteenth century was of considerable complexity even in small states. Everywhere routine business and minor matters were left in the hands of properly constituted authorities, 'Behörden', which generally decided differences of opinion among their members by a vote. But the reins of government were still in the hands of the prince, who received advice from these boards of officials but acted as he thought best, without being effectively controlled, except in a very few states, by assemblies representative of his subjects.

With one exception, these boards or committees of state had branched off from the older council of the prince and his advisers, which in a simpler society had decided all problems alike. The exception was the body created in Protestant lands to carry out the new function of Church government, the *Konsistorium*, on which laymen sat along with clerical members. From the beginning the princes reserved important affairs of state such as foreign policy for their own private control, perhaps making use of a small inner council or *Geheimer Rat* of three or four favourites. Of the committees of the main council, the chief was the one that dealt with finance, and this was naturally the first to become a separate department, the *Treasury* (Hof-, Amts- or Rentenkammer). The council was then left with the administration of justice (sitting as one body it was the court of appeal for the state), of defence and of home affairs, including 'police' in the broad sense indicated above. It had to draft any new legislation that was considered necessary. The working of the whole system depended on the character and business methods of the prince. He might at any time upset the plans of his permanent officials, and against his decision there was in practice no appeal. What was particularly resented in the eighteenth century was the increasing use made by princes of their privilege of Kabinettsjustiz, a summary form of jurisdiction intended as a check on the often cumbrous normal procedure of the courts, but one used more and more irresponsibly by despotic rulers in their own interest. It was, for instance, by the exercise of this power that Karl Eugen of Württemberg was able to imprison the poet Schubart and the publicist J. J. Moser for years without the semblance of a trial.

Lang's description of Prince Wallerstein at work may be a little overdrawn, but it is certainly true in the impression that it gives of the capriciousness inherent in absolutism of this stamp. The prince used to open all reports that came to him from his permanent officials and heap them up on the floor beside his desk, until the pile was as high as he could reach. Then one day, in the midst of walking up and down the room and chatting to his secretary about everything under the sun, he would go to the pile and take out a document at random. He would quickly consider its contents, not neglecting any opportunity of doing the opposite of what was recommended, and finally indicate his wishes in a brief marginal note. It was Lang's business to make a formal draft of the decision. When he brought some thirty of these drafts back to the prince next morning at his lever, they were thrown on to a second pile at the other side of the desk, and there they remained until the prince was going away on a long journey, leaving town for his summer residence, or having the room decorated. Then he would begin to think it was time to clear out his study and would send the signed documents down pell-mell into the chancellery. To counteract his dilatoriness at least in matters of justice, his officials got into the way of sending up the same matter for his consideration once a month, often revising their own recommendations, so that before long several different sentences were hanging over the head of the person concerned. One poor man arrested for stealing was kept in prison for years, it is said, while the courts waited for the prince to choose between the many decisions they had suggested to him, which included hanging, the lash, penal servitude, expulsion from the country, or an immediate pardon in view of his long detention. In the end, according to this well-invented story, he solved the problem for himself by escaping from prison.

This description indicates how true a picture Lessing has given us of a German prince in the first scene of *Emilia Galotti*:

Emilia? (Indem er noch eine von den Bittschriften aufschlägt, und nach dem unterschriebenen Namen sieht.) Eine Emilia?—Aber eine Emilia Bruneschi—nicht Galotti. Nicht Emilia Galotti!—Was will sie, diese Emilia Bruneschi? (er liest). Viel gefordert; sehr viel.—Doch sie heisst Emilia. Gewährt!

Or in scene 8:

CAMILLO ROTA. Ein Todesurteil wäre zu unterschreiben.
Der PRINZ. Recht gern.—Nur her! geschwind.

In fact to understand any work with a political bearing (*Götz*, *Die Räuber*, *Fiesko*, *Kabale und Liebe*, *Don Karlos*, *Egmont* are only the most famous of them) as it was understood then, we need always to remember that almost every German state was ruled by an autocrat, often as irresponsible as Prince Wallerstein.

The territorial princes had not always been in a position to govern without troubling to consult their subjects, but after the Thirty Years' War they had not kept up even the forms of the old assemblies representing the 'Estates' of the territories, in particular the country nobility and the townspeople, that had formerly claimed some control over at least the finances of the state. These provincial diets (Landtage) had always met unwillingly and never shown any initiative or political sense, principally, no doubt, because the two Estates had scarcely anything in common, far less than the squires and burghers in the English Commons, who had never formed themselves into closed castes. In England it often happened that the children of merchants married into the gentry, and the younger sons of country gentlemen engaged in commerce, but not in Germany. By the eighteenth century, apart from four or five exceptions that will be discussed separately, the Landtage, if they met at all, were only picturesque survivals.

With the decay of the Landtage the majority of princes had no one to remind them of their responsibilities. Aping the French court in externals without trying to rival the French government in efficiency, they held it to be their chief duty to their people to make a splendid display. The rather unreal magnificence that was then the ambition of so many princes is expressed in the art they inspired and paid for—architecture, opera, literature, painting, above all, in their portraits by court painters. One of the finest of these, Rigaud's picture in Dresden of Augustus III as crown-prince, presents to us the incarnation of refined pomp and power. We read it in the proudly poised head, the over-erect figure, and in every feature of costume and background, the leonine state wig, the incongruous shining armour, the silk and ermine cloak that swells in the breeze against a stormy sky. It would have been lèse-majesté for a court painter to suggest that a king was no more than a man. The note is not 'What care these roarers for the name of King?' The troubled elements only serve to make more admirable the unruffled majesty of that royal brow. With one hand on his marshal's staff, the other on his sword-hilt, Augustus stands there like a baroque Jupiter. In life, of course, he (and still more his father, Augustus the Strong) most resembled the god when, like the Jupiter of Molière's *Amphitryon*, he was assuring his courtiers and their wives that

> Un partage avec Jupiter
> N'a rien du tout qui déshonore,

but there were strangely few men of the time who ever looked behind the façade. One of the few was Frederick the Great, who as crown-prince directed his *Anti-Machiavel* against such rulers. It is true that his own statecraft later was nothing if not Machiavellian, but he never made himself ridiculous, and his chief charge against the petty despots of Germany was that they were never anything else. 'Most small princes', he says, 'particularly the German ones, ruin themselves by reckless extravagance, misled by the illusion of their imagined greatness....The youngest son of the youngest son of an appanaged dynasty imagines he is of the same stamp as Louis XIV. He builds his Versailles, keeps his mistresses and has an "army" at his beck and call—perhaps strong enough to fight an imaginary battle on the stage at Verona.'

There were, it is true, a few states where more or less representative assemblies still had some influence. The most famous of these assemblies (the only one in Europe considered by Fox to be comparable with the English House of Commons) was the Landtag of Württemberg. It survived because it was a homogeneous body of burghers only, that had established its position amidst the anarchy of Herzog Ulrich's reign in the early sixteenth century. The nobility in Swabia had made itself independent (reichsfrei) and if undisturbed on their small estates the free knights cared little what happened to the duchy in which their lands formed enclaves. Eberhard Ludwig (1677–1733), Karl Alexander (1733–37) with his unscrupulous financial adviser 'Jud Süss' Oppenheimer, and Karl Eugen (1737–93), Schiller's 'tyrant', defied the Estates and for a long time contrived to raise money enough without them, but in a prolonged struggle with Karl Eugen the Estates proved the stronger. Led by J. J. Moser, who did not shrink even from forming alliances with foreign powers, at the risk of civil war, they not only maintained their constitutional rights but established them more firmly than ever. Similarly in Mecklenburg-Schwerin the Estates persuaded the emperor to depose one duke (1728) and forced his successor to grant their demands (1755). In Hanover, in the absence of the Electors (as kings of England), the nobility maintained an oligarchical rule through the Estates (powerful, as in Württemberg, because one strong party took the lead), but though they ruled in their own interests, there was at least no extravagant court to be maintained, the English connection made for freedom of thought, and the people were comparatively contented. In Saxony too the older nobility predominated and at least succeeded in maintaining Protestantism as the state religion even after the Electors, as kings of Poland, had turned Catholic, but they took no steps against the reckless extravagance of Augustus II and his successor, agreeing to any taxation if they themselves were exempted from it. 'Rabiosus der Jüngere' (Rebmann) described the Saxon Diet in 1795 as 'a farce performed every six years, in which all the actors have to say is "Yes".'

If after the middle of the century there was a change for the better in the government of many German states, it was due (except in Württemberg, and even there in part) to the spread of humane ideas in the Age of Enlightenment and to the example set by Frederick the Great in Prussia, rather than to any pressure from below. It will be of interest then to see how the rulers of Prussia differed in aims and methods, as well as in native ability and energy, from those discussed above. It is difficult to exaggerate the effect of the personal qualities of the Hohenzollerns on the fate of their country. Their lucky inheritances would only have made the already ramshackle state still more unstable if the fragments had not been welded into one whole by this line of capable and ambitious rulers. There is no need here to dwell on the statesmanlike rule of the Great Elector and Frederick William I, or on the military genius of Frederick II—these are matters for the political historian. But to understand why the life of the ordinary man was different in Brandenburg-Prussia from that of similar men in other states we must know what those who ruled him were striving for and how they moulded the institutions of their land.

It was not so much in their general aims that they differed at first from their contemporaries, though they were more determined and consistent in their pursuit of military power, as in their energy and efficiency. Every prince aimed, as we have seen, at absolute autocracy, and a Machiavellian Realpolitik was the order of the day. But the Great Elector and his successors were of tougher fibre than most of the would-be 'princes', and encouraged by the dour nature of their subjects, taught by their experience in defending scattered and backward dominions, they came to believe that all their resources must be systematically exploited by an efficient bureaucracy, and all their energies bent to the building up of a strong army, if their land was to survive as a political unit. Bismarck was expressing an age-old maxim of Prussian policy when he said (1888): 'The pike in the European fish-pond prevent us from becoming carp'. Personal ambition and presently a dynastic tradition made the Hohenzollerns ready to sacrifice even what were elsewhere the most treasured values of civilisation to the pursuit of power.

In their administrative methods their great principle was

unification, concentration, 'rationalisation'. The councils that had existed in every province were replaced in the Great Elector's time by the central Geheimer Rat of Brandenburg when, by various devices, the provincial Estates had been, if not in all cases abolished, at least deprived of their importance. The functions of the Geheimer Rat resembled those of the councils of the other states already discussed, the greater, not the inner councils, for it did not handle foreign affairs, but its main business, and this is characteristic of Prussian developments, was to finance the military power of the state. 'It was the necessity for a standing army that provided a motive for the reform of taxation, etc. and the bureaucracy developed in the main out of the military commissaries' (Schmoller). The 'military commissaries', at first agents appointed by the Kurfürst to negotiate with the colonels, who at that period raised regiments privately as a kind of speculation, became permanent officials when standing armies came in. From about 1660 there were commissaries in every corner of the land to negotiate in matters of excise, taxation, billeting and so forth with the local authorities, the beginnings in fact of an anti-feudal bureaucracy, hated by the Estates, but given ever increasing powers by the Electors. There was a separate set of officials concerned with the management of the crown lands, the collection of rents, regalities and the like. These corresponded to the 'Kammer' or treasury officials of the other states and were at first responsible to the Kammern of the various provinces, but by 1689 these had been brought under a central Hofkammer, and it was possible for the first time to budget for the whole land. By gradual stages the two sets of officials were brought under one control, the Generaldirektorium, which lasted with few changes from 1723 till 1806. The Generaldirektorium had at first four departments, each of which, besides looking after the special affairs of a province, had to take over specialised duties for the whole state ('Grenzsachen', army supplies, post, mint). Frederick the Great added five more to the number of these special departments or embryo ministries (trade and industry, military administration, customs and excise, mines, forests). The Geheimer Rat, deprived of so many functions by special committees, had become by this time merely a department for justice and religion. Frederick William I had already set up another advisory body, the Kabinettsministerium, as a sort of Foreign Office.

It was a complex system, but here as in the other states the monarch was the real mind of the state, because he alone was responsible for the co-ordination of the work of all these special bodies. From the time of Frederick William I all important business was dealt with by the king in his Kabinett or office, where by marginal notes on the departmental reports, letters or petitions submitted to him he indicated his decisions to his Geheimsekretär, who then had to draft them as Lang did Prince Wallerstein's. Frederick the Great simply continued his father's system, avoiding whenever possible the audiences which in smaller states were considered so valuable a means of protecting the individual against bureaucratic tyranny. It was his pithy marginal notes that were imitated, with a difference, by the Emperor William II.

The Generaldirektorium directed the activity of a well-planned system of local organs, which may be more briefly described. The land was divided into circles (Kreise) and these again into districts. In the developed system (from 1723) there was in each circle an intermediate authority between the local organs of the Generaldirektorium (called Kriegs- und Domänenkammern) and the central government, in the person of the 'Landrat'. The Landrat, generally a big landowner, who served rather for the honour than for the small salary he received, had as Landrat no judicial functions like the English Justice of the Peace, whom he might seem to resemble, but exercised a general control over the civil service of the various districts of his circle and was responsible for the maintenance of roads and bridges, for military provisioning and for 'police' in the broad sense defined above. The interests of the state were represented similarly in the towns by 'Steuerräte', each of whom supervised in the king's name some six to fifteen towns, keeping an eye both on civic administration and economic development. The 'Kriegs- und Domänenkammern' finally, with large staffs, managed the royal demesnes, collected taxes and dues, and exercised all the functions included under 'police'; they were even concerned with the fostering of industry, in so far as it increased the royal revenues. To this end they were given considerable powers of jurisdiction in matters affecting the revenue, powers that remained a bone of contention until late in the reign of Frederick the Great.

This was by no means the only objectionable feature in the administration of justice. 'Cabinet justice' was still not unknown in Prussia in Frederick's day, and the patrimonial jurisdiction of aristocratic landowners often proved a source of petty tyranny. Procedure was clumsy and very slow, and equality before the law was far from being a reality, though the ideal was more nearly approached in Prussia than elsewhere in Germany. Many improvements were made in the second half of the century, their general tendency being, in Schmoller's phrase, towards a 'nationalisation of justice' parallel to the nationalisation of the army, taxation, police and administration, through the substitution of whole-time trained officials for amateurs with an inherited (or purchased or transferred) right of jurisdiction and claim to its rewards in the way of fees, fines and authority. Sustained and largely successful efforts were made by Frederick's minister Cocceji and his successor Carmer, helped by the great jurist Suarez, to expedite normal procedure and to codify the law. A 'Prozessordnung' was published in 1781 and the 'Preussisches Landrecht' and its supplements a few years after Frederick's death (from 1794 on). The supreme instance was the Geheimer Rat. Next came the provincial 'governments' (this was now practically their only function) and finally the town councils, the owners of manorial estates (Rittergüter) and the king's agents on the royal demesnes.

The Prussian system of government was still despotism, but under Frederick the Great and his father before him it was efficient and 'benevolent' in the sense that, though the king insisted on holding the reins of power and brooked no interference, he did not use his authority and wealth for his own personal gratification and that of his court. The various territories he had acquired and the people he ruled formed an entity Prussia, that came before the royal house in importance and gradually became conscious of itself as a state. Frederick William called himself 'the field marshal and finance minister of the King of Prussia', Frederick the Great 'the first servant of the state', and their actions proved that they were moved not only by personal and dynastic motives but still more by a feeling of community of interest with a larger whole, a strong *esprit de corps*. So Frederick William would line up with his regiment before his palace at Potsdam every Easter, even if snow was on the ground, to be bled with the rest of them, and for years would have no other doctor than his regimental surgeon. His son was pursuing the same aim when he encouraged his young officers to think of themselves as Prussians, from whatever province they came, and made his officials realise that they were civil servants and not servants of the king. Yet even the philosopher on the throne did not escape the penalties of absolutism. He still had much that reminds us of Schiller's picture of the absolute monarch in *Don Karlos*. Like Philip he could trust no one, he could not believe that any of his servants was animated by a sense of duty and honour like his own. And his sense of duty blinded him often to ordinary considerations of morality, because the narrow interests of his own state came for him before everything, while his determinist philosophy could at a pinch shift the responsibility for his actions from himself to the First Cause, just as Philip's scruples could be overcome by the Grand Inquisitor.

Moreover, Frederician absolutism would have required for continued efficiency a succession of Fredericks, a clear impossibility, while it made continuity of policy from reign to reign difficult and left too little room for the natural expansion of the functions of the government. The Stein-Hardenberg reforms were urgently necessary when they came, as a halfway house between despotism and representative government.

In the second half of the eighteenth century a number of German princes tried, generally somewhat half-heartedly and never with much success, to imitate the benevolent despotism of Frederick the Great. Maria Theresa and her advisers instituted many reforms in the administration of Austria after the War of the Austrian Succession, and paid less respect than Frederick to the rights of the nobility. The most pressing practical problems were solved in a way that allowed for the vast differences between the various parts of the Austrian dominions. Joseph II, however, in his impatience to see results and his doctrinaire idealism, introduced with excellent intentions an immense number of ill-considered reforms that could not easily be put into effect by the bureaucracy at his disposal. In him centralisation and government-guardianship overreached themselves, and most of his good work was later swept away with the bad.

Influenced by the spread of humanitarian ideas as well as by Prussia's example, a number of smaller states attempted to reform their administration, particularly after the Seven Years' War. Saxony did so under Kurfürst Friedrich August III, 'der Gerechte' (1768–1827), Baden under Markgraf Karl Friedrich (1746–1811), Weimar under Karl August (1775–1827), Anhalt-Dessau under Leopold Franz (1758–1817). A number of ecclesiastical states imitated them. These states, however, in their attempts to improve the conditions of trade and industry, to economise at court, to reform justice and education and abolish serfdom, were not aiming at power but at the individual welfare of their subjects. Poor-relief was reorganised, new poor-houses, prisons, hospitals established, and in every way the governments showed themselves conscious of their responsibility for what would now be called social services. The subjects of these true 'Landesväter' certainly did not envy the Prussians their military power, with its concomitants, compulsory service and high taxation. Mirabeau sums up the current view concerning these smaller progressive states well in *De la monarchie prussienne*[1] when he says that though small states cannot prevent invasions of their territory, undertake great public works or remove the hindrances to trade and intercourse that are caused by customs duties and the diversity of weights, measures and coinage, their rulers have on the whole too little power to be tyrannical, they are very close to their subjects, who often look upon them as their father, and they keep each other in check, because dissatisfied subjects can so easily emigrate to a neighbouring state. Each state needs good professional men, they are as it were sold by auction to the highest bidder, and for similar reasons the press tends to be freer than in larger states.

As an example of the smaller enlightened states Weimar under Karl August is particularly interesting, because of Goethe's share in its government. The mature Karl August earned universal praise from his contemporaries. In Goethe's well-known summing up of his character and achievements (Eckermann, 23rd Oct. 1828) and in Alexander von Humboldt's description (quoted there) of a day passed with him just before his death, we see a man of strong and generous character, a good judge of men, who had enriched his native endowment of common sense and vigour of will and intellect by profound cultivation. Goethe himself was of course responsible for evoking not a little of what was most attractive in him. He had shown the sulky headstrong boy whom we see in the early portraits that the real world of nature and men was an inexhaustible source of interest for

[1] 4th edn., London, 1788, III, 677 ff.

one not attracted by the empty pomp of courts and not overmuch by literature and art. When Goethe first knew him, his tastes and habits were those of a country squire. His relationship to his small land was, until well into the nineteenth century, very like that of the squire to his manor. He got to know every inch of it by shooting and hunting over it. Every expedition gave him a fresh opportunity of acquainting himself at first hand with the life of his people, and these interests were stimulated by Goethe, the admirer of Möser (who praised patriarchal government with its close personal contacts) and the frequenter of the craftsmen's workshops in his native Frankfort.

It was Karl August's rural rides that suggested his many attempts to improve agriculture, forestry and mining, most of which were, however, too amateurish and sporadic to have much permanent effect. In agriculture it proved extremely difficult to get rid of the old open-field system. The landlords and even the duke's Kammer did not wish all the fallows to disappear, over which they had valuable grazing rights, the peasants were heavily taxed and had no capital, and no faith in new-fangled ideas, the only result of which was to lower the price of corn. But interesting discoveries were made at the experimental farm (run at a loss) and by Batty, the English bailiff, in his small district up in the Thüringer Wald, while forestry was put on a scientific basis and introduced as a subject of university study at Jena before the end of the century. It proved impossible in the long run to do much for mining (at Ilmenau), stocking-weaving (at Apolda) or any other industry. Industry and trade were both crippled by the protectionist policy and old-established rights of neighbouring states, which prevented for instance until 1804 the diverting through Weimar of the trade-route from Frankfort via Erfurt to Leipzig.

Karl August's reign illustrates in fact admirably both the strong and the weak points of patriarchal government at its best. The duke was in close touch with his subjects and was always ready to help them in any practical difficulty of which his own senses convinced him. He took an active part in fighting village fires, he led rescue parties when Weimar or Jena were in danger from floods, and once at least (unlike the count pilloried in Bürger's *Lied von braven Mann!*) he was nearly the victim of his reckless bravery. His curiosity in practical and scientific affairs was insatiable. 'Now he would be in the conservatories, where he knew every plant and moss and flower, now in the gardens and park, now with the professors of Jena, now at one of his farms, now parleying with artists, now exchanging views with poets, now buying antiques, now viewing pictures'[1]—so Frau von Heygendorf describes his versatility. But wide interests and good intentions were not enough without some of the hardness with himself and others that made Frederick truly Great, without a more methodical attention to detail and a much larger measure of the gifts of fortune. The day for tiny states was over. They could not be self-contained and they could not effectively demand what they needed from outside. The more one knows of them, the more one sympathises with Frederick's Machtpolitik, that at first appears so brutal.

Karl August's comparative ineffectiveness was not, however, altogether due to fate and his good nature. Although he was 'ein Mensch aus dem Ganzen' he was an absolute prince and a man of his time, not a martyr to duty. His personal tastes, it is true, were very simple. On his hunting expeditions he would sleep in the meanest cottage or beside a camp fire; he liked a hard bed and plain fare (see for instance Goethe's instructions to his mother for their reception in Frankfort in 1779). Even at court, though appearances had to be kept up, there was nothing sybaritic about the life at Weimar if, as a former page tells us, four bottles of champagne, on the rare occasions when it was served (perhaps four times a year), had to suffice for 50 or 60 people. But the duke wasted far more money than his little land could afford on

[1] Kar. Jagemann, *Erinnerungen*, p. 139.

field sports, on a merely decorative army, on parks and palaces and on women. In his delight in the chase he did not shrink from causing inconvenience and more to his subjects. Goethe had to protest, diplomatically but firmly, against wild boars being allowed to roam freely on the Ettersberg, to the annoyance of neighbouring squires and peasants and the ruin of agriculture. Before this Karl August had arranged pig-stickings in the riding-school, till the spectacle had proved too much for the nerves of his court. His smart keepers and foresters were as dear to his eye as his little army, and he never lost his passionate love of hunting. His favourite dogs had to accompany him everywhere; they were allowed all sorts of liberties at table; they frequently interrupted court concerts with their howls when the tenor sang. When old citizens of Weimar later called up memories of the duke, it was on horseback that they saw him, riding recklessly surrounded by dogs to the chase, or as in his later years, driving out in his old two-horsed almost springless Droschke.

Another even more expensive hobby (for Parforce and Treibjagden, smart keepers and thoroughbred English horses were expensive) was his 'army'. When he came to the throne he pensioned off the senior officers, took command himself and brought in a Prussian officer to train his hussars. There were only some thirty-six of them, but they were given a new riding-school and new stables and were drilled with all due solemnity, a trumpeter playing the cavalry march every day as Rittmeister von Lichtenberg led his men out to parade. In spite of Goethe's protests against 'militärische Makaronis' (Tagebuch 1 Feb. 1779) Karl August increased the army after his visit to Berlin in 1778, set up a company of grenadiers and dressed his men very much like Prussians. He would often get up at four o'clock to drill his battalion himself. It was now 800 strong, infantry and cavalry. In 1783, however, being 200,000 Th. in debt, he had to promise his Landtag that he would economise. He was left with 38 hussars and an officer, and 136 infantry under six officers, but he soon tired of drilling this handful of men. From 1788 he began to satisfy his military tastes by acting as Major-General of a Prussian regiment of cuirassiers stationed at Aschersleben. It was in this capacity that he served in the campaign in France on which Goethe accompanied him in 1792. He resigned his commission in 1794.

Among the duke's cavaliers many extravagant tales were told about his amours. He was unhappily married, and certainly made no secret of being attracted by Corona Schröter, Emilia Gore, Gräfin Jeanette Luise von Werthern, Kammerrätin Crayen and others. From 1802 he had an official mistress in Karoline Jagemann, the brilliant actress and singer, whom he ennobled, with their children, in 1809, with the title of Frau von Heygendorf. Her memoirs present the lovers in a sympathetic light. Though the neglected duchess put a good face on the matter, the usual consequences of Maîtressenwirtschaft, extravagance and intrigues, were not lacking. It was apparently because of Karoline Jagemann, for instance, that Schiller's *Jungfrau von Orleans* was not, like the rest of his later plays, given its first performance in Weimar (Karoline was the only actress for the title-rôle, and the duke and the court were very well acquainted with Voltaire's *Pucelle*), and that Goethe retired from the management of the theatre, after the dispute about the staging of the *Chien d'Aubry*.

Karl August was not free, then, from the usual defects of absolute monarchs, but his peccadilloes were no more than was expected of a German princeling. At bottom he was a man of good sense. But he was decidedly fortunate in chancing on the greatest German of his day and just the educator he needed. Can anyone but a patriotic German historian believe that without Goethe Karl August's name would have been remembered for more than a generation? He was fortunately not spoiled by too much of the conventional education of a prince before he came under Goethe's influence—one has the impression that Graf von

Goerz and his assistants had found him very intractable—and possessed by nature a sense for realities and an impatience with shams to which the genuineness of Goethe, his outstanding moral quality, made an immediate appeal. But under other influences, one fears, he might have become something very like another prince who was considered unusually promising as a young man, Karl Eugen von Württemberg.

The machinery of government in Weimar was of the type described above, modified a little by the influence of Prussia. There was no nonsense about the rights of the people. The Diet of his Estates, or rather a committee of it, was summoned regularly but at long intervals, about every six years. It represented only a small minority of his people and was thoroughly under his thumb, because the nobility were so dependent on court favours. It scolded him mildly for extravagance but agreed to the proposed taxation, its only real function. It never initiated anything. The attitude of the court towards it is reflected in Karl von Lyncker's description of the 'comical' sights that were seen when the country squires and mayors had been well plied with liquor at the banquet of welcome to the duke's first Diet. The Estates Treasury (the office that collected the special taxes agreed to by the Estates) even considered itself a government department and took the duke's part against the Estates. It is not surprising that the duke did not think highly of such an elected assembly. When different views prevailed after the Napoleonic Wars, he was ready as usual to make a fair bargain, and was the only prince in the Deutscher Bund who kept his promise to grant a constitution.

The central organs of government were the usual ones. At the head was a 'Konseil' of three ministers and the duke (from 1776 it consisted for several years of Herr von Fritsch, as 'Erster Minister', Schnauss and Goethe), each member of which made himself responsible for particular departments. Goethe for instance was entrusted at first with mines, roads, and waterways and later with recruiting, Herr von Fritsch with 'police'. Then there was the supreme court of justice and chief administrative body, called as usual the 'Regierung', with a Chancellor as its president. There was a 'Kammer' or treasury, presided over by a Kammerpräsident. Goethe was given this office also temporarily from 1782, when Herr von Kalb proved unreliable. Finally, for Church government and education there was the 'Oberkonsistorium', with the Oberkonsistorialpräsident, a layman, at its head and Herder, 'Generalsuperintendent' or chief of the clergy, as vice-chairman. The various parts of the scattered territories of the duke, some 33 Quadratmeilen (c. 700 sq. miles) in 1775, had been inherited by the dynasty at different times and were still to some extent separately administered. So the Fürstentum Weimar and the Fürstentum Eisenach each had its separate Kammer and Konsistorium, though they shared a Regierung, and even the Landesportion Jena and the 'hennebergische Ämter' (of which Ilmenau was the chief) were separate for purposes of taxation. The work of these various bodies was co-ordinated only by the duke or his immediate advisers; their decisions needed his approval and could be set aside by him. Every morning he received petitioners in person, a practice that contributed much to his popularity, for in times when there were no real newspapers and no organs of public opinion, direct access to the 'Landesvater' was the subject's one hope of redress. One might briefly describe the system of government in Weimar as patriarchal bureaucracy; patriarchal, by tradition and because of the smallness of the state, and not very efficiently bureaucratic, in imitation of greater states. In both these respects it was an unusually good specimen of the commonest type of German state in the later eighteenth century.[1]

[1] For Karl August's rule consult the studies by F. Hartung named in section B iii of the bibliography, the memoirs of K. von Lyncker and Karoline Jagemann (bibliography, section A), and the letters of Goethe and Karl August.

It would be beyond our scope to consider the efficiency of every department of state under German benevolent despotism, but we must at least enquire how the princes raised their revenue and who bore the chief burden of taxation, for the administration of finance already affected every person in the land.

We are not surprised to find that rational forethought played a much smaller part in this matter then than now, that the courts of those days lived very much from hand to mouth. The problem of finance was constantly increasing in difficulty, not merely because of the extravagant personal claims of the princes and their entourage, but because of the new responsibilities that governments were forced to take upon themselves as the structure of society became more complex, the simple machinery of the Middle Ages broke down and more central control, involving fresh expenditure, became necessary. With the disappearance of feudal services, and the consequent need for paid armies and paid officials, the princes had to imitate the Free Towns and buy the services they needed with the revenues from their crown lands and royal dues, or with money raised for the purpose by taxation or loans.

The revenue from crown lands was still the most important item on the credit side of German state budgets in the eighteenth century. Even under Frederick William I half of the state revenues of Prussia came from this source. Frederick the Great too found it necessary to devote much attention to the development of the royal demesnes. This source of income was only unimportant in states where the prince had been forced through reckless borrowing to mortgage his family possessions.

Regalities ('Regalien') were a second important source of income, one that had grown since the Middle Ages because the territorial princes had concentrated these rights in their own hands, depriving the towns, for instance, where they could, of the customs and currency rights which many had formerly possessed. The customs barriers of the towns were replaced by new ones on the boundaries of the state, on roads, bridges, rivers, that crippled German trade until the establishment of the Zollverein. There were few princes who did not also abuse their currency rights, overcoming crises temporarily at the cost of debasement of the coinage. There were sound economic reasons of course for the action of the governments against the towns, larger economic units being urgently needed. The trouble was that even the states were not large enough, and that the protectionist policy of the greater European states was being imitated by them in entirely different conditions.

The economic theory prevailing in these greater states was what is known as 'Mercantilism'. It advocated self-sufficient national units in which trade and industry were fostered by tariffs and made to give financial support to the state whose protection they enjoyed. It was a policy that could not be successfully pursued, economists think, except by countries owning undeveloped colonies which they could exploit; it may in fact be considered as the extension of the old policy of the medieval towns, which aimed at exploiting the country districts around them. In the same way the new nations used their colonies. It was a policy demanding larger units than any to be found in Germany. Even Prussian mercantilism, as we shall see later, was not a success, still less that of the average small state. It was in pursuance of this theory (particularly as put into practice by Colbert in France) that porcelain, tapestry and cloth manufactures were established in a number of states. They were nearly always worked at a loss, and provided for the most part only luxuries for the court or equipment for largely ornamental armies. They sometimes proved the starting-point for important later developments, and enriched the world with many beautiful things, but they were no more economic than the average amateur gardener's home-grown vegetables.

The only kind of export that brought in a really considerable sum to the German princes was that of men, the troops whose services were lent in return for subsidies to England, France and Holland. By this means the Landgraves of Hesse-Cassel, for instance, maintained a magnificent court for more than a century. They built themselves an elegant capital, and a palace at Wilhelmshöhe, one of their many homes, that astonished all visitors with its artificial cascades and other expensive glories. They formed one of the best collections of pictures in Germany. Sixty persons sat down with the Landgrave to dinner every day.[1] And the first of the Rothschild dynasty, Meyer Amschel, laid the foundations of his fortune by assisting Landgrave William IX.[2] Brunswick, Württemberg, Bavaria, Saxony, the Palatinate, Hanover (in 1776 under our George III), as well as smaller states like Ansbach, Hanau, Waldeck were all concerned in varying degrees in this trade, particularly at the time of the American War of Independence, a struggle watched with enthusiastic sympathy for the colonists by thinking people in Germany, when 30,000 German troops, 12,500 of whom never returned, were 'lent' by their princes to England for over half a million pounds. In Frederick I's time even Prussia lent troops, for subsidies, to the Dutch. There is ample justification for the celebrated scene in Schiller's *Kabale und Liebe* (II, 2).[3]

Taxation, the last resource of the prince's treasury, demanded, in order to be productive, a more equitable distribution of the burden and a more effective system of collection than had yet been devised. It was indirect taxation that was favoured, and in some states (particularly in Prussia under Frederick the Great) it became a serious burden. Taxes of this kind became common from the end of the seventeenth century (in imitation as usual of France). The usual form, the

[1] In 1779, when Dr Moore was there.
[2] Corti, *The Rothschilds*.
[3] Biedermann, I, 205–7, 225; v. Boehn, I, 222 ff. The standard book on the subject is: F. Kapp, *Der Soldatenhandel deutscher Fürsten*.

'Accise', was a levy on all goods offered for sale. Frederick the Great developed the system into the notorious 'Regie', managed by a host of French customs officers, armed with powers of search that extended even to private houses. But even this elaborate system was very ineffective because so much of the proceeds stuck to the Frenchmen's fingers. These indirect taxes were raised almost entirely at the expense of the common citizens of the towns. The direct taxes, where they existed, were provided almost wholly by the peasantry. Conditions varied so much in the different states, and even in different districts of the same state, that it is impossible to summarise accurately the details that are known. The one important fact that emerges is that in the country (and for that matter in the Free Towns too), the people best able to pay, being also best able to resist payment, contributed least. The country nobility were practically exempt from taxation. They paid a so-called 'Donativ' to the prince, a substitute for feudal services, which was in no sort of proportion to the taxes paid by others. Landowners who were not nobles, and peasants, paid a land tax to the prince, at rates which varied in different parts but were usually high (up to 50 per cent. of the income for instance in Bavaria), though not so high as they sound, because they were based on very old land-valuations, since the making of which the land had greatly increased in value.[1] Similarly the rich patricians of Ulm and Nürnberg, whose capital was in land, paid a very low rate in comparison with the ordinary citizens whose capital was in trade and industry; while in Frankfort the tax on capital was a small fixed sum on large fortunes, and a comparatively high rate on those below 15,000 gulden. In some provinces there was a poll tax levied at a uniform rate on every person over 14 years old, which also weighed most heavily of course on the peasant. We hear also, it is true, of special levies graduated according to capacity, in Weimar for example, but these always bore hardest on the peasant, who had so

[1] Details in Biedermann, I, 209 ff.

little ready money. It must be remembered that we are speaking here only of payments to the prince; the peasant had also to satisfy the very high demands of his landlord (Grundherr) for services and dues. There is a striking passage on the exploitation of the peasant in Weimar, a comparatively well-governed state, in one of Goethe's letters. Writing to Knebel (on 17th April 1782) he compares the peasantry, wresting a bare living from the soil, with the plant-lice he has observed in his biological studies, for as soon as these creatures have fed themselves full and green on the rose bushes, they are sucked dry in their turn by ants. 'Things have gone so far now', he adds, 'that more is consumed in a day at the top than can be produced in a day at the bottom.'

A concrete example will give a better idea of the finances of an average German state than necessarily vague general statements. As Weimar is one of the few states of that time whose finances have been competently studied (so far as they can be at this distance in time), we may conveniently take it again as our type,[1] and study the financial policy of Karl August in the first decade of his reign. When Karl August came to the throne the land was at least free from debt. His grandfather, Ernst August, and his father, Ernst August Konstantin, in his brief reign, had been extravagant, while Anna Amalie, during her Regency (1758–75), had only managed to make both ends meet because the Seven Years' War, at first a source of expense and debts for Weimar, which had to furnish a 'Reichskontingent', had proved in the end profitable through providing opportunities for selling the treasury's stocks of inferior wheat, its tenants' tithes, at an exorbitant price. But profiteering of this kind was not a permanent remedy for financial difficulties. Unfortunately there was not much wealth in the country to tax. It was an almost entirely agricultural province, and the backward farming methods practised, the so-called three-field system, kept the peasants moving in a vicious circle of constantly

[1] See for the following the works by F. Hartung referred to above.

diminishing crops and increasing burdens of debts and interest. If there was by chance a good harvest, there was no sale for the surplus, because Weimar was so far from the sea that for its wheat to reach a buyer prohibitive tolls and costs of carriage had first to be paid. When the experiment was made, later, of sending wheat to Bremen, the government lost 8000 Thalers in a very few years. There was, as we have seen, scarcely any industry or trade of which toll could be taken by the government.

The only remedy that the Konseil could suggest, at the beginning of Karl August's reign, was economy. They persuaded the young duke to agree to a fixed allowance for the expenses of court and mews (till now the treasury had been considered, as in most small states, as a glorified Privy Purse for the reigning family); they had to fix the amount at 54,000 Thalers, 10,000 more than had been so far needed, and to provide this additional sum they eventually decided on a personal levy, rejecting the alternative proposed by the treasurer, Kalb, of an indirect tax, or 'Accise', on the Prussian model. Though the poll tax was graded, from 16 Thalers for a Geheimer Rat to 4 Groschen for day labourers and rag gatherers, it bore hard on the poorer country people. By this measure and a stamp tax the situation was temporarily met, but in 1782 the duke was obliged to dismiss his treasurer for incompetence and peculation, and after his flight the treasury was found to be deeply in debt again. Goethe was now temporarily given the additional office of treasurer. He persuaded the Estates to pay off the debt by inducing the duke to accept their suggestion of a reduction of the 'army', involving the curtailing of his allowance to 30,000 Thalers. It was possible to balance the budget now without the poll tax, but the financial position was still precarious and continued to be so. None of the government's attempts to improve the economic state of the country had much effect. The duke's subjects would not or could not themselves make any serious move to improve their condition (by adopting improved methods of agriculture for instance) and the government's half-hearted measures could do little with only indifferent local officials to enforce them. Goethe complains in a report for the year 1786 of the 'pettiness' of conditions in small states. It was impossible even to keep the duke down to his allowance (says Vehse). It was Goethe's pent up disgust at the futility of his uncongenial labours in this atmosphere, as much as anything else, that drove him to Italy in 1786, for an activity that produced no results, as he said, made him furious.

PART II

THE OLD ORDER OF SOCIETY
NOBILITY AND PEASANTRY

Chapter I

THE NOBILITY IN GENERAL

The loose political structure of Germany naturally favoured the utmost variety in its social life. State differed from state, and class from class, and though there were influences here as in other countries tending to level out differences of this kind, the process was slow and frequently interrupted. Goethe speaks more than once of the lack of 'general culture' in Germany, contrasting it unfavourably with France and England. It was one of the difficulties that the writers of his age, with their new ambition to reach a national public, felt most. 'Because no general culture can establish itself in our country, every part keeps to its own ways and prides itself on its oddness', says Goethe. Or again: 'We are a collection of private individuals....Every one is content with the views of his province, his town or his own mind, and we may have a long time to wait before we attain to a creditable average standard of cultivation'. Knigge, contrasting the task of the German writer or actor with that of a Frenchman, with the taste of Paris to guide him and the confidence that his allusions will be understood in every part of France, asks how it is possible for any writer to appeal at once to 'the good-natured, naïve, sometimes rather materialistic Bavarian, the refined smooth-tongued Saxon, the heavy Westphalian, the polite Frenchified Rhinelander, the blunt North Saxon'. And Justus Möser, in a similar passage in his *Patriotische*

Phantasien, declares that the Germans are even reduced to swearing in French for lack of a national oath.

Local differences were naturally most marked among those classes of society that saw least of the outer world, peasants, country gentlemen and the inhabitants of small towns. They were least noticeable in the nobility of the courts, who were not considered educated unless they travelled, and who were influenced by the arbiters of European taste in Paris. What one might call the horizontal cleavages between the 'estates' of society were far wider in fact than the vertical ones between states. A description of the social condition of the country at this period must almost of necessity follow the social strata in its arrangement rather than geographical regions, and it will be convenient to discuss the old-established classes, nobility and peasantry, the relics of feudalism, before the more recent growth, the middle class.

In each state big or small, there was a similar pyramid of social groups rising tier on tier to the ruler. At the base in each was the peasantry, not an undifferentiated mass, as we shall see, but relatively homogeneous. At the apex was the aristocracy, graded from the prince down to the simple country gentleman, who would often lead a life hardly distinguishable from that of a peasant. In between came the middle class of town-dwellers, again with many subdivisions, overlapping both nobility (in its patricians and higher officials) and peasantry (in its semi-agricultural tradesmen), and forming, at least at the end of the century, the backbone of the people.

It was not the first time that the middle class had played a dominant part in the life of the country. In the later Middle Ages the towns had been politically powerful and culturally highly developed, at the culmination of a long period of growth, the history of which we shall glance at later. Economic changes had gradually made it possible for a middle class to break through the old, purely hereditary stratification of society, as the new class of knights had done at an earlier period. 'Towards the end of the twelfth century the re-shuffling of social classes, in progress since the early Middle Ages, was almost complete. New occupational groups on an essentially economic basis had taken the place of the old hereditary classes. What was important now was similarity of occupation and through it of way of living, while the features formerly decisive lost their prominence. In the thirteenth century it is already quite usual to speak of peasants, burghers, knights and clergy as separate "estates".'[1] The corporate feeling of the towns had on the whole tended to obliterate distinctions between classes; serfs had become free, and first merchants and then craftsmen had entered the ruling class of patricians, originally purely aristocratic. It seemed probable in the age of the Reformation that the lower nobility would coalesce with the richer patricians and learned professions—much as they did in England—but the upheavals of the sixteenth and seventeenth centuries prevented it.

At the beginning of the eighteenth century then the medieval estates, nobility, burghers, peasants were still sharply distinguished from each other. In spite of, or perhaps because of, the fact that the basis in reason for these class distinctions was fast disappearing, they had hardened in Germany into something very like a caste system. The French Revolution was the next turning point. Germany began to follow England and France. Within the separate states, as in the towns earlier, men began to lose their consciousness of differences of rank as they became aware of their membership of one community. The legal distinctions between nobleman and commoner were then gradually abolished, though the distinctions in the law of the Empire between Fürsten, Grafen and Herren, Reichsritter, Reichsstädter and Reichsbauern were jealously maintained till the end of the old Reich in 1806.[2]

[1] L. v. Ebengreuth, *Kultur der Gegenwart*, II, 2. 1, p. 297.
[2] Cf. H. Brunner, *Grundzüge der deutschen Rechtsgeschichte*, 1901, p. 222.

The change of view may be seen in such small things as the use of titles in public documents. In the Durlach church registers, Roller tells us, the Hofprediger divided people in the early part of the century into three grades. Noblemen were always referred to as 'der gnädige Herr, die gnädige Frau', their daughters as 'Fräulein'; the 'Honoratioren', that is, the better-class townspeople, higher officials, professional men with university training, etc., were styled 'Herr' and 'Frau', their daughters 'Jungfer'; the rest, craftsmen, farmers, labourers and so on were not even mistered. At the end of the century, however, the predicate 'gnädig' was reserved for persons of princely rank, others, though of good birth, simply sharing the 'Herr' and 'Frau' of the Honoratioren.

Even after the French Revolution Mme de Staël could write with truth: 'En Allemagne chacun est à son rang, à sa place, comme à son poste, et l'on n'a pas besoin de tournures habiles, de parenthèses, de demi-mots, pour exprimer les avantages de naissance ou de titre que l'on se croit sur son voisin'. It seemed to her that in France one rank had not been definitely marked off from another in this way even at the end of the Ancien Régime, when the distinctions between classes were more marked, we are told, than ever before. 'La bonne compagnie, en Allemagne, c'est la cour; en France, c'étaient tous ceux qui pouvaient se mettre sur un pied d'égalité avec elle, et tous pouvaient l'espérer, et tous aussi pouvaient craindre de n'y jamais parvenir.'[1] Lady Mary Wortley Montagu, Lord Chesterfield, Dr Moore and the *Introduction to the knowledge of Germany* all speak in the same strain, but there is evidence enough in the German memoirs and general literature of the time. Knigge speaks of the privileges of the aristocracy, the exclusiveness of the courts, the lack of influence of the merchant class in the national life, von Loen of the absurdity of the view held in Germany that no nobleman may engage in commerce, and there are scores of novels and domestic dramas which take this class conflict as their

[1] *De l'Allemagne*, part I, chap. XI.

main theme. Schiller's *Kabale und Liebe* and Grossmann's *Nicht mehr als sechs Schüsseln* were only the most famous.[1] The nobility were taught from their childhood to look upon themselves as a class apart. They differed from the middle class in legal status, standard of living, social customs and moral code, in their education, their taste in art and literature, in the very language they habitually used.

But the Bürger, the more or less educated middle-class citizen of the towns, insisted equally narrowly on every privilege and tradition that marked him off from the peasantry. There were well-marked social divisions among the Bürger themselves, for the 'scholars' who had attended the Grammar School and perhaps a university and taken up a profession, or entered an old-established firm of wholesale merchants, considered themselves superior to the mere retailers (Krämer) and craftsmen, and eligible to enter, by marriage or otherwise, the ranks of the patricians of their town.

Then there were occupational groups that cut across the older caste-like divisions. The clergy and military formed systems for themselves, though family tradition played a big part in their recruitment and in determining the status of their members. Army officers were almost always aristocrats, private soldiers peasants, or the riff-raff of the towns. As to the churches, a distinction must be made between Catholic and Protestant, and in the Catholic Church, between the higher clergy and the simple priests. The higher Catholic clergy and the members of cathedral chapters and most orders, whether of men or women, were always of good family. In the Catholic south and the Rhineland the Church provided ecclesiastical princedoms for many younger sons of ruling houses, and a life of dignified leisure in religious foundations, by no means severe now in their discipline, for a whole multitude of lesser aristocrats. The lower Catholic

[1] For some titles see K. Brombacher, *Der deutsche Bürger im Literaturspiegel von Lessing bis Sternheim*, Munich, 1920.

clergy would usually and the Protestant clergy of all ranks almost invariably be of middle-class or peasant origin. This explains why the Protestant clergy did not enjoy the same social standing as the Catholic. The Protestant theologians were the poorest and most despised students in the universities, for it was almost impossible for a needy student to maintain himself in any other faculty. When after years of private tutoring they obtained a living, they had usually more book knowledge than their Catholic colleagues, but less breeding, having enjoyed fewer social contacts.[1]

By the eighteenth century, the numerous 'Beamten' in the government service formed a group that was in many ways just as truly a separate Stand or estate as church or army. Its upper categories enjoyed high consideration, resembling the nobility in their way of life and possessing even some of its legal privileges. Most of the higher officials were university men, and throughout the century academically trained men in every profession were steadily rising in social esteem and power. If we take away the contributions to intellectual and artistic culture made by the Protestant clergy, professors, teachers, doctors and 'Beamten', that is, by the various categories of the educated middle class, there is very little left. The prestige of this class was so great by the end of the century that the life of the princes themselves was, in Lamprecht's phrase, 'verbürgerlicht', but as the frock-coated middle class approached the aristocracy, they drew away from those who worked with their hands, and the

[1] Cf. e.g. J. M. v. Loen, *Der Adel*, p. 57: 'The Roman priesthood is respected because many people of good birth and excellent talent devote themselves to the Church, and the Protestant clergy are despised because they are usually of lower class origin and display little magnanimity and Christian love in their doctrinal wranglings', or *Sophiens Reise nach Sachsen*, by the Protestant minister Hermes, where a minister who speaks French provokes surprised comment. Most Prediger, especially if themselves sons of the manse, looked on French, we are told, as a wicked language, being poor and having had little time or opportunity to become acquainted with people of fashion. They are contrasted in this respect with French abbés, who were men of the world.

unity of the 'folk' was more a thing of the past than ever. All the Romantics could do was to dream about it.

We pass now to a consideration of the various classes of society in turn, first to what was left of the feudal organisation of society on the basis of land-tenure, and then to the class that had made itself an indispensable element in society by skilled personal services, whether of hand or brain.

The status of the aristocracy had been defined in the course of the centuries in law. To understand their way of life in the eighteenth century we must first know something of their legal privileges, which were still numerous and important, though the duties that had originally justified the granting of privileges had almost entirely vanished. A nobleman had no longer to furnish and lead a certain number of men in his prince's army. If he served in it or assumed any court or state office, he did so for a material reward or because it suited his own interests, not because it was looked upon as his duty. The sense of duty was only invoked as a motive for state service by Frederick William I and Frederick II in Prussia, supported by other motives and not always successfully.

It was the obligation of military service that had originally justified the exemption of the aristocracy, which still held good, from nearly all rates and taxes and from excise duties. The principle of taxation followed in the eighteenth century, as we have seen, was to tax those who were powerless to resist. A gentleman was not only freed from the obligation of military service (a privilege that was shared by the better middle class); he was also, unlike the Bürger, relieved of the inconvenience and expense of billeting. His was in fact the only class in the state that was 'free' in the sense that nothing was demanded of it.

This class also enjoyed many prescriptive rights, usually fortified by law. It had an almost exclusive right to the chief offices under the government and at court, only the lower ill-paid posts being normally open to Bürger, though the attempts of the nobility to preserve this so-called Indigenatsrecht were occasionally frustrated, as we have seen, for instance by Frederick William I, in Prussia. It was possible too to give a middle-class man who was desired for high office the necessary standing by having him ennobled *ad hoc* —we think of Goethe in Weimar—but this did not happen very often. The nobleman enjoyed further special privileges ('Schriftsässigkeit') under criminal law; he could generally claim to be tried by the central courts of the state instead of by the local 'Ämter', could more easily get off with a fine or arrest in his own home instead of imprisonment, and was always in practice more lightly treated than others, even serious offences often going unpunished.[1] If the worst came to the worst he could claim to be beheaded instead of being hanged.

There were many rights of the aristocracy connected with the ownership of land. They alone could entail their estates. In most states they alone might own 'adlige Güter' or manorial estates. So Herder was ennobled for instance by the Elector of Bavaria in 1801, so that one of his sons might hold a small estate in Bavaria which he wished to farm. A right usually possessed by the nobility as landowners and very important, especially in colonised lands like East Prussia, was that of patrimonial jurisdiction, with all the power it conferred. The right to representation in the provincial diet was another, hardly so important, as we saw, at this period. Noble landowners could exact dues from merchants or craftsmen making use of their land. They often had the gift of a living in the Church.

In western Germany, as in France, it was their game rights that aroused perhaps the loudest public protest. This is not the place to go into all their complexity, the right to 'hohe Jagd' (stag-hunting, etc.), 'mittlere Jagd' (for roe-deer, wild boar, wolf, etc.), or 'niedere Jagd' (for hares, rabbits, partridges, etc.) and the struggles for their possession between

[1] For examples see von Boehn, *op. cit.* I, p. 541.

prince and squire and peasant. It was the peasantry that always suffered. J. M. von Loen tells us how they were constantly being requisitioned to act as beaters, as well as forced to lie out all night in the fields like beasts, to keep the game off their crops.[1] Literary protests, like this passage and the satire *Die Parforce-Jagd*[2] by Freiherr von Gemmingen, were not entirely due to the excessive humanitarianism of the age. Complaints occur in almost every state. We saw above how Goethe for instance had to urge Karl August, in December 1784, to do away with the wild boar that he allowed to roam freely on the Ettersberg, to the annoyance of the whole neighbourhood and the hurt of the peasantry, but Karl August was by no means a bad offender compared with monomaniacs like the Landgraves of Hesse-Cassel in the early part of the century.

Not the least prized—and resented—of the privileges of the gentry were the 'prééminences honorifiques', as the French called them, the symbolic marks of distinction that a man of birth could claim. The peerage and gentry had the 'pas', took precedence, before the commoner on all public occasions. They were constantly squabbling among themselves about precedence, as Lady Mary Wortley Montagu discovered in Ratisbon and Vienna. There is at least one instance of a 'war' between two tiny states resulting from such contentions (amusingly described by Gustav Freytag).[3] The aristocracy could claim, in addition to their titles and the use of *von, zu, auf, aus* before their surnames, the superscriptions *Edelgestrenge, Hochwohl-, Wohl-,* or *Hochgeborene, Ew. Gnaden, Gnädiger* or *Gestrenger Herr*, and the other uncouth formulae that had to be mastered by every complete man of the world. The insistence of the Germans on these minutiae already provided amusement for their neighbours. Lord Chesterfield tells his son that he had known many a

[1] *Freye Gedanken vom Hof*, 3rd ed. p. 28.

[2] Printed e.g. in *Deutsche Literatur*, Reihe Politische Dichtung. I.

[3] *Bilder aus der deutschen Vergangenheit*, IV (Der Wasunger Krieg).

letter returned unopened because one title in twenty had been omitted in the direction.

Like the English *Esquire*, many of these appellations later suffered a social decline. A modest visitor to Bavaria may now discover to his surprise that according to the envelopes of his letters he is *Wohlgeboren*. The normal modern use of *Fräulein* is also strictly irregular. It was only beginning to lose its original sense, in which it was applied only to young ladies of good birth, about the middle of the eighteenth century. 'Twenty years ago', says J. M. von Loen in 1752, 'the daughters of Augsburg patricians were addressed as *Jungfer*, but now they are no doubt *Fräulein* like the rest.' 'In Breslau', he adds, exaggerating, no doubt, 'the young women in small shops and at herring stalls are styled *gnädiges Fräulein*.' Even in 1816 one might read in a German newspaper that the post-offices in a north German town had been instructed not to deliver letters to middle-class girls if the writer had called them Fräulein on the envelope.[1] Hence Gretchen's retort to Faust: 'Bin weder *Fräulein*, weder schön' and Marthe's remark: 'Der Herr dich für ein *Fräulein* hält'.

It was impossible in the long run to prevent other classes from imitating the aristocracy in externals by sumptuary laws, however elaborate. Strictly, only the gentry were entitled to wear swords, though well-to-do citizens and anyone who wished to pass as a man of fashion imitated them in this as in the wearing of silk stockings and powdered hair. Even the little sons of better-class townfolk wore them with their Sunday clothes, as we see for instance from Goethe's tale, *Der neue Paris*. They could further distinguish themselves by the use of plumed hats—we hear of many a duel on this point between nobleman and commoner at the universities—by putting their servants into livery, displaying coats of arms, using special seals, wearing pink dominos at masquerades, and a thousand and one such trifles.

Most of these badges of rank were the outward signs of

[1] *Anno Dazumal*, II, p. 318 (? *Vossische Zeitung*).

a special standard and manner of living. It was often impossible to imitate the one without the other. This was true for instance of dress. The fashions for both ladies and gentlemen, extravagant in both senses of the word, were a tolerably effective mark of distinction when rank and wealth still went together and the aristocracy were the only people who lived a life of leisure and could avoid exposing themselves to the elements. No one else could afford these brocades and silks and damasks, the lace and embroidery and jewels, and all the skilled work that went to the making of the lady's hooped skirts, long trains and towering coiffures, or the gentleman's fancy vests, lace cuffs and powdered wig. And no one leading an active life out of doors could have worn them. To be 'natural' in Rousseau's sense was in any case too dull and plebeian. In the absence of other occupations, a game was needed that had complex rules. In classical French tragedy, as in the absolutism of Louis XIV, the pride characteristic of the Renaissance in man's control through reason over what happens to exist finds noble expression, and we may find a remnant of it even in eighteenth-century fashions. Man, as the measure of things, had to improve on nature, whether it was in trimming gardens into formal patterns, or forcing a girl's waist into V-shaped corsets. Native grace and art could turn life even under these conventions into a second nature in conformity with reason, as reason was then conceived.[1] The Revolution reminded the world that it was a reason in blinkers, for the foundations of this life, beautiful as it might sometimes be, had long been insecure.

In Max von Boehn's books on fashion the 'systematic exaggerations that are the essence of women's fashions' can be followed in detail.[2] At the end of the seventeenth century it was the headdress that was inordinately high (the *fontange*),

[1] See for instance Goethe's praise of the countess in her finery, in *Wilhelm Meisters Lehrjahre*, Book 3.

[2] *Die Mode, Menschen und Moden im* 17., 18. *und* 19. *Jahrhundert*, 6 vols., Munich, 1913 and later.

then from about 1720 coiffures were low and skirts began to expand, with the return of the hooped skirt in its various forms (it had been common in the sixteenth century, as we see from Velasquez portraits). This remained an item of ceremonial court dress in France till the Revolution and abroad even longer, but for more general use it began to go out in the 60's, and coiffures rose again, rose as high as chandeliers would allow them and higher, to the great profit of ladies' hairdressers, a new necessity in court towns. As visits to the hairdresser were expensive, even great ladies often could not afford to have their hair done more than once a week; others went for as long as a month, we are told, though it is difficult to believe it in view of the practical difficulties, not to speak of the lack of cleanliness this entailed, but cleanliness was not a strong point even with the most refined. The hair was always powdered, and this necessitated the liberal use of rouge, for white hair 'killed' the natural complexion. Of course it was impossible even for the most fashionable to live always in parade dress. More comfortable costumes were invented for everyday occasions. Many forms of négligé are heard of, of which the loose *Andrienne* (originally a maternity robe) and the tight-fitting *Caraco* (imitated from a tail-coat) were perhaps the best-known types. In both of them the lower part of the dress formed one whole with the jacket, whereas in full dress the upper skirt or manteau was separate from the tight-fitting bodice. The manteau was open in front to show the highly ornamented hooped skirt, and it had a train behind. The négligés, being of the nature of long coats. were open in the same way. In England the *Andrienne* came to be closed in front, giving the *robe anglaise* worn by the sitters of Reynolds and Gainsborough, while the *Caraco* developed into the tailor-made costume. The English ladies were the first to give up elaborate coiffures and rouge (from the 60's), but both were still fashionable in Germany in the 80's.

There were few changes in the dress of gentlemen throughout the period. At first they wore the long, closed, wide-sleeved *justaucorps* over a long vest, with knee breeches and silk stockings. Later, coat-tails were stiffened and coats worn open, then vests, sleeves and coat-tails were reduced, following military fashions, and the prototype of modern evening dress was already recognisable. But the same bright and delicate materials were used as for ladies' dresses, with braid and embroidery on coat and vest and a lavish display of lace at neck and sleeves. For travelling and ordinary occasions 'English suits' became more and more popular. In these, coat and vest were of comfortable cut and heavier material; the colours were more sober, though brighter than what is worn now; leather breeches and top-boots completed the costume for out-door wear, but it was only the 'genius' of the 70's who insisted on wearing them on all occasions, as a sign of the return to nature. Wigs, of various shapes according to the status of the wearer and the particular occasion, held their own until the 80's. Long before this a good many had begun to follow the Prussian army fashion and wear a pig-tail (whence the expression 'Zopfzeit'), and from the 70's the younger men, even in good society, infected by the passion for the natural, began to wear 'their own hair', so that by the time of the French Revolution wigs were already old-fashioned and by 1800 a mere survival. The Protestant clergy, the last class to adopt them at the beginning of the century, were the last to leave them off at the end.

It was impossible of course for the nobility to avoid all intercourse with the vulgar, but they made every effort on public occasions to keep social inferiors at a distance. In the theatre they sat apart from the common man, either in the front seats or in boxes, a device for securing their privacy first thought of in Paris. At public concerts too a space was left between the chairs of the quality and the rest. At ceremonious court concerts, on the analogy of the solar system, the very great were left surrounded by a number of empty chairs in direct proportion to their rank. In the village church, the local nobility would of course have separate pews and a family vault. In the council chamber and in lecture-rooms (like the law lecture-room at Leipzig), where noble and commoner met for a like purpose, each class was assigned its separate benches. Even at the few schools like the Karlsschule in Württemberg, where boys of good birth and others were educated together, the nobles wore distinctive silver epaulettes, dined at different tables, slept in separate dormitories and used bathing places at the river parted by a raised bank.[1] The fashionable world had its separate assemblies and balls, to which the common citizen was not admitted. From the emperor down to the penniless widow of a ruined Reichsritter, the nobility considered themselves in fact, with rare exceptions, to be a different race from the untitled mass. There were even those who thought that in a future life too they would receive differential treatment.[2]

If so much deference was due to any of the gentry, it can be imagined how much was expected by even 'duodecimo' princes. When Karl August visited a village in 1776, the peasants received him, Goethe tells us, 'with music, salutes of mortars, rustic arches of honour, garlands, cakes, dancing, fireworks, serenades and so on', and this kind of welcome was no more than what was expected.[3] Because the Fürst von Wallerstein's secretary, who had been sent ahead to prepare his master's coming, did not have all the bells of a village rung to greet him, but merely arranged a procession of notables, accompanied by the blare of trumpets and the firing of pistols, he was severely reprimanded, and reminded that 'nothing was to be neglected, that might bring home to a subject, through outward signs, the majesty of his lord'.[4] This lord ruled 36,000 people in a province about 320 sq. miles in extent, and the village in question was not even in his own lands.

[1] Berger, *Schiller*, 1; Nicolai, *Reisen*, vol. 10.
[2] Freifrau Karoline von Wöllworth Pahl—quoted by v. Boehn, 1, 545.
[3] Letter to Aug. zu Stolberg, 20 May 1776.
[4] K. H. von Lang, *Aus der bösen alten Zeit*, p. 147.

What made these aristocratic privileges particularly galling to those among the middle class who did not accept the position unquestioningly was the fact that the historical justification for them had vanished. Hereditary privileges had not seemed arbitrary when they involved hereditary duties. Institutions had lagged behind the development of the life of society to such a dangerous degree that it was not only Mephistopheles who thought:

> Es erben sich Gesetz' und Rechte
> Wie eine ewige Krankheit fort.

The various ranks of society had never in reality been closed castes made up of a limited number of families, though they all tried to make themselves so in times of declining prestige. No very profound study of the history of the different grades of the aristocracy is required to prove that each grade had been very considerably diluted in the course of time.

It is not necessary for the present purpose to attempt to trace the history of the nobility back to its obscure origins amongst the Germanic tribes, but it is of interest to note the source of the distinction, carefully made in the eighteenth century, between 'hoher Adel' and 'niederer Adel'. The 'hoher Adel' were all those who had the right to a seat and vote in the Reichstag, from the Kurfürsten down to the Reichsgrafen. They claimed descent from those free knights of the Middle Ages, who besides being of noble descent had held fiefs in return for military or administrative services. In the Middle Ages a subordinate class of knights grew up in Germany, recruited from the Ministeriales, men not of noble birth and usually not freemen, who as direct servants of the king or some great lord gained the reward of a fief. As influential associates of the great, resembling them in their way of life and particularly in their tenure of considerable feudal estates, they soon came to be looked upon as a free feudal nobility. Their lands and privileges became hereditary in their families and in a generation or two they succeeded in closing their ranks to newcomers. A candidate for knighthood had now to be himself the son of a knight. This is the origin of the 'niederer Adel' of modern times. The 'lower nobility' in the eighteenth century was further subdivided into the 'Reichsadel', or 'Reichsunmittelbare Ritterschaft', mostly to be found in Swabia and the south-west corner of Germany, acknowledging no lord but the emperor and no court but the supreme courts of the Empire, and the 'Landesadel', who were subject to the prince of the territory in which their estates lay. As the feudal system decayed, it became usual from the time of Karl IV on for the emperor to raise commoners to the nobility even if they possessed no land and performed no feudal services. The higher nobility saw to it that the emperor did not abuse his privilege, at least as far as the higher ranks were concerned, and insisted that all candidates should be in possession of estates held from the emperor direct. They could insist that even if the Kaiser conferred a title, its holder would not be given a seat as a peer in the Reichstag unless they approved of him, and in point of fact only half a dozen men were so dignified during the last century and a half of the Empire.[1]

The lower nobility tried to be equally exclusive, but they could not so easily prevent the Kaiser from making use of his power. The Kurfürsten of Saxony and Bavaria, when Reichsvikare, were particularly generous with letters-patent, and other princes, for example the kings of Prussia, claimed and exercised the same right. The Catholic 'Stifte', cathedral chapters, and any other aristocratic bodies which had the power in their own hands, retaliated by refusing to admit anyone to their ranks with less than a certain fixed number of noble ancestors, generally four, but a claimant for admission to the cathedral chapter of Trier, and even to the masked balls in Mainz, had to prove the blood of every one of his ancestors back to his great-great-grandparents to have

[1] R. Koser, in *Kultur der Gegenwart*, Teil II, Abt. V, I, p. 248.

been blue beyond reproach, a pedigree of sixteen quarterings (*Ahnen*) being demanded.

For a time doctors of law were considered to have the rank of noblemen, and there was the possibility of the development of a *noblesse de robe* as in France, but the Jurists did not manage to consolidate their position, and by the eighteenth century a doctorate did not carry this privilege any longer. It was in fact not 'standesgemäss' for a young man of rank, if he had passed the examinations for the doctorate, to make use of the title. The title of Hofrat was far more highly rated at court than any doctorate.

Though educated people in Germany, as in France, were coming to value personal merit more highly than birth, there were rich merchants who were ready to pay large sums to the Imperial treasury for titles, in spite of the knowledge that they would not be recognised by the existing nobility. Joseph II made financiers into noblemen by the dozen; in his time it cost in all about 20,000 Gulden to become a count (5952 Gulden in fees), 6000 to become a baron (3015 Gulden in fees), and 386 Gulden in fees to be a mere Adliger ('von-').[1] J. M. von Loen tells us that in the large Free Towns like Frankfort-on-Main and Nürnberg, the new nobility were not highly esteemed, while in Hamburg, Lübeck, Bremen and Basle, towns with a really active trade, a title of nobility was not esteemed at all and the nobles had been excluded from the council.[2] If this is true, it had not always been so, for in the flourishing days of the Free Towns, in South-west Germany particularly, a great many retired merchants had purchased themselves estates and titles of nobility; the consequent loss of brains and capital is even one of the causes suggested for the decline of the old Free Towns in trade and industry.

The political developments sketched in Part I had removed

[1] v. Boehn, I, 544. It cost Schiller, in 1802, 428 Gulden 30 Kr. when through Karl August's recommendation he was raised to the nobility by the Emperor. (Berger, *Schiller*, II, p. 596.)

[2] *Der Adel*, 1752, pp. 128, 129.

most of the rational grounds for the privileges still enjoyed by the aristocracy in the eighteenth century. The lower nobility in particular, as such, had almost ceased to perform any useful military or administrative functions since the breakdown of feudalism and the development of paid standing armies and a paid permanent civil service. Many of their number were to be found in the state service, but for the same material rewards as attracted the middle class too. If they insisted on the local nobility's first claim to high office ('Indigenatsrechte'), it was to maintain their privileges and in the hope of obtaining lucrative posts or sinecures. They became less and less conscious of having any duties in this respect, though it was clear to anyone who looked into the history of the matter that they had been exempted from taxation, for instance, because they served the state in arms, just as their ancestors had been given fiefs for administrative or military services rendered. In both cases the reward had become hereditary, but not the duty. It is true that in Prussia the Great Elector and his successors made excellent use of the nobility, but the severe measures needed to re-establish a tradition of state service are a sufficient indication of the unwillingness of their subjects to serve them. No other rulers attempted anything of the kind. As to the higher nobility, they had become, as we have seen, rulers in their own right, and were as little mindful of any obligations to the emperor as the Landadel was of any to them. They assumed, however, full responsibility for the government of their own states and in so far justified their position.

Those of the country nobility who still managed their own estates had on these grounds a good claim to a privileged position, one almost as good in its way as that of the petty princes, who were often little more than glorified squires themselves. Even if not directly useful in a military or administrative way they were, as landlords, an essential factor in the economic system and had important functions to perform. In the management of their estates, the encouragement of good husbandry, the maintenance of order and dispensing of justice in the squire's court, they could if they liked be princes in small, with a vast power for good—and of course for evil—over the peasants on their land. Moreover, they had as landlords the right to a seat in the Landtag and, if it ever met, they could, in combination with their fellows, bring some pressure to bear on the government of their small state. There were here and there German Sir Roger de Coverleys—we find a similar type described in Eichendorff's reminiscences, and occasional references to patriarchal squires occur in books of travel, and essays in publications like the Moral Weeklies and Möser's *Patriotische Phantasien*, as well as in novels and dramas. On the whole we should perhaps not expect the good squires to be so often mentioned as the bad, who are certainly numerous enough in literature. But there were no village Hampdens amongst the squires of Germany. They never played the same political rôle there as in England. One of the main reasons for this, and for the neglect of their estates by so many absentee landlords, was the attraction of the courts. As in France in the age of absolutism, the courts offered, to those who had the *entrée* to them, political power and wealth, social esteem and display, the society of their fellows and refined luxury. No wonder that so many noble families preferred to spend most of their time at the capital. But though occasionally a source of gain, court life was too extravagant for the resources of most noble families, and necessitated the delegation of their responsibilities as landlords to paid servants. Extortionate demands on the tenantry by the extravagant lord and his often irresponsible bailiff, mismanagement and debts were the result.

Besides the more than occasional inefficiency of the aristocracy as landlords there was another reason that weakened their claims to privileges on economic grounds, namely that there were many other citizens who were just as important in the economy of the country but who enjoyed no such social rewards. J. M. von Loen draws an interesting contrast between the life of a Frankfort merchant's wife and that of a country lady, and asks pertinently which of these is the real 'lady'.[1]

If the merchant of the towns challenged the exclusiveness of the nobles on economic grounds, the cultivated middle classes generally, and particularly those academically trained, could claim that they were the real leaders in many branches of intellectual culture and art. In the age of chivalry, the knights had been the creators and patrons of literature, as well as the indispensable defenders and local governors of the country and owners and controllers of most of its real wealth, the land. The towns and the princes had taken one after the other of these functions from them, until only those concerned with the ownership of land were left. It might at least have happened, as it did to some extent in Italy, France and England, that the privileged and sheltered aristocracy would maintain spiritual, intellectual and artistic values in an increasingly materialistic world.

The nobility as a whole did not, however, contribute very much to intellectual life either creatively or by encouraging the work of others. Over and over again we are told that their badge in the first half of the century was ignorance, and in the second half they only slowly followed in the footsteps of the bourgeoisie. The phrase which Goethe uses in his notes for the continuation of *Dichtung und Wahrheit* about the Weimar court as he found it in 1775 is: 'Gutmütige Beschränktheit, die sich zur wissenschaftlichen und literaren Kultur emporzuheben sucht'.[2] Their peers in England and France

[1] J. M. v. Loen, *Der Adel*, 1752, pp. 134 ff.

[2] *Goethe-Jahrbuch*, 1907, XXVIII, 9. For the earlier period cf. *Wilhelm Meisters Lehrjahre*, VI, where the Schöne Seele is made to say: 'Die Leute, mit denen ich umgeben war, hatten keine Ahnung von Wissenschaften; es waren deutsche Hofleute, und diese Klasse hatte damals nicht die mindeste Kultur'. Cf. also J. M. v. Loen, *Freye Gedanken vom Hof*, 3rd ed. Frankfort and Leipzig, 1768, p. 21: 'Die Unwissenheit ist beinahe das Kennzeichen einer vornehmen Geburt'. See further Knigge, *Umgang mit Menschen*, 3. Teil, 3. Kap., Biedermann, *op. cit.* II, 73, and M. v. Boehn, *op. cit.* I, 543.

looked on them for the most part as ignorant boors, and this judgment seems to be borne out by their poor record in literature and science.[1] The phrase put into the mouth of Olearius in *Götz von Berlichingen*: 'So gelehrt wie ein Deutscher von Adel' hid, like so much else in the play, a contemporary reference. It was fashionable indeed at most German courts to take a mild interest in literature, especially of the lighter kind, and as there was no German literature of general interest to speak of till late in the century, it was natural enough that French should be favoured. But German noblemen really cultivated even in French literature were rare exceptions. The majority were content if they could carry on a conversation in passable French, or at least lard their German with 'French' words,[2] and appear not to be ignorant of popular French writers. Almost all considered it beneath the dignity of a nobleman to desire any genuine scholarship. It was particularly difficult for women to cultivate their minds without losing in esteem. 'Learned women had been made ridiculous', says the Schöne Seele in *Wilhelm Meister*, 'and people could not bear even well read ones, probably because it was thought impolite to put so many ignorant men to shame.' Of course there were brilliant exceptions at Darmstadt, Brunswick, and Weimar, which we shall deal with later, and in encouragement of the fine arts and architecture the nobility had a better record—though

[1] Biedermann (II, i, 133) mentions a few names of aristocratic scholars and writers from the first half of the century, none of them very eminent: Herr v. Tschirnhausen, H. v. Seckendorff, H. v. Bünau-Dahlen, Baron v. Boyneburg, Graf v. Manteuffel, Frh. v. Münchhausen. In the second half there were of course more. In literature one may mention the Stolbergs, M. A. v. Thümmel, the Humboldts, and the less distinguished Weimar wits, H. v. Einsiedel, S. v. Seckendorff. There were many cultivated men of birth in high office: Hardenberg, Stein, Vincke, Schön. A certain number of salons were not without importance, such as those of Graf Stadion at Biberach and Fürstin Gallitzin at Münster.

[2] A young lady in Weimar for instance was capable of saying that she had received a 'grande gronde' from her mother because her 'terrière coiffure' was not 'goûteuse' (v. Lyncker, p. 16).

here again they were no more creative than an American millionaire. The German aristocracy could not therefore have rationally defended their privileges in the eighteenth century on the grounds of their services to culture.

As to their influence on manners, the evidence is almost wholly unfavourable, but it must be remembered that many of our witnesses were scarcely impartial, as bourgeois themselves. Everywhere in these middle-class writings we read of the vices of the courts and their disintegrating influence on the life of the country. The wicked aristocrats were contrasted with the virtuous middle class in one 'bourgeois drama' and novel after another. Courtiers are represented as being, for the most part, selfish, unprincipled, extravagant, licentious, addicted to gambling and drink and every kind of excess. Mephistopheles is made to tell us 'Den Bösen ist man los, die Bösen sind geblieben. Du nennst mich *Herr Baron*, so ist die Sache gut'. But of course the majority of courtiers could not claim to be so distinguished even in iniquity. What is probable is that, through the influence of the Thirty Years' War, the weakening of religious sanctions, the growth of materialistic thought in France and England, and the enjoyment by the aristocracy of power without responsibility, the moral standards of the age of the Reformation (never of course observed by everyone in Germany) had lost most of their meaning for the court classes. Except in pietistic courts, it was decidedly bad form to be 'virtuous'. Most of us would not condemn the life of the eighteenth-century aristocrat quite so strongly to-day as our grandfathers did, as Biedermann does for instance in his *Deutschland im achtzehnten Jahrhundert*, both because the bourgeois values have been rather shaken since then both by thinkers and by events, and because we have learnt to see morals themselves in evolution. Even the bourgeoisie of the time were divided in their attitude towards aristocratic ways of life. What one half of them condemned, not without a hint of concealed envy in some cases—one notes the eagerness with which backstairs scandal was sought after—the other half, particularly in court towns, fostered with all their might if it served their own interests. They had too little independence for their criticism to possess much force. One must in fact realise that it was only in theory that the same ethical ideals held for the whole community. In practice a working balance had to be reached between the very different ideals, different in historical origin and different in social background, of quite distinct classes of society.

We can form some idea of what the German aristocracy in the eighteenth century consciously aimed at in life, from a study of the type of education which was given to their sons in that age. This was the same in all essentials for the higher and the lower nobility, and was imitated by the patricians in the towns. In the course of the seventeenth century the education of the nobleman had come to resemble less and less that which was given to the sons of the better middle class in the town grammar schools. Court circles wanted their sons prepared for life in the here and now. Latin and religion, the main subjects of instruction in the grammar schools, were therefore largely replaced by modern utilitarian subjects or by training in the accomplishments which made a young man welcome in good society. In the official instructions, drafted in French, for the education of Karl Eugen of Württemberg and his brother, for instance, though the traditional phrases are repeated about bringing up the princes in godly and virtuous ways, the main stress is laid on modern languages and the arts of dancing, fencing and riding. The elder prince was to learn a modicum of Latin, 'because he might occasionally need to understand a few sentences in that language'.[1]

The curricula of the special boarding-schools which had been set up for the nobility, the 'Ritterakademien', and those recommended in the numerous handbooks for tutors, follow much the same lines. The indispensable subjects of study are,

[1] Quoted in Biedermann, II, i, 75.

first, languages. French and Latin are usually advocated. French was taught conversationally from a very early age, if possible, and Latin was not made a 'pedantic' discipline. Other languages sometimes taught were Italian, English and Spanish. German was not entirely neglected. Next in importance came the study of the modern world, history (modern political history, and the reading of the reviews), geography, genealogy and perhaps some snippets of natural science, the 'curiosities' of botany, anatomy, physics and chemistry. Philosophy was considered pedantic, but time might be found for a little ethics. Law was important for future rulers and officials, and 'politics', in the special sense attached to the word then, was of value to all. It meant the art of self-advancement by 'finesse' and civility, the 'suaviter in modo' praised by Lord Chesterfield. The 'politic' man or 'Politikus' who figures so largely in literature at the beginning of the century, is the master of the 'lesser talents', whose *savoir-vivre* wins him favour with the great.

A more specialised study was mathematics, in which such great advances were being made at this time. It was important for future officers. Rhetoric, the art of persuasive speaking and writing, was chiefly restricted to letter-writing. For many pupils much the most important item in the curriculum was 'Exercitien', which took the place of the older knightly exercises and led up to modern sport. The exercises included dancing, fencing, riding, shooting and 'Ballspiel', an early form of tennis. Among minor accomplishments, the art of carving at table was still taught, drawing was encouraged, and music was thrown in along with card games and chess. Then apart from the formal studies, sports and pastimes there was the 'science' of manners and deportment, 'Conduite', to be mastered, with all its prescribed forms for various occasions—how to pay compliments, how to dress, to pay calls, to behave in company, at table, on travel and so on.[1]

[1] Curricula from Steinhausen, 'Die Idealerziehung im Zeitalter der Perücke', in *Mitteilungen der Gesellschaft für deutsche Erziehungs- und Schulgeschichte*, IV, 1894.

For final polish, the young man went on his grand tour to foreign courts. The Netherlands, England, France and Italy were the countries most commonly visited, but a long stay in Paris was the one indispensable feature of the journey. Elizabeth Charlotte, the German-born duchess of Orleans and mother of the Regent, whose letters give an entertaining though scarcely edifying picture of life at the French court, sometimes had twenty or thirty Germans of high rank at her parties at once. At foreign courts the young aristocrat was supposed to continue his education by studying the national character and conditions of life, making the acquaintance of leading statesmen, and above all by endeavouring to shed his native rusticity in the company of ladies and gentlemen of refinement. Of course there were many less desirable things he could and often did learn too at pleasure-loving courts, so that in spite of the many advocates of travel as a form of education, from Montaigne onwards, there were never wanting those who saw in it the source of all evil.[1] It was certainly an expensive and often fatiguing and dangerous part of one's education in those days. No young man of birth could go on his travels without a tutor and a man-servant; a young prince of any consequence might have a whole suite of followers. Friedrich III of Gotha for instance (born 1699, reigned 1732–72) made two great tours. On the first, which lasted eighteen months, he took a Hofmeister, two gentlemen-in-waiting, a secretary, a chaplain, a doctor, a treasurer, two pages, a Kammerdiener and lackey, a cook and two other servants. It cost 6500 Thaler.[2]

Naturally an education like this served to deepen the gulf between the lesser aristocracy and the middle class by the stress it laid on the court as the model in all things and a career at court as the goal of all ambition. It was quite openly a 'class-conscious' education, not even modified, as in the English public schools, by friendships between young men of birth and the richer bourgeoisie. Dr Moore noted

[1] See e.g. Biedermann, II, i, 79.

[2] Vehse, vol. 29.

in 1779 the deference paid to boys of rank in the schools of all the countries of Europe, except England, and considered the English public schools 'peculiarly useful to boys of high rank and fortune', because they avoided this 'mean partiality'. In the sixteenth century nobles and bourgeois had attended the same schools, where there were good schools available, the grammar school in a town, for instance, and the 'Fürstenschulen', the new state boarding-schools, in the country. But with the intensification of class distinctions it became usual to educate boys of good birth privately until about the age of eighteen, when many of them (though not, as we have seen, those of the highest rank) would go to the university with a tutor. It was absurd, they said now, to send members of the ruling class to 'scholastic monasteries' to learn Latin and mingle with boors, but they were often sent, especially if destined for the army, to special 'Ritterakademien' reserved for the nobility, small boarding-schools with a score or two of pupils. A few of these had been founded by princes in the sixteenth century,[1] but most had sprung up with the demand for a 'gentleman's education' after the Thirty Years' War.[2] The usual curriculum has been outlined above. These schools were almost all in court towns and provided their pupils with opportunities of mixing in court society and using the prince's stables. Otherwise they seem to have been expensive and inefficient institutions in the eighteenth century, their pupils being too ill-prepared and too proud to learn. By the middle of the century, it may

[1] E.g. the Academy at Selz (Palatinate), 1577, followed by the 'Collegium Illustre', Tübingen, one at Mömpelgard, and the 'Court School' of Moritz von Hessen at Cassel.

[2] In the seventeenth century: Lüneburg, Vienna, Wolfenbüttel, Brandenburg, Berlin, Kolberg, Erlangen. In the eighteenth: Hildburghausen, Kloster Ettal (Bavaria), Liegnitz, Brunswick and a second in Vienna, the 'Collegium Theresianum'. The 'Karlsschule' of Karl Eugen of Württemberg, founded in 1778, may be regarded as the last of these foundations, but it was already more on the lines of a university. See Paulsen, *Gel. Unterricht*, I, 501 ff., and Steinhausen, *Kulturgeschichte*, p. 495.

be noted, the distrust of schools had spread to the better bourgeoisie. It is in this way that Goethe, in *Dichtung und Wahrheit*, explains why he was educated privately.

In their educational ideals, as in so many other things, the nobility were influenced by the Italian Renaissance, modified by Spanish and French currents of thought. The ideal courtier sketched in Castiglione's *Cortegiano* (1528) was brought down to earth and made a little more middle-class by the court of Louis XIV, and more frivolous and 'arriviste' by the Regency. The proper study of mankind was how to please the great. This is almost the whole theme of the many books on 'Lebensklugheit' (ultimately derived from Gracian) that sold so freely in eighteenth-century Germany. The last one of note, Knigge's *Umgang mit Menschen* (1788), strives valiantly but in vain to introduce a note of middle-class independence. Gottsched, in his manuals, like most scholars until the second half of the century, is still frankly servile. One of his reasons for keeping noblemen out of comedy, for instance, is that it is not fitting to display the great as ridiculous.

It seems impossible to avoid the conclusion that the life of the German aristocracy, considered as a whole, was intellectually and morally at a low ebb in the eighteenth century. Yet the picture must not be made too black, and we must not assume too easily that every cultural feature of which we now approve came from the bourgeoisie. The fact remains that the German classics, Goethe in particular, not only found generous patrons at court, but were profoundly affected in their outlook on life by the court atmosphere. They found something so valuable in the essence of aristocracy based on inherited privilege, however many defects the existing aristocracy might have, that in spite of radical beginnings they desired no imitation in Germany of the French Revolution, and showed themselves in their mature outlook decidedly conservative. We can hardly believe that Goethe would have written with such warmth of the ennobling influence of a court as he did in *Tasso* if his own experience suggested the opposite. *Tasso* then might be cited as evidence in favour of the courts and of the claim of the aristocracy to privileges as guardians of a precious standard, of what Korff calls 'the perfection of courtesy', a necessary corrective to excessive individualism. The spirit of 'noblesse oblige' which is taken for granted in everyone here, and expressed in cultured conversation, perfect manners and social tact, that instinctive deference paid by the individual to the feeling of the group, that moral sensitiveness, on which an action out of keeping with the inherited code jars like a false note—this is the fruit of a long tradition, of which Goethe must have found at least traces in Weimar, in Gräfin von Werthern perhaps, the model for the Countess in *Wilhelm Meister* in her grace and charm, and above all in Frau von Stein. The instinctive feeling for decorum which Goethe praises in Frau von Stein was not an individual quality, but one which she shared with the best type of great lady. Where Goethe probably goes beyond his model, and creates a new ideal of society, Korff thinks—and this view is confirmed by a study of the letters and memoirs of the time —is in giving the society so strictly bound by convention the appearance of perfect freedom, in making 'feinste Gesittung' second nature for its members. One's impression is that it was usually, in Germany and, as may be seen from Lord Chesterfield's *Letters to his Son*, in England too, a very much more external affair, not a convention freely and joyfully accepted but one enforced by social conservatism and above all by a snobbish exclusiveness, of which there is no hint in *Tasso*. Goethe was consciously aiming, as in *Wilhelm Meister*, at the imaginative creation of an ideal aristocracy of mind and heart, for which the old aristocracy of birth could only furnish hints.

Chapter II

COURTS AND COURTIERS

Having considered the position of the German nobility in a general way, we may now look at the way of life of each of the two great categories, court and country nobility, separately. About the life of the eighteenth-century courts whole libraries have been written, and in this outline only a few bare details can be touched upon. A great deal of what has been written recently about this matter is neither true nor edifying, being worked up from the more scandalous memoirs of the time, which are about as reliable, it would seem, as the society news in our modern cheap newspapers. These books are almost wholly concerned with the pleasures of court life. Although pleasures were taken very seriously, there was, as we have seen, another side to the life of princes and their following. They did still perform certain useful functions in society, though not enough to justify their privileged existence. We turn now to their more decorative aspect.

The 'court' meant the ruling family and its immediate entourage, all those, let us say, who were regularly invited to official receptions. They would include, in larger states, some representatives of foreign powers, and in all alike the nobility, with holders of court or government offices and their families, and all those aristocratic families from the country or from other states who had chosen to take up their residence in the capital. For foreigners the rules were often relaxed, but in general much more stress was laid on rank as a prerequisite for the *entrée* to good society in Germany than in France or England, where men of letters at least enjoyed high standing, though here too it was a precarious one if not backed by good birth and powerful connections.

Madame de Staël's impression was that in Germany it was only the court that counted as good society, and that one could only enter it with letters of nobility. Two famous examples may be given in support of her statement. Charlotte Schiller, though herself of good birth, was not invited to court functions in Weimar until her husband had been ennobled, and long before this, elaborate management had been necessary before Goethe, the author of *Götz* and *Werther* and a close personal friend of the duke of Weimar, could be allowed to play cards with the young duchess, who took the rules of etiquette seriously. He had to create a precedent for this high privilege by first playing whist with the duke and duchess of Meiningen, a still smaller state, where manners were easier. Then, one evening when Herr von Stein was playing cards with the Duchess Luise, Stein, by arrangement, was suddenly called away and Goethe asked in to take his place. The dowager duchess, it is true, was far less stiffly ceremonious and regularly invited the literary men to dine with her. It can be understood, however, how indignant the old-fashioned courtiers were when Goethe, an upstart bourgeois, was made a Geheimer Legationsrat. It was for his own comfort that it was necessary to have a title of nobility conferred on him.[1]

The court officers, paid and unpaid, were quite numerous even in small courts. Taking Weimar again as a convenient example, we find that in 1806 the ducal household consisted of four groups of people, those in attendance on the duke, the duchess, the crown prince and the dowager duchess respectively. The court proper included a Hofmarschall, thirteen gentlemen-in-waiting, fifteen gentlemen of junior rank (Kammer-, Hof- and Jagdjunker), five pages and ten teachers for them (!), an equerry with two assistants and some fifty underlings, four valets, one chief huntsman, twenty-eight lackeys, two heiducks, two running footmen (Laufer) and two negroes. Thirty-six musicians were attached

[1] Vehse, XXVIII, 107; Karl v. Lyncker, *Am Weimarischen Hofe*.

to the court. The duchess had her Oberhofmeisterin and three ladies-in-waiting. The crown prince and princess had an Oberhofmeister (Herr von Wolzogen, Schiller's brother-in-law) and Oberhofmeisterin, one gentleman and three ladies-in-waiting. The dowager duchess finally had an Oberhofmeister (Herr von Einsiedel) and two ladies-in-waiting (Fräulein von Göchhausen and another).[1] These were the court offices, as distinguished from government and army.

The majority of these offices, though not all, were paid, and they involved perquisites which were a great source of expense to the duke. They are surprisingly numerous when one considers how simple and 'bürgerlich' so many features of life at this court were. The best reminder of this is the charming sketch by Kraus of an evening with Anna Amalie, where we see the dowager duchess and her three attendants sitting with half a dozen guests at a plain square table littered with paint-boxes and sketch-books. The ladies are painting or embroidering, Goethe seems to be reading aloud to the party, and the painter Heinrich Meyer has evidently been showing them prints. The other guests are Herder and a retired English merchant, Mr Gore, with his two daughters.[2] At the official concerts of the Duchess Luise, on the other hand, there was a good deal of ceremony,[3] and she was far more representative of the usual tone in German courts than her mother-in-law. Though entertaining was on a modest scale, even Weimar needed a kitchen staff of twenty-two. Only one or two people dined with the duke every day, but there was a large 'Marschallstafel' to be maintained for the court staff. In some courts of moderate size, dozens of people had the privilege of dining regularly at court—at Cassel, as we saw, some sixty persons dined with the Landgraf every day. At Munich, von Lang tells us, there was not only a large daily company, but vast quantities of food and drink were taken from the court kitchens to persons outside who

[1] Vehse, XXVIII, 308 f. [2] See frontispiece.

[3] Kar. Jagemann, *Erinnerungen*, p. 93.

made claim to this bounty. This was quite in the old tradition of the courts. The ruler's purse was looked upon as bottomless; if he was the father of his people, he was still more the father of his court, and it was his duty to provide generously for his own. In the older records we find quite astonishing figures. At Brandenburg in 1537, for instance, a decree had to be made that not more than four hundred persons should be fed at court. There were four grades of dinner in the common hall, for noblemen, councillors, clerks, servants. It was as noisy as an inn and the Marschall had all his work cut out to maintain order. In addition to these there were numerous 'Abspeiser' who took food out. The sentry at the gate was more necessary for preventing misuse of this privilege than for keeping out intruders. Vast quantities of beer and wine were regularly allowed to the residents at breakfast, dinner, supper and as a night-cap, some two litres of beer a head for instance at Küstrin.[1] It can be understood that any departure from the customs of the good old days was fiercely resisted and that much survived even in the eighteenth century. It must be remembered of course that the court treasury received vast quantities of consumables from court estates and as dues paid in kind.

The Weimar list of court officers looks very modest when compared with that of other small states, let alone the greater or more extravagant ones, such as Saxony in its palmy days. At the neighbouring court of Gotha for instance in 1767 there were the following higher offices: Oberkammerherr, Oberhofmarschall, Hausmarschall, Hofmarschall, Oberschenk, Oberstallmeister, Stallmeister, Oberlandjägermeister and Landjägermeister, in addition to the duchess's Oberhofmeisterin and an Oberhofmeister for the prince.[2] Even Ernst II, in the following reign (1772–1804), after severe economies, needed seventeen Kammerherren and eleven

[1] Kurt Trensch von Buttler: 'Das tägliche Leben an den deutschen Fürstenhöfen des 16ten Jahrhunderts' in *Zeitschrift für Kulturgeschichte*, 1897, an article based on old 'Hofordnungen'. [2] Vehse, vol. XXIX.

Kammerjunker, as well as a Directeur and a Sousdirecteur des plaisirs. As an example of an extremely elaborate court we may take Saxony under Augustus the Strong and his successor. In the order of precedence drawn up in 1716, ninety grades of rank at court were distinguished. In the Saxon State Calendar for 1733 (says Vehse) the list of court offices (Hofétat) takes up fifty-three pages. There was an Oberhofmarschall and ten other 'Obers' (Kammerherr, Stallmeister, Schenk, Küchenmeister, Jägermeister, Hofmeister der Königin, Falkenier, Kämmerer and Generalpostmeister). Then came eighty Kammerjunker, twenty pages (with a tutor and six teachers), a French choir of twenty with a French composer, André, in charge (at a salary of 1300 Thalers), a musical staff of forty-eight led by Hasse (at 6000 Thalers), a separate Polish orchestra of seventeen, a ballet of sixty persons, all French, a court company of eleven (French?) actors and sixteen actresses. The lower servants included about eighty lackeys, the staff of sixteen palaces and sixteen cooks.

This does not represent anything like all that had to be paid for by the Kurfürst's subjects, for his ministers had households of their own like princes' courts. They were in fact, so long as they remained in favour, 'more truly lords of the land than the king himself', as a contemporary tells us. With a recommendation from one of them or some other favourite one could obtain money, offices, estates, or almost anything. It goes without saying that they provided well for themselves. Graf Flemming, for instance, Generalfeldmarschall under Augustus the Strong, the soldier and diplomat who secured for his master the throne of Poland, at first an obscure Pomeranian count, had, according to a description of his 'Hofhaltung' made in 1722,[1] about a hundred domestics

[1] K. Biedermann, 'Aus der Glanzzeit des sächsisch-polnischen Hofes', in *Zeitschrift für deutsche Kulturgeschichte*, Neue Folge, I, 1891. Title and salary of every servant are given, together with much precise information about the household equipment.

of different grades. There were twenty-three 'superiores', from an Oberhofmeister, secretaries and tutors down to an equerry responsible for ninety-two horses; and over seventy 'inferiores', from the five pages and a 'Polish gentleman' who played the Bandor and waited at table, the eight musicians and their Italian leader, through various skilled tradesmen and lackeys to the chambermaids and kitchen-maids. The count's salaries and wages bill came to 13,534 Thalers a year (nominally 40,000 M., but in pre-war values at least three times that amount, so about £6000). The appointments of the count's palaces were correspondingly magnificent; he lived on a scale that would make the life of a Hollywood millionaire look tawdry. He could, and did on occasion, entertain a hundred and ninety people to dinner without requiring to borrow any table ware; for state occasions only silver, silver-gilt or fine porcelain services would be used.

It will be understood that the standard of elegance in Dresden was high. Several other notables would rival Flemming in display and the other noblemen would ruin themselves in trying to do the same. Later, under Augustus III, we hear similar tales about Graf Brühl, who was particularly famous for the magnificence of his wardrobe.

It would be a waste of time to accumulate lists of court offices in Germany, but in discussing Germany as a whole, the infinite variety of conditions there must always be remembered. This makes a description of court life in Germany a very different matter from one of contemporary France or England. A full description could only be wearisome, yet no selection of details can do justice to the complexity of the theme. The only method is to indicate the range of variation in each particular, and we have seen now how great it was in the matter of court staffs. We find a corresponding variety in the activities of the various courts, though again there is a similarity in the ground plans which makes a summary description not impossible. We are not dealing now of course with the court as an instrument of government (this concerned a particular set of officials, who would however partly share the social life of the rest), but with the courtiers as the ruler's social companions and friends. This function of the court soon became largely an end in itself, and an elaborate traditional round established itself, constantly influenced by the examples of foreign courts. It is obvious that the existence of such a large number of courts in close proximity enormously strengthened the prestige of the courtier as a type and gave a special character to German society.

The prince was the sun of the court world; everything that happened there was regulated by his actions. Yet he himself was not quite free, he was bound by long established custom and etiquette, in some courts very completely, in others much less. At the imperial court in Vienna, for instance, the court year and the court day were alike regulated by ancient custom, inherited mainly from Spanish sources. On a certain date the emperor regularly went into residence at Schönbrunn, on another fixed day to Laxenburg, on another he returned to the Hofburg. The order of procedure on saints' days and at recurring festivities (such as birthdays), at banquets and receptions, and to a slighter extent, the activities of an ordinary day were all governed by time-honoured custom, just as much as the election and coronation ceremonies. One can well understand that much of this had to be so. Ceremonial functions at the imperial court would have been meaningless if they had not been dignified, and dignity and improvisation are incompatible with one another. On such days the consciousness of continuity with the past and future had to be awakened. For more ordinary occasions, the established routine served a useful function by making thought and new decisions unnecessary. It was as salutary as habit, the 'flywheel of society', is in everyday life. It was particularly necessary for a society that was freer than most from the imperious demands of material conditions. The farmer is bound by the weather and the seasons; he must, if he is to live, do certain things at certain times, and so it is in varying degrees with all engaged in useful work. Experience seems to teach that a society which does not need to work has to invent for itself artificial restraints to replace the pull of external necessity. The ceremonial, even of the imperial court, was probably not felt as a cramping influence but as a welcome support, though custom, like law, could become tyrannical here as everywhere. That the strict rules of etiquette could, however, be relaxed on occasion for strangers is indicated in a letter written by David Hume from Vienna in 1748. The rather corpulent philosopher, in a uniform which he was said to wear as awkwardly as a grocer of the trained-bands, accompanied General St Clair to court and was introduced to the empress dowager.

'You must know', he says, 'that you neither bow nor kneel to emperors and empresses, but curtsy, so that after we had had a little conversation with her Imperial Majesty, we were to walk backwards, through a very long room, curtsying all the way, and there was very great danger of our falling foul of each other, as well as of tumbling topsy-turvy. She saw the difficulty we were in, and immediately called to us: Allez, allez, messieurs, sans cérémonie. Vous n'êtes pas accoutumés à ce mouvement et le plancher est glissant. We esteemed ourselves very much obliged to her for this attention, especially my companions, who were desperately afraid of my falling on them and crushing them.'

The various courts were bound by custom in different degrees, but in all there was some norm, the chief features of which were usually laid down in black and white in a 'Hofordnung'. One important matter that had to be dealt with in such a document was the order of precedence—we saw how elaborate this was in Dresden, with its ninety grades. It was a very important matter everywhere, as foreigners like Lady Mary Wortley Montagu discovered. Freytag's essay on the serio-comic 'War of Wasungen', mentioned earlier, shows how far disputes about precedence could go.

The Hofordnungen also defined the duties and privileges of important court officers and the customary rights of all grades, and laid down rules for the conduct of the court, particularly the immediate household, in the interests of order and dignity. But there was much of course that was governed by unwritten laws.

Regulation and custom lightened the burden of the prince and court officials, but if they took their duties seriously many of them still had plenty to do. The greater number of the residents at courts however had no serious functions. Their duty was pleasure, and their enemy ennui. We have glanced at the day's activities of a few ruling princes above. It may be of interest to describe the activities of the court now more systematically. The great outdoor amusement for men was hunting, especially at the smaller courts in wild country. Innumerable stories are told of the extravagance and excesses of German princes in pursuance of their favourite sport. 'Treibjagden' called for the services of hundreds of beaters, usually peasants for whom this work was part of their 'Frondienst'. Crops were trodden down in 'Parforcejagden', and game was so jealously protected that the crops and poultry yards were always in danger. Great sums were spent on horses and equipment. From the point of view of the outsider it was all very wasteful and cruel. Protests were naturally not lacking in the humanitarian age. One outspoken one is L. F. G. von Göckingk's poem *Die Parforcejagd*, written about 1771, a description of a stag-hunt in verse dialogue, in which the physical pain of man and beast and the indifference of court circles to the sufferings their pleasures cause to others is expressed in lines such as the following:

Ein Bauer

Jesus Maria! Was ist das?
Ach weh! mein schön Getreide,
Und meiner Wiese langes Gras!
Da seht mir nun mal beide!

Wer gibt für mich nun Martinshahn,
Zinskorn und Steuer? Keiner!
Der gnäd'ge Fürst hat das getan?
Ach Gott! erbarm dich meiner!

Ein Reitknecht

Hundsfött'scher Bauer, halt das Maul!
Um solchen Quark solch Lärmen anzufangen?
Ihr Lumpenpack seid so so faul:
Wär' ich der Fürst: ich liess euch alle hangen![1]

But the hunting man himself had a different point of view. His unbounded delight was shared by the large staffs of keepers and foresters. Rude energy found an outlet here that had formerly often spent itself in feuds and faction fights, and the health and pleasure it gave were positive goods to be set off against the damage that was done to others. A hunting prince, like a hunting squire in England, was not the worst type of man and ruler. We have seen how Karl August, for instance, was led in his hunting expeditions into every corner of his lands and given a direct acquaintance with the life of his people, and though hunting rights were a jealously guarded privilege of the aristocracy, the enthusiasts had some reason on their side when they claimed that hunting helped to maintain something of the primitive unity of the folk, and to prevent pampered courtiers from losing touch with the roots of things.

Hunting was not usually considered in those days a fit sport for German ladies, though one hears of some Dianas, and ladies might be asked to pig-sticking displays. Their open-air pleasures were drives and walks, usually by prescribed routes and in full dress, and undertaken in the bigger towns rather with a view to meeting other people than to enjoying the charms of nature. Every court town had its promenade, and extensive gardens, at first exclusively formal gardens in the manner of Versailles, an extension of baroque architecture

[1] Reprinted in *Deutsche Literatur*, Reihe Politische Dichtung, Band 1, 1930.

into the landscape, extravagantly adorned with artificial fountains, waterfalls, orangeries, and later, with the spread of the fashion of the picturesque from England, 'English parks' with carefully planned prospects, of little hills, woods and rivulets, curving lawns and artificial ruins. Almost the only outdoor game we hear of, except some winter sports, is the 'jeu de paume'. Winter sports, however, were very popular. In the long continental winters sledging was a great delight. The court would sally forth to the tinkling of bells in a long procession of sledges carved and painted to resemble peacocks, dragons, swans, fish, each holding two or three ladies and driven by a cavalier.[1] In Vienna they would even cart hundreds of loads of snow into the town to make this amusement possible.[2] In some places (Weimar for instance) skating became all the rage and gay parties and masquerades were held on the ice, but the delights of skiing remained to be discovered.

But one does not think of German court life as mainly lived out of doors. So much more is heard in that age of the theatre and opera, of card parties, concerts, balls and redoubts. The chief resource of the courtier in his idle hours, which were many, was cards. If the imperial court drove out in sledges to Schönbrunn, they played cards there before returning. Even in summer the goal of their drives would often be a quiet country retreat where card tables had been set out for the court in tents and arbours. There were few games that were not played for money, and gambling was one of the vices most commonly laid to the charge of courtiers as a class.

Almost every day, in the season, there would be organised entertainments held at the prince's expense. Amongst these the opera and the drama took the first place, and they were as lavishly supported in all courts as the prince's resources would permit. It had long been customary to invite foreign

[1] See for instance Göckingk's charming poem, *Als der erste Schnee fiel*.
[2] Wraxall, *Memoirs of the Court of Berlin*, etc. I, 316.

troupes of players to German courts. There had been Italian comedians at various courts in the sixteenth century, even before the English players first began to tour the Continent in 1586. The Thirty Years' War had interrupted these visits, but soon after it was over there were French and Italian troupes to be found again at the courts of the Tirol, Bavaria, Saxony, Austria and elsewhere. From the middle of the seventeenth century opera, already well established in Italy and France, found a footing in the German courts too, some of which soon began to maintain permanent Italian companies of their own and to build theatres to house them. The first specially built theatre in Germany was the Ottonium put up by Landgraf Moritz von Hessen at Cassel in 1605. It was followed by many others, especially in the second half of the century, after the war, each bigger and more luxurious than the last. The most spacious of all in the eighteenth century was the Ludwigsburg theatre built in 1750, which had a stage across which squadrons of cavalry could gallop, and was so arranged on the bank of a lake that elaborate nautical spectacles could be displayed.[1]

In Germany, as in France and England at an earlier date, there was a period when the courts were the sole support of opera and almost the only support of the spoken drama. It

[1] For details see e.g. Nestriepke, *Das Theater im Wandel der Zeiten*, Berlin, 1928, and *Deutsche Literatur*, Barockdrama Band v, Die Oper, ed. W. Flemming, Leipzig, 1933. Amongst the earliest court theatres are, in the seventeenth century: Vienna (Hofburg), 1626, Innsbruck (2, *c.* 1650), Munich, 1657, Vienna (opera), 1666, Dresden (opera, 1667, holding 2000 people), Brunswick (1691, opera for 2500). Hanover followed in the early eighteenth century (described by Lady Montagu, 1716), Berlin in 1741, and additional theatres were built in Dresden and Vienna. Almost all the smaller courts gradually followed suit. The courts were imitated by Augsburg (1630 and 1665), Ulm (1641), Nürnberg (1667), Hamburg (1678), Leipzig (1693), the *city* of Vienna (1708). Frankfort-on-Main did not possess a theatre till 1782, though a concert hall had been used as a theatre since 1756. Before that time travelling troupes coming to Frankfort put up their own temporary wooden building, as they had to do in most towns.

was the ambition of every court to have an Italian opera and a French comedy of its own, an ambition seldom realised, it is true, for lack of means, but the German courts were slower than the French or English in encouraging a native drama and opera. Their influence was more beneficial on the technical side of stage production than on the drama as literature. The revival of the literary German drama in the Sturm und Drang and the classical period owed very little to the courts directly. The smaller courts sometimes accepted the services of German players when a French troupe was beyond their means or not easily available, but it was with the same air of condescension to the second-best that is displayed by the count and countess in *Wilhelm Meister* when they engage the German actors to entertain an illustrious visitor. The half dozen German touring companies that existed in the first half of the eighteenth century would all occasionally play in court towns, but they were seldom engaged for a long stay. It is only in the third quarter of the century that we hear of German troupes enjoying the patronage of courts for longer periods (Schönemann in Mecklenburg-Schwerin, Döbbelin, Koch and Seyler in Weimar). Gotha was the first court to have a regular court theatre for German plays directed by a court official. The experiment did not last long there (1774–7) but Gotha was imitated in turn by Vienna, Mannheim (under Dalberg, Schiller's first patron), Munich (for German and French plays), Berlin (from 1786, with Iffland in control from 1796), Weimar (from 1791 under Goethe), and by the courts of Cassel, Mainz and Stuttgart. The first of these 'national' theatres (i.e. German repertory theatres) had been the one founded at Hamburg in 1767, the history of which can be followed in Lessing's *Hamburgische Dramaturgie*. Hamburg, the greatest commercial centre in Germany, could not support its repertory theatre for more than a couple of years. Similarly Frankfort-on-Main, a little later, was glad to share a troupe with the Elector of Mainz. It was only the courts that were willing to spend money on these unprofitable enterprises.

The courts then kept alive a taste for acted drama at a time when other classes had lost interest in it, providing models later for private enterprise in the towns, and they accustomed people to the idea that good drama (like opera, and music generally) ought not to have to depend on box-office receipts. They thus prepared the way for those German state and municipal theatres of to-day which are the envy of other countries. In the eighteenth century, there was perhaps too much decentralisation. Material resources and the available talent were too widely scattered to produce notable results, but on the other hand there was a spirit of rivalry that maintained standards, here and there (as in Weimar) a man of genius was given free scope, and a far larger proportion of the people were educated to the more expensive forms of art than in England. The general public was usually admitted to performances at court theatres, though they had to pay for their seats (the court usually did not) and be quiet and unobtrusive. The court theatres had an atmosphere of their own, far from democratic, but none the worse artistically for that, if the taste of the élite was good. At Cassel, Dr Moore says, the front gallery, with a convenient room behind, was reserved for the court. When the prince or princess stood up, between acts or during the performance, all the audience, pit, box and gallery, did so too. Elsewhere we read that if the ruler was present no one might applaud before him, and even in Weimar Goethe would stand up and shout 'Do not laugh' if the audience did not take a poor tragedy (like Schlegel's *Alarcos*) as it was meant, and they would accept the reproof with perfect good humour.[1]

Opera owed everything to court encouragement, as in Italy and in France. It was a form of entertainment that went admirably with baroque palaces and despotic government,

[1] For an interesting impression of the Weimar court theatre see *Crabb Robinson in Germany*, pp. 100 f.

for it expressed better than any other the love of power and magnificence that filled its patrons, and their exclusive claim to culture. Nothing could have been less 'of the people'. It was a great temptation for extravagant princes. In Vienna, Dresden, Munich, Ludwigsburg and many other capitals vast sums were spent on it, especially on spectacular staging, for spectacle was of the essence of opera as then conceived, and it was for opera that all the tricks of the producer were devised. Lady Mary Wortley Montagu writes from Vienna, describing an opera performed on a Sunday in the garden of the Favourite:

> Nothing of that kind ever was more magnificent; and I can easily believe what I am told, that the decoration and habits cost the emperor thirty thousand pounds sterling. The stage was built over a very large canal, and, at the beginning of the second act, divided into two parts, discovering the water, on which there immediately came, from different parts, two fleets of little gilded vessels, that gave the representation of a naval fight....The story of the opera is the Enchantments of Alcina, which gives opportunity for a great variety of machines, and changes of the scene, which are performed with a surprising swiftness. The theatre is so large, that it is hard to carry the eye to the end of it; and the habits in the utmost magnificence, to the number of one hundred and eight.

The only drawback was the cold. Later, as we have seen, covered opera houses were built with stages almost as large, and they too sometimes made good use, as at Ludwigsburg, of the natural landscape behind. The spectacles of the naturalistic stage and the modern music-hall, with their 'real' waterfalls and living animals, or, on a higher plane, the crowd effects at Oberammergau and the enchanting view of the hills through the central stage—all these things were anticipated in the operas of that time and were no doubt more important for most of the audience than the music. One is reminded in this connection of the remark of an English traveller to Germany in the eighteenth century, made about the Heidelberg tun, that 'what the Germans seem chiefly to aim at in their undertakings is the surprising or the prodigious'.[1]

It goes without saying that what the poor courts could offer was only an inferior imitation of all this splendour. Even in the big courts there was little opera outside the carnival season. If the smaller courts could support a professional theatre or opera at all they usually had to combine the two in an unsatisfactory way, using many of the actors as opera-singers. This was so in Weimar under Goethe's management. It was in such conditions that the 'Singspiel', the forerunner of the Operetta, became a popular genre, with its combination of spoken dialogue with songs and instrumental accompaniments. From the memoirs of Karoline Jagemann, the Weimar court singer and actress, one learns with mingled amusement and admiration how limited the resources of the Weimar court theatre were in Goethe's day. In *The Magic Flute* the Genies were three seminarists, awkward country boys in brick-red tights several sizes too large, and soiled tunics not long enough to hide their muddy boots. They wore clumsy rose wreaths round their unruly hair and their cheeks were painted as red as Easter eggs. In the same performance the Queen of Night, being unfit to appear in public, sang her aria from the wings while a substitute performed her actions on the stage. Stage knights were content with cardboard helmets and armour, and the velveteen coronation mantle of the Jungfrau von Orleans, obtained after difficult negotiations, served for many years as the state robe for stage princes or princesses of any time or country.[2]

Though instrumental music and singing naturally benefited enormously through the patronage of the courts, conditions were far from ideal for the great composers whom Germany

[1] The anonymous *Introduction to the Knowledge of Germany*, London, 1789, p. 184.

[2] Karoline Jagemann, *Erinnerungen*, 1926, p. 90; Nestriepke, *op. cit.* p. 352.

now produced, as a study of the life of J. S. Bach, Mozart or Beethoven teaches us. We feel it was an ignoble thing for men of genius to be dependent on such crotchety, tyrannical private patrons, but dependence on the general public can hardly be said to have proved better. The courts provided great artists with the indispensable instruments for their training and development. What Mozart learned by his stay in Mannheim almost justifies in itself the huge sums (200,000 Gulden a year or more) that Karl Theodor spent on his opera and theatres. In providing for the fashionable pleasures of the moment the princes were indirectly enriching the world's permanent treasures of art. Even quite small courts engaged a permanent Kammermusiker or two, and any virtuosos who happened to pass through on their tours, to supplement the performances of talented amateurs in the regular concerts which every court expected.

In the second half of the century a perfect craze for amateur theatricals spread from the French to the German courts and all of them soon had their 'théâtres d'occasion', usually for French plays, but occasionally, as in Weimar, for German, though in Weimar too French plays were more popular with the majority of courtiers proper.[1] It was only a step to acting from the masquerades that had been popular since the Renaissance. One elaborate kind of masquerade called a 'Wirtschaft', a kind of picnic in costume, or pastoral in action, centred round an acted scene, written in verse by the court poet. The notables dressed up as peasants at a village wake or wedding, as shepherds, fishermen, millers, gamekeepers, waggoners, knife-grinders and all kinds of characters 'of the people'. It was found delightful (though expensive for the cavaliers, who, in Vienna at least, had to provide costumes for their partners) to escape from ceremony and etiquette by such a change of costume. In Bavaria the courtiers in costume would drive in from Nymphenburg and be received at the Residenz in Munich by the Kurfürst

[1] See v. Lyncker for contemporary descriptions of these plays.

and Kurfürstin dressed as village innkeepers (whence the name 'Wirtschaft'). The Georgensaal would be turned into an inn, at the sign of the 'Bavarian Lion', and provided with rough tables, painted chairs, and earthenware beer mugs and plates.

Even Goethe at Weimar did not escape the duties of the Renaissance court poet. He provided original plays and adaptations for amateur performances, some of them rapid improvisations, some the product, in whole or in part, of his best powers. The first version of *Iphigenie* itself was written for a court entertainment, in which Goethe took the part of Orestes. The 'Singspiele' and 'Maskenzüge' are lighter works of the same nature, uneven but full of delightful details, and in his old age Goethe made supreme poetic use of the Masquerade in the second part of *Faust*. All this work would have been inconceivable without the court background. It gives us a vivid idea of what this festive poetry and poetic festivity could be at their best.

Receptions, banquets and balls were the standing form of entertainment apart from plays, operas and concerts. At ordinary receptions cards were played and the ladies often brought their 'work'. Fashions in ladies' work were led by the French court. Under the Regency, it was cutting out scraps for screens and candle-shades; towards the middle of the century 'les nœuds', netting, came into fashion, and from about 1770 the ladies kept their hands busy with 'parfilage', the unravelling of gold braid. That their tongues were not idle is suggested in the neat verses sent by Mme du Deffand to a friend:

Vive le parfilage!
Plus de plaisir sans lui!
Cet important ouvrage
Chasse partout l'ennui.
Tandis que l'on déchire
Et galons et rubans
L'on peut encore médire
Et déchirer les gens.

In Germany the more bourgeois sewing and knitting were not despised, either at court or at the assemblies which the gentry arranged among themselves. An assembly held in Hanover in 1769 is described by J. G. Zimmermann as follows:

Last Friday I was at one of these gatherings, one in which about eighty people meet every week, and to which my wife and I have a standing invitation. The company assembles in four fine long rooms that form a suite and are lighted by some hundreds of wax candles. Of these eighty people thirty or forty will play cards. Of the rest some sit and work at their 'entoilage' or 'réseau' while others of us entertain them with our conversation, or they walk hand in hand and arm in arm from sofa to sofa and room to room. At the end of this suite of rooms there is an anteroom where musicians are usually playing. Both ladies and gentlemen are attired in all their finery, the ladies in satin dresses, deeply décolleté and richly trimmed with 'blondes' and lace, and with shawls of Flemish lace over their shoulders. They all wear diamond hair ornaments, earrings and necklaces, their coiffure is in the latest Parisian fashion, their gowns are imitations of the latest models from Paris. Not a word of any language but French is spoken. You flirt and rally and kiss all à la Française.[1]

Dancing was never more important as a social accomplishment than in the eighteenth century, and balls of every degree of magnificence and formality were frequent in all court towns. The usual German ball from the 70's onwards (like the one in *Werther*, 1774, or Mozart's *Don Juan*, 1787) included three types of dance, one French and stately, like the minuet, pavane, coranto or quadrille, one English and less formal, the 'country dances' in which couples arranged themselves face to face in two long lines (whence the name 'contredanse'), and one German and still more individualistic and intimate, consisting almost entirely of waltzing. Even dance programmes mirrored the influence of country on

[1] Quoted by E. Buchner, *Anno Dazumal*, II, p. 81. 'Entoilage' is the cutting and mounting of scraps, 'réseau' or 'filet the making of a net-like lace.

country and class on class, for the minuet was essentially of the court, while the waltz had descended from a vigorous peasant's 'Ländler' and only gradually made its way into good society. When Goethe was in Strassburg he found he must learn to waltz; he makes Werther and Lotte 'revolve round each other like the spheres', but they are the only couple in the party who can waltz well. It was many years before the waltz displaced the older stately dances, especially at court, where it was at first considered vulgar and rather shocking. The queen of Prussia averted her eyes when it was danced at a Berlin court ball for the first time (in 1794) and the young duke of Devonshire, when he saw English girls dance it, vowed he would never marry a girl who waltzed, though he had been charmed with it on the Continent. A similar remark had been put into the mouth of Werther thirty years before. 'Redoubts' were in great favour. At these masks were worn, with either 'dominos' or fancy dress. In many court towns, especially in the Catholic south and west at carnival time, the young people of good society formed exclusive dancing clubs to supplement the regular balls.

Not the least among court entertainments were the pleasures of the table. German cooking had not a good reputation with foreigners (Lord Chesterfield calls it 'execrable') but every effort was made in high circles to temper its grossness with French art. In smaller towns it was abundance that was aimed at rather than subtlety. In Treves, for instance, at big dinners 'the dishes were heaped so full of meat and game that the tables were near to sinking; often ten large fowls, three roast geese, or two huge turkeys in one dish'.[1] Everywhere it was usual to serve several dishes at each course, as much as would suffice now for half-a-dozen meals. To offer 'not more than six dishes' to nobility was a gross insult (see Grossmann's play of 1777, *Nicht mehr als sechs Schüsseln*). The middle-class Viennese, we are told,

[1] Graf Boos von Waldeck, quoted Buchner, I, p. 366.

offered ten or twelve, and at a banquet twenty-four were expected. It was like Schlaraffenland.

In the matter of drink too the Germans had an unenviable reputation. Even in 1789 the writer of the *Introduction to the Knowledge of Germany*[1] says that in some courts a visitor 'is initiated and purchases in a manner his freedom by submitting to drink till he has lost the use of his reason'. This was especially the case now, he added, in ecclesiastical courts, where gallantry was taboo. The account that Baron von Pöllnitz gives of the heavy drinking at Würzburg, Fulda and other ecclesiastical courts is borne out by many other descriptions. In Würzburg Pöllnitz could not avoid being drunk twice a day, so numerous and well-honoured were the toasts.[2] Every contemporary would understand why in Goethe's *Götz* the Bishop of Bamberg and the Abbot of Fulda when we first see them are drinking together after dinner, and why Liebetraut is made to speak of 'Das Weinfass von Fulda'.

At the greater courts there were gourmets as well as gourmands. Vast sums were spent on the elaborate preparation and on the elegant serving of banquets, though to judge by all we read the 'prodigious' had a way of creeping in. Lady Mary Wortley Montagu was impressed by the magnificence of the tables of Viennese people of quality. She was more than once 'entertained with fifty dishes of meat, all served in silver, and well dressed; the dessert proportionable, served in the finest china'. She was particularly surprised at the variety and richness of the wines. A wine list was laid on each guest's plate, often to the number of eighteen exquisite varieties. Vienna was already famous for good living. The Berliner Nicolai could not conceal his astonishment at the variety and excellence of the food even in the restaurants. It was in Vienna that à la carte meals first became usual, and for 45 Kreuzer, Nicolai says, one had (in 1781) six courses, with a choice of seven soups, five kinds of

[1] London, 1789, anon. [2] *Mémoires*, I, 224.

fish and other things in proportion, and this on a fast day. There were cafés, always crowded, resplendent with mirrors, hangings and pictures, and Nicolai considers it worthy of mention that in the Kohlmarkt you could buy ices. It will be remembered that Frau Rat Goethe poured away the ices sent down to her children from Count Thoranc's table (in 1759). Food was a more important matter to the Viennese, Nicolai thought, than it was even to the Bavarians, Swabians or Swiss.[1] Vienna was already the 'Phäakenstadt', but so was every court town in a greater or lesser degree, though they could not all be instinct as Vienna was with the spirit of the warm south.

The serving of meals on special occasions was so elaborate that one could almost speak of a new mixed art, comparable with opera, combining the pleasures of the table with those of the concert-room, the sculpture gallery and the theatre. There was nothing new in dining to sweet music, but the art of the court confectioner was quite a new development. The Konditor at a great court had had the training of a sculptor, and it was his function to produce sugar ornaments for the table that would have put into the shade the most elaborate of modern wedding cakes. The 'Dresden china' figures, debased versions of which are to be found on the humblest mantelshelf in England, were at one time used as ornaments for the tables of the great, but earlier still the rococo shepherds, dairy-maids, huntsmen and so on were made by the court confectioner in sugar. There might be a formal garden the length of the table, with a little fountain of perfumed waters in the centre edged with statues, avenues of trim trees, beds of flowers in natural colours and little sugar ladies and gentlemen promenading on the paths. Or a sugar castle might be shown from which in the course of the evening a miniature firework display would be given. The chef often rivalled the confectioner with his surprise pasties, from which a dancer might emerge to delight the company.

[1] Nicolai, *Reisen*, v.

The 'town' in any little Residenz was an extension of the palace. Several of the German capitals in the eighteenth century were creations of the recent past, and it is easy to follow the process by which a whole town grew up to provide for the needs of a court. There is an instructive example in miniature in the memoirs of the court painter and architect Mannlich. A relative of the mistress of his patron the duke of Pfalz-Zweibrücken (Karl II August) owned a farm near Homburg (Pfalz) that she wished to sell. The duke was accordingly persuaded to visit it one day. It was made to look very attractive. The farmer and his family and all their servants were working in their picturesque Sunday clothes, the finest of cattle were brought there for the visit, delicious cream and butter were served and by good fortune the weather was glorious. The court doctor assured the prince that it would be impossible to be ill in such surroundings, and the ladies and gentlemen-in-waiting could not sufficiently praise the view. The duke easily fell a victim. Next day Mannlich was summoned to him. The stables and byres had to be enlarged, a cottage for the farmer and his family had to be built, the rooms needed structural alterations, decoration, and furnishing. An English garden had to be made of the woods, valleys and meadows near the house. In a few weeks the farm had already grown into quite a village, for the crowds of workmen who were needed had been accommodated, with their families, in specially built huts, where you saw their wives washing their linen out of doors and their children playing and dancing. The 'Luisenhof' had become the 'Karlsberg'. At first the duke just drove over every afternoon, but presently he wanted to dine there. This necessitated further alterations—a new kitchen wing, a large dining room. And so the farm grew and grew until the duke was living there permanently. Soon a regular Schloss had been built, with stables for a thousand horses, kennels for a thousand dogs, an enormous riding-school, with quarters for the equerries, grooms, keepers, cooks and servants; an 'orangerie' with rooms for the gentlemen-in-waiting, pages, officers, doctors, chaplains and gardeners; a picture gallery and library, a theatre, a zoological garden, and barracks for 1400 men. Finally a whole town had to be called into being, to accommodate all those whose services were required by the duke and his court. All this happened in about ten years (1777–86). It is said to have cost the duke fourteen million Gulden—the income of the duchy was 800,000! The new town was burnt by the French in 1793 and now dense woods cover the site of it.

It was in a similar way that bigger capitals like Mannheim (1606), Karlsruhe (1715), and Ludwigsburg (1704–33) had been built at the whim of a prince—that is why their streets are laid out in some clearly planned symmetrical pattern, a chessboard or a cartwheel—and the older established capitals, though not so obviously built to order, were similar to the new ones in the make-up of their population. It consisted, besides the court proper, of officials and personal attendants, a garrison, and craftsmen and shopkeepers catering for the wants of all these. If there were any 'manufactures', they were almost always of luxury articles for the court (ribbons, gold braid, lace, various fine stuffs and hangings, silk stockings, hats, snuff and playing cards are the items which recur most frequently in the lists of manufactures in court towns given in Reichard's *Guide des Voyageurs*), or of fine porcelain, some of which would be made to order for foreign patrons and some sold in the open market, after the requirements of the prince, for court use and for presents, had been met. There were such factories for instance in Meissen, Nymphenburg, Berlin, Vienna, Ludwigsburg, Cassel, Ansbach, Gotha and Fulda. Even in Prussia the chief manufacture subsidised by the state, apart from porcelain, was blue cloth primarily intended for soldiers' uniforms, though for a time the citizens of Berlin were forced to wear it too.

The craftsmen of these towns worked mainly to order for the aristocracy. Nicolai contrasts Stuttgart, with its 250 tailors to 18,000 inhabitants, with the Free Town of Ulm, with only 31 to 13,000. In Munich, he says, there were sixteen goldsmiths and seventeen wigmakers, but only fifteen clothmakers. In all these capitals there was a considerable trade in luxuries imported from France and England, for court circles despised German work. Early in the century Lady Mary Wortley Montagu had remarked on the contrast between the free towns of Germany and the capitals.

'In the first', she said, 'there appears an air of commerce and plenty. The streets are well-built, and full of people, neatly and plainly dressed. The shops are loaded with merchandise, and the commonalty clean and cheerful. In the other, a sort of shabby finery, a number of dirty people of quality tawdered out; narrow, nasty streets out of repair, wretchedly thin of inhabitants, and above half of the common sort asking alms. I cannot help fancying one under the figure of a handsome clean Dutch citizen's wife, and the other like a poor town lady of pleasure, painted and ribboned out in her head-dress, with tarnished silver-laced shoes and a ragged under-petticoat, a miserable mixture of vice and poverty.'[1]

Weimar, tiny as it was, was a typical court town in this respect too. In the market-place, in addition to the apothecary's, the proprietor of which also practised as a doctor, there were only two shops. One of them sold fine cloth, velvet, gold and silver braid for ladies' and gentlemen's clothing, and the other, kept by a Frenchman, perfumery and cosmetics. (Until the eighties, as we saw, ladies at court generally rouged very heavily.) There were butchers and bakers, of course, a shoemaker or two, a smith, and all the other tradesmen required, but they would not have shops with goods displayed in a window. They would either use the front room of the house to receive customers, or sell their goods (particularly consumables like bread) at a counter formed of the shutters to the front window, or at special stalls. The butchers had booths arranged side by side under

[1] Letter of Aug. 22nd 1716.

the arcades of the town-hall, and the smith worked under an old gate arch. In Dresden or Vienna there would be dozens of shops, but there would be the same distinction between luxury and everyday goods, a preponderance of the luxury trades, and consequently an increased dependence of the citizens on the patronage of the court.

It is difficult to obtain statistical information about the proportions of the various elements in the population. Some figures quoted by Reichard for Vienna are instructive so far as they go. Out of a total population of about 260,000 (in 1795) there were 3253 members of the aristocracy, 6000 lackeys and 34,000 other servants. In Berlin in 1783, out of a total of 141,000, the garrison with the men's families made up no fewer than 33,000. Officials and families accounted for 14,000, and personal attendants on these and the court another 10,000, so that 57,000 persons, well over a third of the population, were directly dependent on the king.[1] There were only some 10,000 citizens with full rights. Similarly in Dresden in 1791, out of a total of 58,000, about 20,000 were not subject to the jurisdiction of the town but to that of the electoral prince's agent. They included 6621 officials and soldiers. We get an idea of the figures in small capitals from the very careful statistics compiled by Roller for Durlach. In the first ten years of the century, while it was still a Residenz, the proportion of servants to the whole was over 12 per cent., but in the last ten years, when it was a country town again, only 2 per cent. The number of those following the learned professions declined in the same period from 12 to 6 per cent. There was a correspondingly greater number of persons engaged in agriculture (25 instead of 15 per cent.), while the figure for handicrafts remained fairly constant at about 40 per cent., for the garrison at 8 to 10 per cent., and for trade at 5 per cent.

It was useless to expect civic spirit from the inhabitants of any such town. A very large proportion of the inhabitants

[1] Preuss, *Entwicklung des deutschen Städtewesens*, p. 172.

were 'gefreite Bürger', exempt from the ordinary rates and taxes and often subject to special jurisdiction. They included, in Durlach for instance, all connected in any way with the court, the nobility, the officials down to the lowest, the official court purveyors, the servants of the nobility and officials; and almost all the 'Intelligenz', the ministers of the state religion and their subordinates, teachers, doctors, apothecaries, artists and scholars, rich rentiers, manufacturers and their chief staff, the Bürgermeister and council and in fact all the 'better class' or 'Honoratioren'. The citizens of the court towns were naturally extremely conservative and loyal in their attitude to the court. They would accept the existing order of society as one ordained by God, and would be very chary of criticising even the worst extravagances of their ruler, for they would take a pride in the magnificence of his palace, and have a share even if merely as onlookers in court festivities.

The poet Justinus Kerner, in his reminiscences of his boyhood in Ludwigsburg (*Das Bilderbuch aus meiner Knabenzeit*), gives us a vivid impression of what the pageantry in such a little capital might be.

During my earliest childhood [he says], Duke Karl Eugen was still reigning. He resided in Ludwigsburg during the summer months, and then the broad streets of Ludwigsburg and its avenues of limes and chestnuts, usually so empty, would be thronged by courtiers with silk coats, bagwigs and swords, and by the ducal military in brilliant uniforms and grenadiers' caps, beside whom the townspeople in their modest civilian clothes formed an inconspicuous minority. The splendid palace with its spacious squares and gardens, the neighbouring park with its palace, the 'Favorite', the shady avenues that led to the town and made delightful cool promenades full of blossoms and perfume in the town itself, the great broad market-place with its arcades, often provided the scene for the pleasures of this worldly-minded prince, the scene of festivities which seem like dreams of delight when one looks back on them from the present. In the 'Favorite' opposite the main palace firework displays were given that equalled those of Versailles in splendour. Fêtes were held on the lake near the town at which the pretty daughters of citizens had to appear as queens of the sea. In the early years of his reign the Duke, whose birthday was in the winter, often made magic gardens, to celebrate it, like those we read of in the Arabian Nights. In the middle of autumn he had the existing orange gardens, a thousand feet long and a hundred broad, enclosed in a huge framework of glass to protect them from the winter cold.

It was a select company to which concerts and plays were given, in a setting of eternal summer, in these 'winter gardens', but the whole town could witness the 'Venetian Fairs' held in the market-place.

The whole market-place was covered with an awning, buyers and sellers were all in fancy dress. It was a motley throng of gaily costumed figures that moved there in procession and played the maddest pranks. There was one of the Duke's Heiducks, a perfect giant, who was dressed up like an infant, wheeled about in a cradle, and fed with bread and milk by a wet-nurse who was a dwarf, and this was only one strange sight among many.

It was not in the little capitals themselves then that independent critics of the princes were to be found, for these circles were kept loyal by 'bread and circuses'. But they were to be met with in the Free Towns, in proud republicans like Goethe's father, as well as among disgruntled state servants like J. J. Moser or Freiherr von Knigge. To the typical Aufklärer the 'slavish submissiveness' of the inhabitants of towns like Dresden already appears ridiculous. Rebmann in 1795 for instance quotes derisively passages like the following from a Dresden weekly paper:

'*Hofbegebenheiten.*' Dienstag den 31. Januar und Freytag den 3. Februar brachten Seine Kurfürstliche Durchlaucht einige Stunden im Grossen Garten mit Fasanenschiessen zu. Nachmittags fuhr unser Landesvater nebst seiner teuersten Gemahlin einige Stunden aufs Fischhaus.

Montags den 24. May erlustigten sich Seine des Prinzen Anton Hochfürstliche Durchlaucht mit Spazierengehen in der Friedrichstädter Allee, und geruheten darauf bey des Prinzen Max Hochfürstlicher Durchlaucht einen Besuch abzustatten.

The Bürger proper are accustomed to subservience, he says. They look on with equanimity when the carriage of a nobleman is driven through the streets at such a pace that the lives of pedestrians are every moment in danger. When the servant of some bankrupt count strikes out with his burning torch amongst well-dressed people at a gate, because the crowd has held up the carriage a little, they wipe the burning pitch off their clothes and go quietly home. For anyone who is not a member of one or other of the two privileged castes, nobility and army, seems to be here merely on sufferance.[1] Nicolai comments on the pleasure-loving easy-going way of life of the people in capitals, such as Vienna, Munich, Stuttgart, but he admits that the citizens of the Free Towns are far too stiff and ceremonious. In many of the capitals, especially in the south, one can find something of the old spirit even to-day. The people are more often in holiday mood; they cannot live without their theatre and their music; popular festivals (like the Munich Oktoberfest) are still celebrated with gusto and the sense of pageantry is not dead. They are interested in the appearance of their town, its public buildings and streets and fountains. They are not absorbed in the making of a living, they still find time to live. The general level of art and taste in Germany would be much lower without them.

The multiplicity of little courts certainly favoured the diffusion of a taste for luxury and certain kinds of art. It is more doubtful whether court patronage was a benefit to creative art, especially to that of native artists. Since the Renaissance the 'artist' in the modern sense had gradually come to be distinguished from the craftsman, not only in consequence of increasing specialisation, but still more because the men whose services were sought after by the

[1] *Wanderungen und Kreuzzüge durch einen Teil Deutschlands,* von Anselm Rabiosus dem Jüngeren (G. F. Rebmann). Altona, 1795.

condottieri of Italy and their later imitators, to express their personal pride and glory, naturally became 'personalities' themselves, not patient anonymous workmen executing prescribed tasks by a routine method. It is true that they were often exploited by their patrons, and with our modern romantic ideas of the respect due to creative genius, we cannot help being painfully conscious of this fact when we contemplate certain forms of rococo art. Even a Renaissance picture, as Mr Clive Bell says, 'was meant to say just those things that a patron would love to hear', and 'in the eighteenth century painters are, for the most part, upholsterers to the nobility and gentry'. The career of J. C. Mannlich was probably typical of that of the general run of court painters in Germany. His father, descended from a family of Augsburg goldsmiths, was court painter to the duke of Pfalz-Zweibrücken (Christian IV), and as the boy showed talent for painting while still at school, the duke had him trained at Mannheim. Later he accompanied the duke on his annual visits to Paris, had lessons from Boucher and became acquainted with all the young French artists of note. After this education had been completed by four years' residence in Rome he became chief court painter to his patron (1771). Finding that serious and tragic subjects like the sketches he made from Homer and the history of antiquity did not please the duke, he had to turn to Ovid's *Metamorphoses*, Guarini's *Pastor Fido* and similar works for motifs that would. Soon afterwards we find him painting scenery for amateur theatricals at court, and as the taste for them grew and he expressed ideas about theatres, he was asked for plans for a court theatre. It was built, earned loud praise, and to his consternation Mannlich found himself appointed chief architect by the new duke, although he had never studied building-construction in his life. His chief task was the planning of the new 'Karlsberg' (see p. 95) with all its decorations and furnishings. Finding that Mannlich had a good collection of pictures, the duke informed him one day that he would pay him whatever he liked for it, and had already given orders for its removal to the palace. Soon he was entrusted with the supervision and the cataloguing of the duke's growing collection of pictures, though still acting as chief architect and superintendent of the theatre. In his capacity as 'Director of all the Fine Arts', his duties included even such things as the planning of court festivities. He ended up after the French Revolution as Director of the Bavarian Picture Galleries in Munich. What is particularly striking in his well-written autobiography is the absolute dependence of even a highly placed official on the whims of his duke. It also reminds us how much of the artistic energy of the day went into applied art. The artist was not there to express himself, but to give appropriate and agreeable forms to everything that surrounded his patron, from his palace and its gardens to his snuff-boxes and walking-sticks.

This social fact is important if we would understand the character of German baroque and particularly rococo art. Art had become a luxury. Of course great personalities would not have let themselves be suppressed by any patron, but except in architecture Germany did not produce any artists of outstanding genius at this period, and the lesser men were content, like Mannlich, to adapt themselves to the taste of their patrons, who in their turn followed the prevailing fashions of France and Italy. But the glorious use that architects like *Neumann* (Würzburg, Residenzschloss) or *Pöppelmann* (Dresden, Zwinger) made of the opportunities given them by extravagant princes shows that not all the blame for the rather weak and characterless art of the age is to be laid at the door of the patrons. The general run of them had no doubt no more taste or understanding than the count, the patron of the actors in *Wilhelm Meisters Lehrjahre*, but an artist with ideas could usually contrive to express them much as Wilhelm does in his *Vorspiel*. For the true artist, a patron was simply a necessary evil, one element in the situation that he had to master in his art, and one advantage of Germany's separatism was that it offered the man of genius at least a considerable choice of evils, so big a choice, if he was of outstanding merit, that he could hardly fail to be appreciated at something like his true value somewhere, as we see from the lives of the great musicians of the age. They suffered greatly, but perhaps not more than artists in other ages. Of the necessity of the evil there was, however, no doubt, for no art but literature, and that only in part and only late in the century, was able to dispense with the support of the higher aristocracy. Even a theatre with pretensions to art could not, as we have seen, maintain itself without their help. Art inevitably owed much to aristocratic patronage, if only for the reason that the aristocracy controlled such a large share of the resources of the country.

It can be readily understood that at every court the suitors for the favour of the prince were as thick as flies round a honey-pot. 'Antichambrieren' was raised to the level of a fine art by those sufficiently well connected and well dressed to secure entry. It was a subject of instruction at the Ritter-akademien. This was the golden age of adventurers. Casanova and Cagliostro were only the most famous of a host of plausible knights of fortune with assumed titles, unbounded self-confidence and the external appearance and manners of gentlemen, who maintained themselves by making themselves agreeable and by scheming and gambling, while many like Herr von Pöllnitz, with better claims to their titles, were hardly distinguishable from adventurers in their way of life. Knigge's description of the type is perhaps worth quoting:

Wherever there is a rich widow to be married, a pension or office to be had at any court, they are quickly on the scent. They baptise themselves, give themselves titles, re-create themselves, as often as they please, and as the matter in hand requires. What they cannot pull off as a simple nobleman they attempt as Marquis or Abbé or officer. There is no enterprise or state department between heaven and earth which they would not be prepared to take charge of, no branch of knowledge about which they cannot converse with a self-confidence that puts even scholars to confusion. With admirable adroitness, with a *savoir vivre* that better men might learn from them with advantage, they obtain things which honest and capable men have not the courage to desire. Without profound knowledge of human nature they have that quality which, in the world as it is, enables men to gain the mastery over the truly wise, namely *esprit de conduite*.[1]

They are a real danger, he says, in the small German courts, with their pockets full of projects for the good of the land. Memoirs and letters of the time are full of complaints of the impudence of foreign adventurers at the little courts, with their slavish admiration of everything French. In fact, where externals were so important and self-interest the only motive, even the *honnête homme*, as described for instance by Chesterfield, had something of the adventurer about him.

[1] Knigge, *Umgang*, p. 306.

Chapter III

THE AGRARIAN ECONOMY

From the point of view of the economist, court life with all its splendour was an elaborate superstructure raised on the basis of an agrarian economy. The prince usually derived a good half of his income from his own estates, and the rest was raised in taxes, the burden of which lay chiefly, in most states, on the cultivators of the soil and small landowners. The court nobility lived partly on money rents from their estates and partly on the prince's generosity. As Goethe wrote in the letter quoted above, 'more was consumed at the top in one day, than was produced in one day at the bottom', or in another letter, 'It is always the peasant who has to carry the burden'. In turning now to the conditions of life in the country we shall be studying the principal material foundation of German civilisation in that age and shall be concerned with much the most numerous section of the German people, forming at this time almost three-quarters of the whole.

Among the conditions that governed life and labour in the country in those days two sets of facts are particularly important, those concerning the legal rights of landowners and tenants and those concerning the technique of agricultural practice. To understand the legal aspect of country life is a matter of great difficulty because of the extreme complexity of the conditions of land tenure, yet this was a factor of the highest importance, for it determined ultimately by whose hands the necessary labour should be performed and what every individual's share of the produce should be. The system of land tenure went back of course to a time when money was unknown, but it had been very considerably modified by the rise of towns and the increasing use of money.

The whole available land had long since been staked out and every portion of it was the property of some individual or group. The landlord was in the great majority of cases a ruling prince or a nobleman. There were also landed proprietors of middle-class origin, members of families that had grown rich in the towns, but the restrictions placed at various times on the purchase by members of the middle class of old feudal estates kept their number comparatively small. In the east almost the whole of the land was in the hands of the nobility. Round about the towns of the west and south a number of Rittergüter had passed into the hands of townsmen, but many of these had purchased a title to match their estate and had become, or were on the way to becoming, country gentlemen hardly distinguishable from the descendants of the medieval Knighthood, whose estates, as we have seen, were fiefs granted originally in return for services to the former owner of their land, some prince or great nobleman. Very large estates were still owned by the Catholic Church in the west and south. In Protestant states they had of course been seized by the princes after the Reformation. The Free Towns still owned much land round their walls. So the 'lord' spoken of in what follows might be a city corporation, a 'Stift', bishop or abbot, or a retired merchant, but in most cases it would be a member of the nobility or a ruling prince.

It was not enough for any such lord to own land. It brought him in nothing unless it was worked, and it was necessary for him to give or lend land, or the use or produce of land, in return for labour services. After so many centuries of development, the relations between landlords and peasantry were very various. Some peasants were little better than the slaves of their masters, while at the other extreme we find peasants who have almost complete right of ownership over extensive estates and only pay nominal dues to a landlord.

A true slave has no human rights. He is a kind of human domestic animal, who can be forced to work till he drops, and made to live under any conditions that please his master.

He may even be bought or sold. The serfs of Russia at this time had been reduced to a state very like slavery of this kind. In some parts of Germany too there were peasants who were very little better placed than Russian serfs. Their lord could demand labour from them and their families without limit, he allowed them no possessions of their own and could turn them out of their house and land when he wished. They and their children on the other hand could not leave the estate or even marry without his consent. Being bound to the soil they were turned over to the new owner if the estate changed hands. They were subject without effective appeal to the jurisdiction of their lords, and some lords even claimed and exercised the power of life and death over them. Though this sounds to us an utterly wretched state of life, it might not be so if the lord was generous and just. Besides possessing rights over his serf, he was responsible for his welfare and in his own interest could not afford to neglect this responsibility entirely. A serf had to do a great many things against his will, but he was spared some of the dangers of freedom. He was assured at least of a bare sufficiency.

Serfdom of this kind or approximating to it is found in eighteenth-century Germany east of the Elbe, in the regions, that is, colonised in the Middle Ages by settlers from the older German lands west of the Elbe. In this area towns were far less numerous than in the west, the peasantry could not pay dues in money because there was no market near enough for their produce, and the landlords found it therefore to be in their interest to farm as much of their estate as possible themselves and produce corn for export, instead of letting out their land at a money rent. They accumulated large compact estates by selling or exchanging any inconveniently distant portions of their lands, and by dispossessing, whenever they could, peasants with hereditary rights. They then worked this new land along with their old demesne, the labour for both being provided by the tenants who remained. The estates in this colonised area were no doubt less scattered from the beginning than in the west, and the landowners were always given rights of jurisdiction over their tenants, whereas in the west a tenant's landlord and 'Gerichtsherr' were by no means always the same person. It was the combination of 'Gerichtsherrschaft' and 'Grundherrschaft' in the same person that constituted the 'Gutsherrschaft' characteristic of the east. The 'Junker', as we now call them, were noblemen owning and usually farming for themselves large compact estates, who also administered the law and tried the peasants on these estates not only in civil but in criminal cases. Being a kind of sheriff, magistrate and police-chief in one, the landowner in these parts exercised an almost irresistible authority over his tenants and was able to introduce a system which, though not strictly serfdom or true slavery, came very near to it in its practical working. His peasants were bound to the soil, they could not marry or learn a trade without permission; he could demand unlimited services from them and had the first claim on the labour of their children. One even hears occasionally of peasants being bought and sold or gambled for, but these are isolated and usually not strictly legal transactions (whereas in Russia serfs could be openly put up to auction in the days of Catherine II).

The services demanded varied from estate to estate and were seldom definitely fixed. In East Prussia, we hear, the peasant had to work at least three days a week under the whip of the overseer for his lord, and often up to five or six. He had often only the nights left for work on his own plot. Services were in general very heavy east of the Elbe, but payments in money and kind correspondingly light. In the west it was the other way round, but whatever the system might be, the peasant was seldom left with more than the bare minimum necessary for existence.

In the eastern districts a peasant's tenure of his land was on a very insecure basis. He was usually a so-called 'Lassit'. He was allowed the use of some land in return for services and dues, but the term of his tenure was seldom defined. He was simply 'left' in possession until further notice (Lassbesitz) and could seldom dispose of the land freely or even be sure that his son would succeed him. He usually did not even possess his buildings and farming tools. Holdings were of course of various sizes. The peasants with large holdings would usually perform 'Spanndienste', i.e. supply horse and man for ploughing or carting; those with smaller holdings would have no horses and be obliged to work for their lord with their own hands (Handdienste). There were already a large number of workers who had no land of their own, dispossessed peasants and others, whose position was that of farm labourers.

If conditions in the east closely resembled those in Russia, conditions in the west were very like those in France. Feudal services had usually been commuted for money payments, the peasants being able to sell produce in the towns. Restrictions on the peasants' personal freedom had also almost all disappeared. The 'corvées' were usually fixed; in some places they did not amount to more than a few days' work a year, in others they might perhaps come up to about fourteen days. The peasants usually held their land on a hereditary basis, their rights were well protected, they could generally dispose of their land freely and they owned their buildings and implements.

Nearly all these differences between east and west resulted from the fact that in the east there were extensive Rittergüter run by the owner himself, while in the small states of the west and south-west more and more land and rights had been ceded to the peasants, in return for fixed money payments to lords who spent most of their time in the local capital. Except on the estates of the Imperial Knights, in Baden, and in one or two smaller states, the landowner in the west had jurisdiction only in minor cases, the major being reserved for the courts of the prince. Owing to this fact and to the more scattered nature of their holdings they could not use these rights as an instrument for petty tyranny. Some of the

Reichsritter, however, had a very bad reputation for the way in which they treated their peasantry. The state of Bavaria too formed in many ways an exception in the area west of the Elbe, conditions here being on the whole very like those in the east.

The peasant, it will be seen, besides being dependent on the vagaries of the weather and exposed more than any other class to the ravages of war, was less of a free agent than the average townsman, being more closely bound by the routine of the little society into which he was born. On the other hand he was seldom in danger of actual starvation, as a 'free' townsman might be, and although he had to work hard, he never experienced the still more unhappy situation of being out of work. Naturally his personal dependence was looked upon as a great evil by the liberals of the Aufklärung, while agricultural reformers criticised the inefficiency of forced and therefore scamped labour. We meet with many reflections in literature of the movement for the freeing of the serfs. In the strict legal sense there were no actual 'serfs' (Leibeigene) in Germany like those of the early Middle Ages and of classical antiquity. The feudal dues and services still exacted were a burden on the *land*, not on the *person* of the peasant, and had mostly been commuted for money. Most of the restrictions on their freedom had had their origin not in medieval serfdom but in later developments, particularly in the 'Gutsherrschaft', described above, of the lands east of the Elbe. But even if the peasants were at worst only what Knapp has called 'erbuntertänig' (hereditarily subject) it was natural that the reformers should use the familiar word serfdom for a relationship which in practice was very little better than slavery. The movement for the freeing of the serfs made little progress in Germany until the nineteenth century.

It was only from the prince of the territory that the peasant could hope for relief. He did not always look to him in vain, for in Prussia and Austria the state needed a flourishing peasantry, to provide healthy recruits for the growing armies, and billets in their houses and barns for the soldiers. Actuated in the main by these motives the Prussian and Austrian rulers endeavoured by a number of ordinances to prevent the confiscation of peasants' land (Bauernlegung), but they were not so successful, or perhaps so desirous of success, when they joined in the attempts at the abolition of serfdom that began to be made in Germany in this century. The demesne peasants were freed in Prussia in 1798 and the following years, but the rest did not obtain their freedom until between 1808 and 1816, and then only at the cost of concessions that made the landowners' position even better than before. In Austria, in spite of Joseph II's humane attempts, the peasants were not freed till 1848, but other German-speaking territories were not so backward. In the north and west, where conditions were better to begin with, it was only a small step to release the peasant from feudal dues and give him an independent holding, yet here too it needed the impetus of the French Revolution to induce the peasants to assert their claims.

To pass now from the legal to the technical aspect of country life, we may note that there are two extreme types of agricultural system, the primitive or self-sufficing one and the modern capitalistic type, in which the agricultural unit, a larger and more highly organised one than before, produces mainly for export, and is consequently obliged to purchase many of the commodities it requires, instead of producing them itself. In eighteenth-century Germany the former type prevailed almost exclusively, and it continued to do so till quite the middle of the nineteenth century. The main aim was, both on small holdings and on large estates, to grow what the owners and their families and dependents themselves needed for their upkeep. Any surplus there might be would be sold in whatever market was available, but commercial considerations were not paramount.

There were of course exceptions to this rule, conditions

naturally varying considerably over so large an area. Three zones may be distinguished, one of small independent holdings in the south-west, one of dairy-farms in Hanover and Schleswig-Holstein, and one of large estates in the colonised east. Of these the dairy-farms, under Dutch supervision, early became dependent on trade owing to their specialised nature, but the small farmers of the south-west were for the most part content if they could feed themselves. Even the large estates of the east only exported a small proportion of their produce. Sombart estimates (*op. cit.* II, 630) that the annual export of corn from Danzig in this century was only about as much as could be grown on 100,000 acres, or half one Prussian 'Kreis'; yet Danzig was the main port for the whole of the eastern corn-land. The agricultural population consumed about two-thirds of their total production even in 1850; out of the remaining third came not only the amount exported, but also the supplies of the towns. The smaller towns very often needed little from outside, for they grew a large proportion of their food themselves, and in the larger towns too (in Frankfort, for instance —see *Dichtung und Wahrheit!*) the citizens had large gardens and vineyards outside the gates, while some kept cattle or pigs on the common and in the woods. There had been edicts since the fifteenth and sixteenth centuries forbidding citizens to allow their pigs to run about the streets at all hours of the day and night, but pig-sties were to be seen in front of the houses in Berlin till nearly the end of the seventeenth century,[1] and small places like Weimar still had their 'town herdsman' at the end of the eighteenth century.

When we know that the claims made on the productivity of the land were so modest, we do not expect to find very advanced methods of cultivation in practice, nor indeed had the methods in vogue in Germany at this time progressed very far beyond the standard of the Middle Ages. In this respect, however, Germany differed little from the rest of

[1] Biedermann, *op. cit.* I, 366.

Europe. England only began to introduce rational methods on a large scale, following Holland's example, in the second half of the eighteenth century. We know from Arthur Young's writings that a large proportion of the English land under tillage lay in open fields, the same rotation being used on all soils alike. These village farms were run by associations of agricultural partners who occupied intermixed strips, and cultivated the whole under common rules of cropping, or 'field constraint'. The obstinate conservatism of the farmers added to the inherent defects of this system. 'In 1768 turnips and clover were still unknown in many parts of the country; and their full use only appreciated in the eastern counties.' 'Turnips remained, at the close of the eighteenth century, an alien crop in many counties.' 'In Middlesex, in 1796, it was no uncommon sight to see ploughs drawn by six horses, with three men in attendance.' 'Traditional methods were treasured with jealous care as agricultural heirlooms.'[1]

The reforms initiated in England by Young did not spread to Germany till well into the nineteenth century. Cultivation remained extensive instead of becoming intensive; deep ploughing was held to be not merely unimportant—it was generally left to the most incompetent labourers or even children—but harmful and unnatural. The open-field system (Dreifelderwirtschaft) with an unvarying succession of spring-sown corn (barley and oats), autumn-sown corn (wheat and rye) and fallow, was all but universal. Only gardens, where vegetables, fruit and fodder were grown, were exempt from 'Flurzwang' or field constraint, the community routine of cultivation. Age-old tradition, unaided by theoretical knowledge, determined all the methods employed, and there was no room for individual experiments, for the 'natural' methods handed down from antiquity had a greater sanctity in the country than even the traditional arts of the craftsmen in the towns. To attempt with impious hand to improve on nature,

[1] Lord Ernle (R. E. Prothero), *English Farming Past and Present*, 2nd ed. pp. 202–3.

in the manner of manuring the soil, for instance, was a crime against God, said an old steward in Bohemia in the early nineteenth century. Conservatism so deeply rooted could only be overcome by interference from high quarters: 'Your burgher or peasant will do nothing unless he is paid for it or kicked into it', said the officials of those days.[1]

Agriculture proceeded therefore in a vicious circle. The open-field system with its large and neglected permanent pasture provided insufficient fodder, so that the cattle were often so weak in spring that they had to be dragged on sledges to their grazing ground; shortage of cattle involved lack of manure, without which an improvement of the yield was impossible. It is not surprising then that J. C. Schubart (1734–87), who in the latter half of the century made great efforts to extend in northern, south-eastern and central Germany the cultivation for fodder of clover, that had been grown in the Spanish Netherlands for centuries, was hailed as one of the greatest benefactors of the century, and ennobled by the emperor, Joseph II, with the title of 'Edler von dem Kleefelde'. The effects of this revolution were slow to make themselves felt, for throughout the century the productivity of the land remained on the whole extremely low. In Silesia for instance between 1770 and 1780 wheat gave an average crop of 5·6 fold, and rye of 5·2 fold, while in England in Young's time wheat and rye already produced a ten-fold crop, bad as methods were, and other crops were twice as good as the Silesian ones.[2]

In parts of northern Germany and in Austria sheep-rearing was carried on for the export of wool and was considerably improved in this century by the Spanish government's consenting at last to the export of merino sheep. These sheep-farms, and the dairy-farms on Swiss and Dutch models, that produced cheese and later butter beyond home needs, were the most advanced types of farming to be found in Germany then, though in proportion to the rest they were of small

[1] Biedermann, I, 168. [2] Sombart, *op. cit.*

account. Before the end of the century attempts were made at the reform of other branches of agriculture, particularly by the above-mentioned clover-Schubart, and by an admirer of Young, Albrecht Thaer (1752–1828), who did much to spread the 'Norfolk System' of rotation in Germany. By this the years of corn-growing were interrupted by the growth of other crops to allow the soil to recover and to supply fodder. With more fodder the stock of cattle could be increased and the land could be more adequately manured. But what was principally lacking was a theoretical understanding of the processes involved, and only the first steps had been made in this direction by Priestley, Lavoisier and others in the last two decades of the century.

The vigorous efforts made by the rulers of Prussia, by some lesser princes (like Karl August) and by a number of individual landowners—for the national importance of agriculture was obvious to all—were not attended by proportionate results. The most useful accomplishment of the Prussian government in this direction was the establishment in the thinly populated eastern districts of religious refugees from France and Holland (from 1685 onwards), and later of emigrants from the southern states like the Palatinate and Württemberg, where agricultural practice was relatively good. It was with the same intention and by the promise of similar privileges that the Russian government attracted South German settlers to the Volga basin, where their descendants still form separate communities to-day. Frederick the Great continued in this respect the policy of the Great Elector and his own father. Frederick William had also gained new land for cultivation by extensive draining operations in the Havel valley, had deepened rivers and improved roads to facilitate the export of produce, and made many efforts to improve methods. Frederick the Great similarly carried out a big drainage scheme in the Oder and Warthe marsh, an area of 300,000 acres. In the matter of methods perhaps his best work was the encouragement of the cultivation of the potato. It was not until the 70's that potatoes were grown in fields, and we hear that severe measures were needed to overcome the apathy and prejudice of the peasants. It was commonly believed for many years that eating potatoes gave rise to scrofula, rickets, consumption, gout and all sorts of diseases. Nettelbeck tells us in his memoirs that when Frederick sent the first cart-load of them to Kolberg in 1744, after a famine, so that citizens might try the crop in their gardens, they could make nothing of them. 'The things have no smell and no taste', they said, 'and not even dogs will eat them (raw!). What is the use of them to us?' But next year a gendarme, a Swabian by birth, was sent with the load to show people how to grow and use them. In the south the potato was better known, though only as a garden plant. Perhaps the greatest single difference between the usual diet of all classes in 1700 and in 1800 was that in 1700 the potato was almost unknown and in 1800 indispensable. For the peasantry the chief consequence was that absolute famine came to be a thing of the past. If the corn crops failed they had potatoes to fall back on, and in time the potato was a more important staple article of diet than bread.

Chapter IV

THE PEASANT

The everyday life and thought of the country dwellers were such as one might expect, given the fundamental conditions of their life outlined above. There were naturally great differences between family and family, both amongst the nobility and the peasantry, according to the economic position and inherited privileges of each. As in France, there were some families of noble extraction whose standard of life was no higher than a peasant's, and there were free peasants here and there, particularly in the south, who were little lords in everything but name.

The average peasant and his family, as we have seen, had never much more than was necessary to keep body and soul together. There could be no question of luxuries in their life. It was necessary for them to buy from the towns only what could not possibly be dispensed with, a few spices perhaps and metal ware. For the rest they depended on what they themselves or their neighbours could grow in their fields and gardens and make with their own hands. Houses and furniture and the clothing of both men and women were the work of members of the household, assisted occasionally perhaps by a neighbour, or more rarely by a travelling craftsman. The following description of English rural life at this period could be applied in almost every detail to German conditions:

> The inhabitants had little need of communication with their immediate neighbours, still less with the outside world. The fields and the live-stock provided the necessary food and clothing. Whatever wood might be required for building, fences or fuel, was provided on the wastes. Each village had its mill, generally the property of the lord of the manor; almost every house had its oven and brewing kettle. Women spun wool into coarse

cloth; men tanned their own leather. Wealth only existed in its simplest forms, and natural divisions of employment were not made, because only the rudest implements of production were now used. The rough tools required for the cultivation of the soil, and the rude household utensils needed for the comfort of daily life, were made at home. In the long winter evenings farmers, their sons, and their servants carved the wooden spoons, the platters, and the beechen bowls; fitted and rivetted the bottoms into the horn mugs, or closed, in coarse fashion, the holes in the leather jugs. They plaited the wicker baskets; fitted handles to the scythes, rakes and other tools; cut the staves, and fixed the thongs for the flails; made the willow or ashen teeth for rakes and harrows, and hardened them in the fire; fashioned ox yokes and forks, racks and rackstaves; twisted willows into scythe cradles, or into the traces and other harness gear. Travelling carpenters, smiths and tinkers visited farmhouses and remoter villages at rare intervals to perform those parts of the work which needed their professional skill. But every village of any size found employment for such trades as those of the smith and the carpenter. Meanwhile the women plaited the straw for the neck-collars, stitched and stuffed sheepskin bags for the cart saddle, wove the stirrups and halters from hemp or straw, peeled the rushes for and made the candles. Spinning wheels, distaffs, needles were never idle. Coarse, home-made cloth and linen supplied all wants. The very names of spinster, webster, shepster, litster, brewster, and baxter, show that women span, wove, cut out and dyed cloth, as well as brewed and baked for the household.[1]

In the matter of clothing the villagers were almost beyond the reach of fashion. They used their clothes until they were worn out. Styles of dress did, of course, change over long periods. The great variety of peasant costumes worn as best clothes on special occasions all embodied features of the town dress of much earlier periods, perhaps of the sixteenth century or earlier.[2] The peasantry had at some time or other adopted modified versions of town fashions, but these had become stereotyped, because the conditions necessary for

[1] *Social England*, ed. Traill, v, 101 (article by R. E. Prothero).

[2] See K. Spiess, *Die Deutschen Volkstrachten*, Leipzig, 1911.

quick changes of fashion, above all a surplus of means and variety of stimulus, were not present in the country. It was the same with many other features of their material civilisation and even of what higher culture they possessed, as has been pointed out by Hans Naumann and those who like him believe in the 'Sinken des Kulturguts'.[1] But the opponents of this theory are no doubt right in claiming a considerable degree of creativeness for the peasant. It was by no means all the features of his culture that had been passively received by him from 'higher' social classes. Many of the most important went back to a time when there were no other classes—the form of the peasant house and of the chief agricultural implements, as well as innumerable customs and beliefs owed little or nothing to either knighthood or bourgeoisie, for they were older than both. And though admittedly strongly attached to tradition, the peasant was no more incapable than any other man of modifying what he borrowed to serve his own purposes, and of having occasionally good ideas of his own.

What prevented rapid change was the strength of community feeling in the village, and institutions like the three-field system, with its rules of common cropping, which both expressed and fostered this feeling. It is now fashionable in Germany to praise the traditionalism of the peasant, by a reaction against the views expressed when the individualistic middle class led public opinion. For the townsman from the Renaissance age onwards, however, the countryman was 'der dumme Bauer'. He was held to be coarse, stupid, dishonest, drunken and quarrelsome, and it was not until the time of the Romantics, after hints from Rousseau and the 'Sturm und Drang', that it was discovered that the countryman was in his own way a completely civilised person who was even superior to the townsman in much that was now held to be important in life.

In reading eighteenth-century descriptions of peasant life

[1] See H. Naumann, *Grundzüge der deutschen Volkskunde*, Leipzig, 1922.

the change of attitude, by which our present-day views have been affected, must be kept in mind. It was not the townsman's feeling of superiority, however, that inspired the following description of the peasant's life by a man revered by Goethe in his youth, J. M. von Loen:

The peasant is brought up in complete ignorance like a mere animal. He is plagued continually with feudal services, running messages, beating up game, digging trenches and the like. From morning till night he must be digging the fields, whether scorched by the sun or numbed by the cold. At night he lies in the field and becomes little better than a beast of the fields, to keep the beasts from stealing his seed, and what he saves from their jaws is taken soon afterwards by a harsh official for arrears of rent and taxes. The countryman to-day is the most wretched of all creatures. The peasants are slaves and their men are hardly to be distinguished from the cattle they tend. The traveller comes to villages where children run about half-naked and call to every passer-by for alms. Their parents have scarcely a rag on their backs. A few lean cows have to till their fields and give milk as well. Their barns are empty and their cottages threaten to collapse in a heap any moment. They themselves look neglected and wretched; one would have more pity for them, if their wild and brutish appearance did not seem to justify their hard lot.[1]

These general impressions are confirmed by such different writers as Laukhard, *Der reisende Franzose*, Nicolai, Knigge and Crabb Robinson. The references to the peasantry by Crabb Robinson in his *Letters* are particularly interesting because he is able to compare German with English conditions. The condition of the peasantry varied greatly in the provinces he visited. He was never in the eastern and northern states, where the lot of the peasantry was hardest. Of those he saw, the peasantry of the Catholic ecclesiastical states like Bamberg and Würzburg seemed the best placed. Even where the material prosperity of the peasant was equal to that of the English villager, he seemed to Crabb Robinson

[1] J. M. v. Loen, *Freye Gedanken vom Hof*, 3rd ed. Frankfort and Leipzig, 1768, p. 28.

to be more subservient, owing to the feudal burdens he still bore, and it seemed wrong to him that so much field work should be left to women. Howitt, writing forty years later, but before the Industrial Revolution had seriously affected Germany, was inclined to minimise the hardness of the German peasants' lot because he was so pleased to find that the majority of them owned the land they cultivated, whereas the average villager in England was a labourer dependent on a master. Howitt too was only familiar with the south and the Rhineland, where it is true that the peasant proprietor preponderated, and where he had, by this time, commuted his services for money payments. His picture would not have been so favourable if based on conditions in Mecklenburg or Prussia. He was struck by the patient laboriousness of the German peasants, men and women, and by the economy they practised, collecting as they did every scrap that could be used for fodder, manure or firewood. These habits he explained as the result of their working for themselves and not for a master. Aesthetically, however, he preferred the English countryside, with its variety of large and small estates, manor-houses and cottages, and the neatness and cleanliness of even the smallest homesteads. The rarity of gentlemen's seats in the country was a point noted by all English travellers—it was due to the attraction of the nobility to the courts. The cottages were less spick and span than in England because the women worked so much more in the fields, and perhaps also because there was no Hall near by to set a higher standard in these matters.

The chief civilising influences in the village were the minister and the schoolmaster. The power of the minister was so largely a matter of personality, whatever the sect he represented might be, that no brief general statements can be made about it. Some varieties of Protestant ministers will be dealt with later. The power of the village schoolmaster can be more usefully discussed at this point. Generally speaking, it was very slight indeed, for though, in an age that believed so passionately in education, country people were not neglected by the reformers, most of their proposals remained on paper. In Prussia, for instance, the most advanced of the German states in this respect, the village schools seem to have remained wretched in most cases until after the end of the century. From official reports of an inspection made in 1802 and 1803 in Cleve, a Prussian province where conditions were favourable, it appears that Frederick the Great's admirable General-Landschul-Reglement of 1763 had remained a dead letter. Theoretically, attendance at school for six hours a day was compulsory for all children between the ages of five or six and thirteen. For the poor no fee was charged. The qualifications necessary for a teacher were defined, classes were to be duly graded and uniform textbooks to be used. But at their inspection it was found that forty-three teachers out of sixty-seven were incompetent. Hardly any had attended the training school set up for Cleve in 1784, they had usually been appointed without being examined and once in office they had neither the leisure nor the books they required to improve themselves. They were so wretchedly paid that all had some other occupation. Many were organists or vergers or both, some were tailors or exercised some other craft, some sold brandy or collected tolls. The school buildings, where regular buildings existed, were almost always in bad repair. Often a room had to be hired for the purpose in a house, and sometimes the teacher slept in the school-room. There were often no separate classes. Each child came up book in hand and said its lesson. The curriculum was extremely narrow, reading, writing and perhaps a little arithmetic, and a good deal of religion. Little was read beyond the Bible and catechism. Attendance was extremely irregular. In summer the schools were empty.[1] If these were the conditions in an enlightened state, it can be imagined what they were like in

[1] W. Meiners, 'Landschulen und Landschullehrer im Herzogtum Cleve vor hundert Jahren', in *Archiv für Kulturgeschichte*, III, 1905.

the average small state. But in the second half of the century a considerable number of peasants could at least read and write, as is indicated by the large sales of the calendars and so forth that were written for them. Of R. Z. Becker's *Noth- und Hülfsbuch*, for instance, a million copies are said to have been sold in just over twenty years.

Chapter V

THE COUNTRY GENTLEMAN

The everyday life of the average German country gentleman in the eighteenth century would not be very different from that of an English squire. There were perhaps greater differences between rich and poor noble families in Germany than in England. There would be many who, like the Reichsritter of the south-west, ruled as little sovereigns over broad estates and perhaps owed allegiance only to the emperor himself, and other *Junker* who, in Freytag's phrase, 'were only distinguished from other country dwellers by their superciliousness and their scorn for work in the fields'. As in France, many of them would have no estates of their own, but only a house in the village and a few acres of land, of which they might merely be tenants. Some again, though of moderate means, would have good connections with the leading courts, whose protection would ensure for their sons good careers in the army or the diplomatic or civic service, while others, buried in the depths of the country, would have no ambitions exceeding those of an English yeoman. They differed from each other immensely, again, in breeding and in intellectual attainments. There were the Hardenbergs and the Humboldts at one extreme, and, at the other, boorish Junkers such as those who figure in so many German stories, or in the memoirs of K. H. von Lang, Friedrich von der Trenck and many more, worthy descendants of the robber knights of the late Middle Ages and the restless *Krippenreiter* of the seventeenth century. In between came the great mass of the country gentry, who, living in peace and comparative comfort on their estates, could count themselves among the most fortunate of their time. Such a country gentleman 'took no more notice of the great world than was necessary, mixed without ceremony at great family parties with the whole nobility of the neighbourhood, allowed himself an occasional caroüsal, bred his foals, sold his wool, and disputed with his parson. If he was not too strict he maintained tolerably good relations with his subjects and seldom had any conception of the harm that he himself suffered through his labourers being serfs'.[1]

The country nobility were still often able to maintain their position, even when they did not administer their estates wisely, because of the many privileges their birth conferred on them. In the Catholic south there were few old families who had not relatives in some cathedral chapter, some wealthy order (like that of the Knights of St John or the Teutonic Knights) or some monastery, convent or other religious foundation, on almost all of which the best sinecures were reserved for the nobility. Where this privilege was not available, as in the Protestant north, families when hard pressed had to be content with mortgaging their lands or seeking an alliance by marriage with one of the many wealthy middle-class families who were eager enough for this honour.

The healthiest and most contented families were usually those who remained independent of lay and ecclesiastical courts alike, living a simple patriarchal life, the essential features of which had been much the same in the time of Horace as they were in eighteenth-century Germany or England. The more attractive side of this life has been charmingly described in an essay of Eichendorff's, himself the descendant of such a family in Silesia. On the rare occasions when they read something about the life of the great world in the newspapers, he says, it seemed to them like a fairy-tale. The monotony of their lives was only broken by frequent shooting parties, which ended with much firing of shot-guns and phantastic huntsman's tales, and by ceremonious visits to the annual fair in a neighbouring country town. In the winter each family in turn would give

[1] G. Freytag, *Bilder aus der deutschen Vergangenheit*, III, 9 Kap.

a ball in its own home, a jolly improvised affair, for which a large living-room, emptied of furniture, would serve as ballroom, and the schoolmaster and a few cronies would provide the music. The ball would be opened, as at court, with the traditional minuet, but strenuous and noisy dances would make up most of the programme.

These fortunate folk lived simply but contentedly in houses that were for the most part quite unpretentious even though always dignified with the name of 'Schlösser', houses which, however lovely the country might be, were not constructed to afford the aesthetic delight of a distant prospect, but to allow the family to see from their windows what was going on in their stables and barns. The ambition of the men was to be sound farmers, and the pride of the ladies was a reputation for good housekeeping. They had neither time nor feeling for the beauty of nature, they were still products of nature themselves. The poetry of life, such as it was, was left as a useless luxury to their young daughters, who did not fail in their few idle hours to strum old-fashioned arias and sonatas on a tuneless clavichord and to brighten the kitchen garden behind the house with choice beds of flowers. As soon as day broke there was so much bustling activity in house and farmyard that the startled visitor would hastily take refuge in the garden. Doors would fly open and bang to on every side, and amidst much unnecessary shouting and disputing they would sweep and milk and make butter, while the swallows flitted gaily over the confusion as if they were part of the household, and the morning sun shone brightly all through the house over the faded family portraits and the brass mountings of the old furniture.

Such a country gentleman's estate was necessarily very little dependent on the outside world. When the nearest main road was itself an ill-defined cart track, as it usually was, things could not be otherwise. Once inside the lane leading to the 'Rittergut', the visitor felt himself to be in a little world apart. Here were the houses of the peasants who had lived and worked on this estate all their lives and never travelled further than the nearest market town, here the fields with their intermingled strips, the produce of which was almost all consumed within the estate boundaries. In the manor house and the adjoining farm buildings not only every kind of food required by the squire's family was stored and prepared, but beer was brewed, much of their clothing was made, and all kinds of common articles now bought in shops were produced by the skilled hands of the ladies of the household and their servants.

Such a large estate could not be run successfully without a great deal of skill and knowledge. All those arts were needed which are now the domain of the pioneer rancher. We can form a good idea of the range of knowledge required by the ideal country gentleman from such works as W. H. von Hohberg's *Georgica curiosa oder adeliches Landleben*,[1] the first of a number of 'outlines of knowledge' for the landed gentry. Here we read for instance of the laws that affect the landowner, the precautions to be observed in purchasing estates and building houses, the elements of agriculture, horse-breeding, gardening, brewing and the cultivation of silkworms, as well as of the duties of the father and mother of a family and the arts of riding, hunting and fishing.

It goes without saying that the more bookish type of education was of little importance for a young nobleman from the country unless he aimed at a career at court or in foreign service. The majority would be taught to read and write by the village schoolmaster or parson and continue their education either at a 'Ritterakademie' or at the grammar school of a neighbouring town, or perhaps they would receive all their instruction at home from the local pastor or some young theologian. The ideal presented to them would be much the same as for the young aristocracy in general, but with less insistence on the refinements of the courts and a knowledge of the great world. They would seldom be submitted to a severe discipline and would make no secret of their being more interested in horses and dogs than in languages or history. From the age of sixteen or so they

[1] Nürnberg, 1687, 2 vols. folio, with many interesting plates.

would turn their back on their studies for good and give themselves up to the occupations and particularly the sports of a country gentleman. It is this type that Knigge paints in his picture of the country squire at court, who, appearing in the antechamber in the embroidered dress that is so stiff and so cold after his familiar top-boots, surtout and smoking cap, trips over his sword and evokes the contempt of the Frenchified cavaliers assembled there by his blunt speech and provincial manners.[1]

It was by no means every member of the country nobility who was as unfamiliar with courts as this. It has been mentioned that one thing which struck English travellers in Germany was the comparative scarcity of gentlemen's country seats, for in the south and west, as we have seen, large numbers of the country nobility were attracted to the courts, often residing almost continuously in the capital and leaving the management of their estates to stewards. Many who lived chiefly in the country would contrive long visits to neighbouring capitals, especially if they had a daughter to marry or a son to start on a public career, and a large number would be in touch with the courts through relatives and friends. It was a privilege of the nobility, including the country families, to send their sons to court as pages, a privilege of which those who had the necessary means and good friends at court still made frequent use. But in spite of all these links between the country and the capital, there remained an easily perceptible gap between court nobility and country nobility. On the whole, the cultivated and much travelled country nobleman, who, while not neglecting his estate or his public duties, maintained an interest in the liberal arts and perhaps contributed himself to science or literature, was a very much rarer figure in Germany than in the England of the Augustan Age.

[1] Knigge, *op. cit.* Einleitung.

PART III

THE NEW ORDER OF SOCIETY
THE MIDDLE CLASS

Chapter I

RETROSPECT

The section of society to which we may apply the vague term middle class was already so large in eighteenth-century Germany, and the differences between its various groups were already so marked, that some study of its historical development is necessary before its complex structure can be understood. Each century since the early Middle Ages had left its mark on middle-class life, but the new features as they appeared had never entirely effaced the old, so that life in the eighteenth century is constantly reminding us of one aspect or another of the life of past ages.

The history of the middle class or 'Bürger' is, as the German word itself suggests, the history of the towns. Towns arose at a certain stage in the economic development of Germany with increasing specialisation, as they had arisen earlier elsewhere. The division of labour was carried much further in a town than in the self-sufficing communities which had preceded it. A large proportion of its inhabitants were craftsmen and traders who could give little or no time to agriculture, and for whom food had therefore to be imported from the surrounding country. In the primitive agricultural communities of the early Middle Ages, on the other hand, almost all the material needs even of great landowners were met by the produce of their own estates and the labour of those living on them. We have seen that many agricultural communities in the eighteenth century still needed very little from outside.

Yet the difference between village and town in this respect, especially in early times, was only one of degree. In medieval towns there were always many citizens following purely agricultural pursuits. Many craftsmen and traders too spent a portion of their time in this way, or at least had gardens, and kept cattle on the common, so that every town in medieval Germany presented a semi-rural aspect, with its cultivated fields within the town boundaries, its barns and pigsties and the cattle straying through its streets. There were hundreds of semi-agricultural small towns of this type still in eighteenth-century Germany, in fact there were few towns which did not produce a fair proportion of their food supplies within the area owned by their citizens. In other respects too there was still much to remind one of the self-sufficient period, for a good deal of work was done in the middle-class home which in England at this period would have been left to a tradesman. Goethe tells us in *Dichtung und Wahrheit* that his father, a well-to-do citizen of Frankfort, chose men-servants who had some skill as tailors, so that clothes could be made for the family at home. In the early nineteenth century all English travellers expressed astonishment at the 'cooking and linen mania of the ladies'. As late as 1842 we read: 'The hoarding of linen and of stockings is a passion with most German ladies. Spinning-wheels abound, and are to be seen in the houses of many people of great pretensions: in still more of the burgher class, and in every house of the common people. Ladies of rank and fortune are still plentiful, who spend their mornings in the kitchen up to the elbows in flour'.[1] Bread, preserves, even soap and candles, were made at home.

Traces of self-sufficiency lingered long, but the medieval town was already a settlement that could not exist without obtaining foodstuffs and raw materials from the surrounding

[1] W. Howitt, *The rural and domestic life of Germany*, p. 233.

countryside, in return for the products of its craftsmanship and for ready money. By the end of the thirteenth century Germany was already honeycombed into economic regions, each one of which had such a town as its centre. These towns dotted over the country would be perhaps three to five hours' journey apart in the south and west, seven or eight in the more thinly populated north and east, so that from almost any village a peasant could go to the nearest market and return in a day. The boundaries of the regions were of course fluid, fixed by convenience and custom, though legal considerations might enter in, because of the rights often acquired by towns to compel the use of certain roads by carriers. In the town market once a week the produce of the country was exchanged for the industrial wares of the town. There was also an active exchange of goods and services between the members of the town population and a certain, usually very limited, amount of trade with other towns.

It is easier to describe the economic function of the fully established town than to account for its origins. Some scholars stress the importance of the market, others that of the castle. Both were essential features of a town. The land on which a town was built belonged to the king or to some feudal lord, lay or ecclesiastical, and all towns began under the protection of some lord. If the legal and political aspects of their history are emphasised, the castle appears more important than the market, but economically it is the market which gives the town its *raison d'être*. Sombart[1] thinks that we must seek the origin of towns in the demand for the services of craftsmen on the part of the only people who could pay for them, lords and bishops living on the revenues of their lands. However this may be, it seems clear that the growth of towns is a phenomenon connected with the development of *Grundherrschaft* and the increasing use of money, as well as with the increasing contacts between peoples and the new standards of life that resulted from the

[1] *Op. cit.* 3rd edition, I, 134 ff.

Crusades. It is clear too that when towns had reached a certain stage their development could not be very rapid, because even apart from the ravages of epidemic diseases three great obstacles limited the range of their trade: unproductive agricultural methods, bad communications and the lack of a sound currency. These checks to the growth of towns had not been removed, in most cases, even in the eighteenth century, so that Germany's towns were still small. They had seldom spread much beyond their medieval walls, and we must remember that even the leading towns of the Middle Ages were very small indeed compared with modern cities. A town with 20,000 or more inhabitants was an exception. There were only ten or twelve of this size in fifteenth-century Germany.

Small as the medieval towns were, they soon became a political force to be reckoned with. In the time of the later Hohenstaufens they came to share the real power with the territorial princes. By the power of combination and by money payments, many of them gained one privilege after another from their original lords. All of them, even if they were under the rule of seignorial officials, were privileged places as compared with villages. They were fortified and comparatively safe to live in. They were sanctuaries invested with the town peace, so that if runaway serfs succeeded in remaining for a year in a town before their lord could establish a claim to them, they became free. They had a monopoly of trade, and held their weekly market under the protection of their lord or bishop. The larger towns held periodic fairs for trade with more distant parts. They aimed at and usually secured the full control of their market and its tolls, and authority to regulate wages, prices, hours and quality of wares in their gild industries. They frequently gained independent jurisdiction, the right to set up a mint, and authority to impose duties and taxes.

It was as a result of this bargaining process that the distinction arose, still a very important one in the eighteenth century, between Free Towns (Reichsstädte) and Territorial Towns (Landstädte). The Free Towns carried the conflict with their feudal superiors one stage further. Instead of owing allegiance to a lord inconveniently near at hand, they succeeded in establishing a communal form of government for themselves and were subject only to the emperor. The Landstädte were not always worse off, for a happy compromise or the weakness of their lord might make conditions very favourable for them.

Both types of town were constantly contending not only with their lord but also with two other forces, the surrounding villages and other towns. The first of these conflicts led to the domination of the organised town over the unorganised country. The town wished to establish a monopoly of industry and trade, and to ensure its supplies of food and raw materials. This policy involved the control of roads, so that all goods in transit should pass through the town market, the prohibition of rival markets within a fixed area, rights of pre-emption (Stapelrecht), the prohibition of industrial activities in the country (Bannrecht), and other similar measures. The second conflict, with other towns, the struggle for monopolies, was carried on partly by the means mentioned above, but mainly by tariffs. All these measures of civic egoism were enforced with greater consistency and success in Germany than anywhere else in Europe except in Italy, because of the lack of a central authority in these two countries. Many effects of these measures persisted down to our period, in innumerable tolls and restrictions on trade—it was owing to an old agreement of this kind that it was impossible, for instance, to divert the main road from Frankfort to Leipzig through Weimar (see above, p. 31)—but many privileges of the towns had been curtailed by the state governments.

The internal organisation of the towns naturally underwent great changes according to the varying success of their policy towards the outside world, and the rate at which their inhabitants grew in numbers and became differentiated in function. The town council of the Free Towns was for long elected from the ranks of the patricians alone, the families of some standing in the town, 'who had exercised no craft and engaged in no petty trading, but had lived on their incomes (from property) or kept themselves honestly by enterprises of some scope, or in some respectable official capacity'. In towns with a large trade, especially in the northern ports, the merchants soon came to be the dominant element in these councils. They generally contrived to maintain their position here against the attacks of the artisans, but in the more industrial towns the craft-gilds successfully claimed a share in the government, or even took it entirely into their own hands, becoming in many cases exclusively political organs. These struggles too had left very clear traces in the constitutions of the German towns of our period, with important results for their social life.

No less important were the effects on everyday life, in the eighteenth and even in the nineteenth century, of the medieval organisation of industry in gilds. Down to the time of Gottfried Keller and later, German literature is full of figures whose life and outlook is still in all essentials that of the medieval gild craftsman, a fact which lends support to those economic historians who hold that the forms of German industry were not fully capitalistic until the second half of the nineteenth century. A brief description of the gild system, in its less controversial aspects, must therefore be attempted.

A gild craftsman was, at least in the early days, one of a small group of people in his town who alone possessed skill in a certain craft, or later, who were officially authorised to practise such a craft. He only needed a few tools which anyone might acquire, but his skill had had to be gained by serving a long apprenticeship. It was handed down from one generation to another. It was very usual for a master's son to succeed him, and a master treated his apprentices, even if they were not his own children, almost as members of the family, for his apprentices and journeymen lived with him in the same house. Though the difficulty of training young craftsmen and the slow growth of the population themselves tended to keep down the number of craftsmen, it was considered necessary that they should be organised in a corporate body. Whether the initiative came originally from the workers themselves or from the lords who employed them, and how much the gilds were influenced by older (Roman) models, are still matters of dispute, but it is clear that the individualistic point of view which comes so naturally to us was then comparatively rare. Men had no desire to stand alone. They instinctively grouped themselves with their relatives in clans, or when that was no longer possible, with fellow-villagers in a village community, or later still, when this tie too was broken, with fellow-workers in a gild. So some see in the gild a kind of artificial family, others the forms of the village community adapted to industrial conditions.[1]

The gilds were therefore nothing if not clannish. Their policy was directed towards maintaining equality and solidarity among the members of the gild, and excluding non-members from the enjoyment of their privileges. Not competition, but co-operation between masters was their aim. All members enjoyed the same rights and advantages. No master might make a corner in raw material; the available resources had to be equally shared. No one might have more than a certain maximum number of apprentices and journeymen, or more than one workshop and stall. The masters fixed prices in common council for all classes of goods, and determined what wages might be paid to journeymen. Uniformity of price was further ensured by their houses being side by side (they had no regular 'shops') and their stalls together in the market. There were no middlemen required in most trades; the craftsman himself sold the

[1] So Sombart, *op. cit.* I, 190.

things he had made. Further, all gilds were exclusive. They were never content unless they had a monopoly of producing their particular kind of wares. No one was allowed to practise the same trade in their town without belonging to the gild. Some gilds had their monopoly recognised in a charter obtained from the town authorities; even when it was not mentioned in their charter, or if the gild had no charter, it was taken for granted by everyone that gild membership was compulsory for all engaged in the craft.[1]

The interests of gild members were maintained not only by active measures against blacklegs (Pfuscher, Störer), but by the various tolls and vexatious restrictions imposed by the town, to protect home industries, on imported goods. It was possible for a long period to prevent competition because of technical conditions, the nature of the demand and the prevailing habits of thought and feeling. However much he might exert himself, a master could only turn out a limited amount of work, because everything had to be done by his own hands or those of his apprentices and journeymen, whose number was strictly limited, both by the possibility (at least in theory) of their setting up for themselves when they had acquired skill, and more effectively, by gild and town regulations. Moreover, one man's wares were usually as good as another's. They were all in a traditional style, and if an individual made any slight improvements they could not be patented. The demand too was steady and conservative, governed by tradition and habit in a society essentially static, arranged in something very like castes.

But the most important factor of all was the mentality of the craftsman in this static society. A man worked to keep himself and his family according to the usual standard of that state of life unto which it had pleased God to call him, to use the phrase that still survives in the English Church Catechism. The characteristically modern desire to 'get on', to be better than one's neighbour, was certainly active in

[1] Kulischer, *Allgemeine Wirtschaftsgeschichte*, I, 194.

some individuals, but it was combated in every way by the 'vis inertiae' of the mass, fortified by the disillusioned wisdom of the Church. Here too the parallel with the village community is striking. As each villager, in the ideal village, had just enough land to be cultivated by a family and to provide food for it, the gildsman was to have enough work to keep him occupied and to furnish him with a maintenance. He made goods for certain regular customers, usually to order, and he was his own salesman.

We have considered the gilds so far only from the point of view of production, as it concerned the masters or independent craftsmen. We must enquire further how the gilds served the interest of the consumer and of the lower grades of workers. The needs of the consumer were satisfied well enough by the gilds so long as he asked for a good solid piece of workmanship in a traditional style. The gildsman wished to live and let live. The danger to the consumer that a monopoly seems to us to bring with it was counteracted by the strong ethical feeling of the gilds, which inspired their efforts to ensure good quality in their wares and to charge a just price, and secondly by the fact that the producers of one class of wares were consumers of others. Living as they did side by side with other craftsmen they were far more vividly conscious of being members one of another than men can be to-day, when the relations between producer and consumer are impersonal and determined only by the 'cash nexus'. The governing body of the town, whether under the control of the lord or not, had not an entirely impossible task in trying to reconcile the views of the various gilds and was usually able to give its authority to their recommendations. Of course there were incessant conflicts between opposed interests, there was corruption and legislation in the interests of a class. In the later days, as we shall see, both gilds and town councils were sometimes instruments of oppression, but in the Middle Ages a good working balance of interests was, it seems, generally attained.

The position of apprentices and journeymen was probably not so ideal, even in the best times of the gilds, as some enthusiasts would have us believe. The gilds were corporations of masters and they seem to have had monopolistic tendencies from a very early date. The older view (of Gierke for instance) that this was the case only in the period of their 'decline' (sixteenth to eighteenth century) is no longer widely held.[1] All the three types of restriction governing full membership of a gild were imposed already in the thirteenth and fourteenth centuries. These restrictions concerned (*a*) the candidate's parentage. They excluded strangers to the town, sons of serfs, illegitimate children or sons of members of the 'unehrliche Berufe' (a motley list: barbers, shepherds, tanners, millers, watchmen, grave-diggers, executioners, etc.). (*b*) Technical training. The apprentice, once admitted, had to 'serve his time', usually four years in Germany, to work as 'Geselle' or journeyman in different towns (this was called his 'Wanderzeit') and produce a prescribed 'Masterpiece'. (*c*) Finally he had to be able to pay for his privileges. At the beginning of each of the three stages (as apprentice, journeyman, master) he paid a fee to the gild; before admission as master he had to prove that he was in possession of a certain amount of capital, and had always to provide an expensive 'Meisteressen'. Many of these conditions could be relaxed in favour of masters' sons, or those who married masters' daughters or widows. It is probably not true, even for the best days of the gilds, that every journeyman could hope to become a master in due time. Some remained journeymen for life, and a great many had to work for many years for a master at a wage fixed by the gild before they could attain independence. There were married journeymen, no longer living in their masters' houses. There were unions of Gesellen and strikes in Germany even in the fourteenth century.[2]

[1] Kulischer, *op. cit.* I, 199 ff.

[2] *Ibid.* 210 f.

The gilds were far more than industrial unions. 'They embraced the whole man', in Gierke's phrase, like all the brotherhoods which were so numerous in the Middle Ages, ranging as they did from associations of lawyers to unions of prostitutes. Men could not detach parts of their personality, as it were, in the modern way, and join an association for one limited purpose. The gild had a particular *raison d'être*, but the members formed at the same time a fellowship for all purposes which they could have in common. Those practising the same craft lived as true neighbours in the same street (as old street names still remind us). In addition to its function in industry, a gild might perform that of a modern friendly society, a freemason's lodge, a social club, a company of volunteers, even a political party. The citizens grouped themselves by gilds on ceremonial occasions, and for some religious purposes; the gilds, not individuals, were represented in the town council.

In the early days of the towns there were comparatively few people engaged purely in trade. It has been calculated for instance that in medieval Frankfort, which had more trade with distant parts than most towns, four-fifths of the population were occupied in direct production (including agriculture).[1] The one type of exchange that was absolutely vital for the towns, that of industrial wares for provisions, took place in the open market on market-day, and no intermediaries were needed here between craftsman and peasant. There were often separate markets for cattle, horses, corn, hay, wood, fish, meat, salt, etc., and even here, where wholesale trade must have been permitted, the private citizen was always given the first chance of buying. The number of middlemen was kept down to the minimum and they were closely watched by the town authorities. The craftsmen sold their wares retail, either in their market booths or in their houses. The butchers and bakers had their booths on or near the market, and here stood also the stalls

[1] G. v. Below, *Das ältere dt. Städtewesen und Bürgertum*, p. 106.

of the Krämer, the only real 'shopkeepers', who were usually prohibited from selling articles made in the town. They dealt in small imported articles, such as dried fruit, dyes, perfumes, imported ironmongery and hardware, hats, gloves, ribbons and finer dress materials. Woollen cloth was sold by the cloth merchants (Gewandschneider). Below the Krämer there were street-sellers of local produce, fruit, fish and so on.

This local trade, almost entirely concerned with the produce of the land and labour of the town and of the country a few hours' journey round, would be almost the only trade that mattered in small towns, and much the most important even in large towns. Except for cloth, salt and some spices, the articles brought from a distance were still almost all luxuries, which would scarcely enter the lives of any but the well-to-do. The products of ordinary handicraft were naturally not exported, unless they were a speciality of the town, like Nürnberg ironware and instruments. The same natural principles governed the export of agricultural produce and raw material generally. Every region was normally self-sufficient in food supply. It was possible to maintain the wheat trade of the Hanse, for instance, only because in every year it was necessary somewhere or other in their area to import grain owing to a local bad harvest. Their herrings, on the other hand, were in wide demand, because they could not be obtained elsewhere. Owing to the predominance of local trade, there was no hard and fast distinction in medieval times between wholesale merchants and retailers. The wholesale merchants were retailers who had extended their scope, and they still sold goods retail too. The merchant (or later his agent) accompanied his goods to their distant destination, just as to the local market. The long distance trade was mostly conducted at the periodic fairs, held at fixed times in convenient centres. Only the bigger towns had fairs of any importance. The imported goods were distributed from these centres by pedlars.

How little an eighteenth-century Free Town had changed since the Middle Ages may be seen from Goethe's description of his native Frankfort in the first book of *Dichtung und Wahrheit*:

The great bridge over the Main was my favourite place for walking. Its length, its massiveness, and its fine appearance made it a notable structure, and it was, besides, almost the only memorial left from ancient times of the protective care which civil government owes to its citizens. The beautiful stream above and below the bridge attracted my eye, and it always filled me with delight to see the gilt cock on the old cross over the bridge glitter in the sunshine. Generally I extended my walk through Sachsenhausen, and for a farthing enjoyed the experience of being ferried at my leisure to the other bank. Back once more on the Frankfort side of the river, I would stroll along to the wine-market, and admire the mechanism of the cranes when goods were being unloaded. But it was particularly entertaining to watch the arrival of the market-boats, so varied were their cargoes, and so extraordinary, sometimes, the figures which could be seen disembarking. If I went on into the city, I always paid a respectful greeting to the Saalhof, which at least stood on the spot where the castle of the Emperor Charlemagne and his successors was reported to have been. I liked to lose myself in the old industrial quarters, and, particularly on market-days, to mingle with the crowd surging round the Church of St Bartholomew. From the earliest times, the throng of craftsmen and retailers had jostled each other there, and because of their right of possession, it was not easy in later times to provide for more space and light. The booths of the so-called *Pfarreisen* were very important places for us children, and we took many a copper there to buy coloured sheets printed with animals in gold. Only rarely, however, did we care to force our way through the narrow, tightly packed and dirty market-place. I call to mind also that I always fled with horror from the disgusting butchers' stalls, standing close together and abutting on the market-place. The *Römerberg*, on the other hand, was a delightful place for walking. The way to the new town, through the *Neue Kräm*, was always cheerful and interesting, though we were sorry that there was not a street leading into the *Zeil* past the Church of Our Lady.... But what chiefly attracted the child's attention were the many little towns within the town, the fortresses within the fortress. I mean the walled monastic enclosures, and several other buildings dating from earlier times and more or less like castles to look at—the *Nürnberger Hof*, the *Kompostell*, the *Braunfels*, the ancestral home of the family of Stallburg, and several other strongholds, transformed in modern times into dwellings and workshops. Nothing of striking architectural beauty was to be seen in Frankfort at that time. Everything pointed to a period long past and full of disturbances, both for the town and its surroundings. Gates and towers, defining the bounds of the old city—then further off, other gates, towers, walls, bridges, ramparts, moats, with which the new city was encompassed—all indicated only too plainly that the necessity for safeguarding the common weal in times of unrest had called for these arrangements, and that all the squares and streets, even the new ones, broader and better laid out as they were, owed their origin to chance and caprice, and not to any regulating mind.... It was one of our favourite walks, which we endeavoured to take several times a year, to follow the course of the path which ran along the inside of the city walls. Gardens, court-yards and out-buildings extended to the foot of the wall; a glimpse was afforded into the home-life of thousands of little families, each shut off and hidden from its neighbours. Passing from the ornamental pleasure-gardens of the rich to the orchards of the ordinary citizen, kept for the sake of their produce—thence to the factories, bleaching-grounds and similar establishments, and even to the churchyard—for a little world lay within the limits of the city—we saw before us, changing at every step, a most strange and varied spectacle, which our childish curiosity could never sufficiently enjoy.

In this description, as in so many others in *Dichtung und Wahrheit*, Goethe has selected and arranged the details in such a way that his picture of Frankfort, without losing its individuality, has become that of a typical town, of an 'Urform des Lebens'. Our attention is drawn first to Frankfort's geographical position at an important river-crossing, its primary *raison d'être*, and to its water-borne trade, then to the Saalhof, on the site of the castle of the first town lords, under whose protection a market had first been established. The congested Old Town, with its industry, its market, its butchers' stalls side by side, reminds us of the chief activities of the medieval town and its gilds, the *Römer* of its self-governing town-council and its struggles with the emperor, the fortifications of its political independence and power of self-defence. The complexity of the social structure of this community, a state in small, is brought home to us by the mention of the strongholds of the patrician families, the monasteries, and the houses and gardens of citizens rich and poor. Finally the growth of new forms of industry is hinted at in the last sentence.

Frankfort was of course not merely a local market. Its fairs had been famous from an early date, for it was marked out by its geographical position as a convenient meeting-place for traders from northern Germany, southern Germany and France. It is important for our purpose to enquire where the comparatively small number of German towns which were more than local centres were situated, because, although many of them had lost ground by the eighteenth century, they were still the strongholds of the old-fashioned middle class, and usually exhibited many features by which they might be distinguished from the court towns, discussed above, and from the newer centres of trade with which the next chapter will be concerned.

These more important medieval towns were to be found for the most part either in the west and south-west of Germany, on the Rhine and upper Danube and their tributaries, or on the Baltic and North Sea coasts. The opening up of Europe that began with the Crusades, and the shifting of the stream of trade between Constantinople and the West from the Roman overland route to the Mediterranean and Italy, together with Germany's political connections with Italy under the Salian and Hohenstaufen lines, were the main external influences favouring the growth of these larger towns in the south, while in the north-east the colonisation of Riga and Reval and the Land of the Teutonic Order,

Prussia, led to an active trade by sea with the northern ports, that was extended before long to Poland, Russia, Scandinavia and England, and became almost a monopoly. The Hanseatic merchants overshadowed the trade of the north of Europe as the Italians did that of the south. In the twelfth century they were allowed by the English king, who still considered trade as a private, not a national, affair, to build the Steelyard in London as a warehouse and inn for their members, and they had soon other centres in Novgorod, Bruges, Bergen, Wisby and elsewhere. This league of merchants grew into a league of towns, at least so far as the towns were represented by their merchants, and included in its prime eighty or ninety places scattered between the Lower Rhine and Livonia. As England gradually attained commercial independence, Cologne, the original leader, and centre of the English trade, gave place to Lübeck, that commanded communications between the North Sea and the Baltic. The sea-ports Hamburg, Bremen, Wismar, Rostock, Stralsund, Stettin, Danzig and the river-ports Frankfort-on-Oder and Breslau were the most important of the other members. These northern towns were engaged in the handling of goods, mostly natural products; wool from England, in return for wine, hardware, woollens, silk and later corn and wood; herrings from the Baltic, where they then abounded; and furs, leather, wood from Russia, for wine and beer, and later for linen, woollens and other manufactured goods.[1]

The prosperity of the southern towns, though originally founded on trade in goods, attained its later proportions chiefly through financial transactions. The first towns to gain importance were those on the Danube route to the east, particularly Vienna and Regensburg (Ratisbon), but as Italy grew in wealth and power, they had rivals in Nürnberg, Augsburg, Ulm and Basle. These southern towns, especially

[1] Monograph by D. Schäfer, in *Monographien zur Weltgeschichte*, 3rd ed. 1925. Selected documents with commentary in J. Bühler, *Bauern, Bürger und Hansa*, Leipzig, 1929.

Nürnberg, were skilled in fine metal-work, both in iron and the precious metals, for which Germany, until the discovery of America, was the chief source for Europe. There were twenty-nine different varieties of iron-workers in Nürnberg in 1363. Their skill was no doubt influenced by their connections with the East and its exquisite workmanship. Augsburg and Ulm exported fustians, Basle woollen cloth, and Constance linen. All four towns were geographically well situated for trade and did not, like most towns in Europe, allow the Italian merchants to come to them with their oriental wares. They themselves went to Venice, Milan, Florence, Genoa and the Spanish coast towns and sold these goods in southern Germany, Austria and Hungary, where they predominated as the Hanse did in the north of Europe. Their Fondaco dei Tedeschi beside the Rialto, the counterpart in Venice to the London Steelyard of the Hanse, is still a monument to their importance. Giorgione and Titian painted its façade. But they could never obtain the same control as the Hanseatic merchants did in undeveloped northern lands, for the Italian towns were themselves too far advanced to allow it. In Venice they were not allowed to sail beyond the lagoon.

It was not till the second half of the fourteenth century and the fifteenth that Augsburg and Nürnberg reached the full tide of their prosperity. The merchants and patricians, having accumulated wealth by mining speculations, trade or ground rents, began, in spite of the Church's ban on usury, to lend money to princes and potentates on a large scale, with results at first very profitable to themselves. The most famous of these early financiers was Jakob Fugger, descended from a weaver of Augsburg who, by financing mining operations in South Germany, Hungary and Spain, and by loans to the Hapsburgs and others, increased his fortune ten-fold in twenty-five years and on his death in 1525 left nearly two million Gulden to his heirs.[1] The money of Augsburg is said

[1] For details see: R. Ehrenberg, *Das Zeitalter der Fugger*, 1896, and the same writer's *Grosse Vermögen*, I. *Die Fugger*, 2nd ed. 1905.

to have played a decisive part in bringing Charles V to the imperial throne, and in the sixteenth century the financiers from southern Germany were amongst the leaders at the new money-market of Antwerp, especially when the Florentine bankers ceased to be rivals through the transference of the bulk of their business to Lyons, the other great financial centre of the time, after Austria's victory in Italy (1530). Their good fortune was unhappily short-lived. Owing to the growth of national feeling in England and France, the finances of these countries became more and more national, and Spain and Portugal were soon the only large borrowers from the South German bankers. Spain proved anything but a reliable debtor. Its first bankruptcy, together with that of Portugal and France, in 1557, is said to have cost Germany the equivalent of 200 million marks, and was felt throughout the South German towns.[1] It was followed by another in 1575, and this and subsequent losses completely ruined many of the financiers of Augsburg and Nürnberg. Even such large houses as the Welser were involved, while the Fugger and some other families of the purse only retained that part of their fortunes which they had invested in landed estates. From now onwards Germany was quite overshadowed as a financial power by the rising national states, who alone were able to keep and increase their wealth by trade and colonial ventures, developing new methods in finance, industry and trade to meet the new situation.

The financial losses of these, the wealthiest towns of sixteenth-century Germany, were no doubt partly responsible for Germany's failure during the next two centuries to maintain the eminence in trade and industry which had been hers at the time of the Reformation, and which is reflected in the thoroughly middle-class literature of that age, and above all in the buildings and art of the great towns mentioned above. But it is generally held that the root cause of her misfortunes

[1] Lamprecht, *Deutsche Geschichte*, VIII, 1. Teil.

was her inability to share in the advantages which accrued to Europe from the great geographical discoveries of that period, the discovery of the sea route to India and of the new world of America. By these discoveries new regions were opened up for European exploitation, and something resembling world trade came to be established for the first time. The old commercial routes and centres were not abandoned. Local trade, and trade between the countries of Europe, was only stimulated by the discoveries, and increased by leaps and bounds, but the old mainly overland route from northern Europe to the East was soon overshadowed in importance by the new ocean routes, which gave commerce an altogether new range and made possible the comparatively cheap and rapid transport of much greater quantities of goods. The leadership in this trade naturally passed from the Italians and the Hanse towns to the peoples of the Atlantic seaboard, the Portuguese, Spaniards, Dutch, French and English.

As the scope of trade was extended, it came to be an object of rivalry not between cities only but between the new national states. The new period is marked by a series of struggles for power between the European nations, struggles in which commercial motives played a very important part, for commerce and political power grew to be interdependent. The Conquistadores, Portugal and Spain, exploited their new discoveries to the utmost, but the less dramatic methods of Holland and England, both supported by well-developed home industries, proved to be more effective in the long run. The Dutch, with their colonial enterprise and their seamanship, were the great models and rivals of the English. England succeeded in asserting naval and commercial supremacy over Spain in the sixteenth century, over Holland in the seventeenth and over France in the eighteenth, and at the beginning of the reign of George III, to quote Mr G. M. Trevelyan's words, 'was held in higher esteem by the nations of the world than ever before or since'.

The position of Germany, or rather of the various states

of Germany, for Germany was not really one country, was very much less enviable. The Germans had had no direct share in the discoveries, or in the trade resulting from them. The Hanseatic merchants were too much occupied with their northern trade, no longer such an easy monopoly as in the past, for they had now to reckon with stronger forces in Scandinavia, England and Russia. They had neither the money nor the organisation necessary for fitting out large expeditions. Their prosperity was founded on the co-operation of a large number of comparatively small traders, with traditional markets and ports of call, and a truly medieval power of inertia to check any undue speculation. One can still trace survivals of this traditionalism in the early chapters of Thomas Mann's *Buddenbrooks*. The financiers of South Germany were, however, more enterprising. Some of them launched expeditions to exploit newly discovered countries (like that of the Welser to Venezuela), but they all came to nothing for lack of the requisite backing of technical knowledge and physical force. A more profitable and less risky line of business was the financing and fitting out of expeditions undertaken by other nations, notably Portugal and Spain. The important German houses soon had branches in Lisbon, and in Antwerp, when it took the place of Venice as centre of the spice trade. But though their Spanish connections brought the fortunes of the Fugger and other German houses to their zenith, about the middle of the sixteenth century, the value of the old trade with Venice was steadily declining, as that city lost her hold over the East. Her decline was indeed slow, for throughout the sixteenth century the transalpine trade was still considerable, but the smaller towns and the smaller merchants began to suffer before the end of the century, and were unable to recompense themselves by ventures further afield.

Though the immediate and direct effects of the colonial discoveries on Germany were small, their wider consequences were of the utmost importance, especially as regards Germany's relation to other countries and to the sources of world wealth. Her geographical position became a hindrance to her, and remained so until the nineteenth century, when the re-introduction of overland transport made her once more the clearing-house of a great part of Europe, and encouraged ideas of an independent 'Mitteleuropa'. Her lack of political unity, further, made it impossible for her to back up her merchants, as the great colonial powers all did, with force of arms. Schmoller sums up the general situation as follows:

> Germany had a good start in processes, traffic, even foreign trade, but no authority able to take advantage of it. The Empire was kept busy in the sixteenth century with maintaining religious peace, and was subservient in the seventeenth to the Austrian and Catholic Hapsburgs....Everywhere economic bodies were becoming political except in Germany, where the advantages it had enjoyed before 1620 were being lost. It was not the loss of men or capital, nor the shifting of trade routes from the Mediterranean to the Atlantic, but the lack of politico-economic organisations, which caused Germany's decay.[1]

The chief factor we have not yet mentioned was the Thirty Years' War. Though it undoubtedly had very serious effects, it is no longer thought to have been so overwhelming in its consequences for German trade and industry as used to be imagined. All the leading powers except England had something corresponding to such a war of religion, yet only Germany was finally prostrated, for the main causes of her downfall were independent of the war and already effective before it. We must not, however, go to the other extreme and shut our eyes to the enormous loss of life, the reckless destruction of the fruits of long labours and the disastrous moral consequences of this most irregular of all modern wars. The peculiar brutality with which it was waged on both sides was due partly to the leaders, who, however ideal their motives at the outset, were in the end fighting for material and political gains, aims which were still more openly

[1] G. Schmoller, *The Mercantile System*, trans. Ashley, 1884.

pursued by their allies, and partly to the nature of the armies they commanded. That they should be made up of mercenaries was inevitable since the decay of the feudal system; they were given their peculiar stamp, however, by the way in which they were recruited. The task was entrusted to entrepreneurs, war-merchants, who were given a fixed sum to provide an agreed number of men in fighting trim. They were left complete freedom in their manner of obtaining them, and Falstaff's methods of recruiting were jests in comparison.

The pay of these rough troops was so difficult to raise that they were frequently given authority to shift for themselves, with the consequence that the direct losses of the inhabitants through their marauding were even greater than the heavy contributions demanded by their rulers for the upkeep of the armies. All armies in those days had a camp following two or three times as numerous as themselves, by whose combined demands the districts they visited were sucked dry of all existing supplies, while they were prevented from cultivating the land by the military operations. The atrocities and the wanton destruction for which these troops were responsible more than equalled even the worst achievements of the twentieth century. Many villages disappeared entirely. In Württemberg there were for instance in 1654 eight towns, forty-five villages and over 30,000 buildings in ashes. Great stretches of cultivated land were nothing but desolate moorland after the war; in Saxony in the years following the war the country was so wild that wolves would attack the villages.

The country population suffered more from direct violence than the townsmen behind their walls, but those who survived the war appear to have been better situated than the average town-dweller, for wheat was cheap for lack of purchasers and there was a great demand for their services to reclaim the damaged lands. The more complicated foundations of town life were very seriously undermined, for the war had made regular communications impossible over the greater part of Germany, completely crippling trade and industry. Many towns had suffered in spite of their walls from direct visitations, and all had felt the still more terrible consequences of famine, and of the plague produced by hunger and unnatural foods. Comprehensive and reliable statistics are not available, but even allowing for great exaggerations in the local estimates, historians agree that the population of towns and villages was frequently reduced to a third, a quarter, sometimes even a tenth of its former number. That of Württemberg was reduced from 313,000 to 65,000 between 1634 and 1645, that of Bohemia from four millions to 800,000, that of Augsburg from 80,000 to 18,000, and so forth. It is generally agreed that Germany did not make good the population lost in the war till well into the eighteenth century.

The material damage that was done left traces till later still, for in nearly all towns there were large numbers of ruined or abandoned houses. The losses of the towns in direct contributions to the state were very heavy, often ruinous. Göttingen for instance had paid over 500,000 Thaler by 1629, and Lüneburg contributed a similar amount in the last ten years of the war. Only the northern ports and the great centres Frankfort and Leipzig retained their commercial importance.

The moral consequences of the war were extremely serious. A whole generation grew up without knowing what peace was like, living from hand to mouth and often driven to desperate remedies, while round about them they saw examples of every imaginable crime, not checked by any authority or any effective public opinion. A general relaxation of standards was inevitable. In their uncertainty of the future men lived for the present, and the most senseless luxury was displayed in a starving country by those who happened to have the means. The parallel with later crises, in 1806 and 1919, is most striking. When their money ran out, men took to the army while the war still lasted, and often to robbery when it was over. A great gulf was fixed between court circles and the rest of the people, for the rulers had for the most part lost all the sympathy of their subjects, while they were led by the foreign models, with which they became familiar through foreign alliances, to consider themselves as a different breed from the common folk. It seems to be a general effect of war to heighten contrasts. Certainly the German aristocracy became from this time on definitely estranged from the mass of the people. The effect of the foreign influences on literature and art in general is well known. They were also of importance in developing a taste for luxuries of every kind, and dissatisfaction with the badly finished work of the German craftsman. The war damaged home industries by hindering the further development of German technique and powers of production, and by leading to connections with foreign countries that opened up the way into Germany for their superior goods.

Throughout all these upheavals in the great world, the gild system of industry had persisted in Germany little changed, but it was already proving inadequate in the new circumstances. Despite all their efforts, the gilds could not escape the effects of the competition that was inevitable as intercourse increased between the various regions of Europe and between these and the world outside. The gild worker was best able to turn out a solid article in a traditional style. One has only to think of an old-fashioned shoemaker or carpenter in a small town to understand his idea of how things should be made. When the courts of even small princes were in touch with the great capitals of Europe there naturally arose a more discriminating demand than the old-fashioned craftsman could satisfy. A higher degree of specialisation, more elaborate tools and plant were required, for any master to keep the quality of his wares equal to that of his foreign competitors, and the old gild organisation was not elastic enough to admit of such developments. The work of the

German craftsman was generally looked upon with contempt by the fine ladies and gentlemen of the seventeenth and eighteenth centuries. Their almost slavish preference for anything made in France, though mostly a matter of fashion, had some real justification in the superior quality of the French goods with which the market was flooded. In the seventeenth century we read: 'No clothes will satisfy us Germans now that do not come from France. French scissors trim our German beards better than any others; our watches go better if the Germans in Paris have made them, for the air there is more favourable for their manufacture than at Augsburg', and so on for such varied articles as combs, ribbons, chains, stockings, boots, shirts, hats, sticks, powder, needles. Moscherosch's *Gesichte* are full of such complaints.[1]

A further disruptive tendency was the inability of the handicraft system to satisfy a mass demand. There were, it is true, no such large towns in Germany as in some other countries, calling for enormous quantities of similar goods, nor had it any colonies to swell the demand, but there were nevertheless articles in common use needed in great quantities, particularly articles of clothing, which the craftsmen could not produce as rapidly and consequently as cheaply as 'manufacturers' who co-ordinated the work of many employees, and used any labour-saving machinery that was available. Here again foreigners stepped in where Germany's organisation failed her. England, that had once exported raw wool to be dealt with in Flanders and Germany, had captured by the seventeenth century almost the whole of the German woollen industry, and supplied Germany with manufactured goods through the 'Merchant Adventurers'. This was a company, at first, in Elizabethan times, a regulated company or gild of independent merchants, that had established itself first in the Netherlands, and then in 1567 in Hamburg, where the city's private interest in the increase of its trade, even though it was under English initiative and

[1] See especially part II, 'A la mode Kehrauss'.

domination, prevailed against the general opposition of the Hanse to any trespassers in its domain. What the English and French did not bring was supplied by the Dutch, whose highly advanced industrialists found a ready market in the whole Rhine region, and established regular Dutch colonies in Krefeld, Mannheim, Hanau and other new towns, especially after their closing of the Scheldt had been legalised by the Peace of Westphalia. The consequences for Germany of the development of this 'passive' trade will be discussed in the next chapter.

Chapter II

GERMAN TRADE AND INDUSTRY IN THE EIGHTEENTH CENTURY AND ITS CHIEF CENTRES

The population figures for Germany in the eighteenth century are a sufficient indication that her economic state was nearer to that of the Middle Ages than to that of the late nineteenth century. The population had indeed begun to increase again, but at nothing like the rate at which it was to grow in the following century. For the preceding three centuries famine, plague and war had kept the population almost stationary. The Thirty Years' War had furnished the last and most effective 'check' on a large scale. Earlier in the Middle Ages, however, between the twelfth and fourteenth centuries, there must have been a steady increase in the population, to judge by the extensive colonisation of the country east of the Elbe. This progress was only resumed in the eighteenth century. Reliable data are difficult to obtain, but from estimates made on various evidence it would seem that the population of several Prussian provinces was doubled or even trebled during the century, though part of this increase was due of course to the vigorous efforts of the Prussian rulers to 'people' the kingdom. It is estimated that by 1740 the population of Prussia had increased owing to immigration by some 600,000, so that these immigrants constituted a quarter of the total number of inhabitants at that time.[1]

It seems improbable that this comparatively high rate of increase prevailed in those parts of the country where the growth of the population depended chiefly on the excess of births over deaths. In the eighteenth century almost every-

[1] *Handwörterbuch der Staatswissenschaften* ('Agrargeschichte').

thing had still to be learnt in hygiene; smallpox, typhus and children's diseases carried away large numbers of victims every year, and even the plague made one last onslaught on Germany early in the century before retreating to the East, reducing the population of the Duchy of Prussia by one-third. England, which was considerably in advance of the Continent in matters of hygiene, had only rid itself of the plague in 1666, and its normal death-rate in the eighteenth century was still 41 per thousand in a fairly good year, to be compared with a rate of about 13·7 before the Great War. In London it was over 50 in the first half of the century, though it fell to about 30 by its close. In all countries the death-rate was so high in the towns that many statisticians believed their numbers only to be maintained by a constant flow of newcomers from the country. In Berlin it was 40 or more per thousand at the beginning of the century, and it did not fall to below 35 at the end. The figures given by Nicolai in his *Reisen* for various German towns range from 50 per thousand for Vienna to half that rate for Coburg. In general, the bigger the town was, the higher was its death-rate. The birth-rate was still high in town and country alike, but infantile mortality was extremely heavy, between a fifth and a third of all children born dying in the first year. In almost all the individual families of which we hear at least four children were born, often six or more, but all but two or three usually died in childhood. The statisticians prove that this was generally the case, both in Germany and the neighbouring countries. Necker estimated that of the whole population of France, one-quarter died before attaining the age of three, another quarter between the ages of three and twenty-five, and a third quarter between twenty-five and fifty. Similar estimates were made for Germany.[1]

At the end of the century the number of the inhabitants of the territories forming the pre-war German Empire must have been round about twenty millions. The first official

[1] Kulischer, *op. cit.* II, 10.

figures are for 1816, and give a total of 24·8 millions. It gives us some idea of the growth of the population since then, and the enormous reduction in the death-rate that the nineteenth century has brought about, when we remember that in the matter of numbers the Germany of 1914 stood in about the same relation to Germany in 1800 as this did to the Empire of Barbarossa.[1] For comparisons it is interesting to note that in 1800 England and Wales had just under 10 million inhabitants (nearly twice as many as in 1700), Scotland 1·6 million, and Ireland over 4 million,[2] while France contained about 24 million people.

More important for the sociologist than the gross number of inhabitants is the density of the population, and its distribution between town and country, a sure index to the nature of its economic life. It is quite clear that the majority of the German people were dependent for their living on the soil even until the first half of the nineteenth century. 'Even in the middle of the nineteenth century Germany was an essentially agricultural land, sprinkled with a few unimportant small or medium-sized towns. The centre of gravity of its social life was still definitely in the country.'[3] In Prussia, even in 1849, only 28 per cent. of the inhabitants lived in towns, in Saxony rather more, about 34 per cent., in Württemberg 20 per cent., in Baden, Hesse-Darmstadt and Hanover 15 per cent., and in Bavaria just under 15 per cent. It should be remembered too that 'town' is here used in a legal sense, so that many of the places included would be extremely small. In Saxony, for instance, at this time only five 'towns' out of 140 possessed over 10,000 inhabitants, and most would be no larger than at the end of the Middle Ages. Statistics from occupations give us the same picture; in 1843 about 60 per cent. of the German population was still engaged in agricultural pursuits, in Austria 69 per cent.[4]

[1] Estimating the latter with Kötzschke at 7–8 millions.

[2] *Handwörterbuch der Staatswissenschaften*, art. 'Bevölkerungsstatistik'.

[3] Sombart, *op. cit.* II, 626.

[4] *Ibid.*

Contrast this with the figures for 1910, when out of a total population of 64·9 millions, 38·9 millions lived in towns of over 2000 inhabitants, and 13·8 in towns of over 100,000, while in 1907 only 28·6 per cent. of the population were engaged in agriculture or forestry, as against 42·8 per cent. in industry and 13·4 per cent. in trade.[1]

In spite of the increase in the population, Germany was far from being densely populated in 1800. On the rich soil of Württemberg there were 72 to the square kilometre, in Saxony with its manufactures 50, in Prussia only 30 (though this was at least twice as many as in 1700). Some of the more densely populated regions, beside Württemberg and Saxony, were (using the names of the modern Prussian provinces) Westphalia (55), Rheinprovinz (50), Silesia (45).[2] In England and the Netherlands the figure was 65.

It is clear then from these figures that no revolutionary changes in industry and commerce had taken place in Germany since the Middle Ages. The revolution came of course in the nineteenth century. In the eighteenth century, though the medieval pattern of economic areas each dominated by a market town had been disarranged, particularly by the activity of the territorial princes, something very like it still persisted. The main body of trade was still local. A glance at the communications then available convinces one that it could not have been otherwise except in a few specially favoured places, for although the amount of traffic by land and water had grown steadily since the Middle Ages, travel had become very little easier or safer since then. A longish journey was still something of an adventure even in the most civilised parts of Europe. Naturally the conveyance of goods and letters was also slow and expensive, in spite of the progress that had been made in the organisation of regular services.

[1] *Statistisches Jahrbuch des deutschen Reichs*, 1913, pp. 4, 5.

[2] Kulischer, II, 7. *Handwörterbuch der Staatswissenschaften*, art. 'Bevölkerungsstatistik'.

For land traffic, the difficulty still only very partially overcome was the provision of smooth hard roads, partly a matter of deficient technique, partly of lack of capital and co-ordination of effort. It seems that none of the European countries had a really good system of roads before the nineteenth century. France was far ahead of the rest. In the second half of the eighteenth century it had a good system of metalled main roads, 'chaussées', radiating from Paris, but the by-roads were still bad. In England the first turnpike trust had been created in 1663, but in spite of dozens of turnpike acts the roads, even the roads leading to London, remained very indifferent, and the side roads often mere unmetalled tracks, with ruts sometimes four feet deep. On a road of this kind Young in 1770 found three broken-down carts between Preston and Wigan. Pack-horses were in universal use till the nineteenth century. When it had been necessary to make good roads they had been made, by Wade, for instance, in parts of Scotland, for military reasons, and near London, but there was little co-ordination of effort, methods were bad and the burden was too heavy for local authorities.

It can be readily imagined what the state of German roads must have been, with a less insistent demand, a greater multiplicity of authorities and even less possibility of co-ordination for large areas. It is true that in autocratic states with a fairly efficient bureaucracy it was easier to overcome local indifference if the prince took it into his head to have good roads. In this way some of the South German states obtained improved metalled roads in the course of the century. The first chaussées were made in Hesse in 1720, in Baden in 1733, in Württemberg in 1772. Nicolai, who travelled all over Germany in 1781, tells us that the roads were infinitely better in the south than in the north, where owing to the lack of stone the material difficulties were very much greater. Even the main roads of Prussia were execrable; sand in summer and mud in winter, in spite of all the efforts of Frederick the Great. At the end of the century Reichard, perhaps the chief forerunner of Baedeker, in his popular *Guide des Voyageurs*,[1] informed travellers that in the south they could go from Frankfort or Nürnberg to Vienna, from Vienna to Switzerland or Italy, and from Switzerland back to Italy without finding an unmetalled main road or a bad service of posts. Nicolai had said much the same in 1781, but had added that it had not long been so.[2] Reichard singles out the roads of Bavaria, Fulda and the Palatinate for special praise, then Würzburg and Württemberg, then Baden and Bayreuth. The pleasantest of all is the famous Bergstrasse from Darmstadt to beyond Heidelberg, highly praised by English travellers too.[3]

In the north, Reichard says, the roads are in general very bad. 'In certain seasons and in rainy weather, one is often obliged to leave the ordinary road.' Even in 1842 Howitt tells of 'ruts which swallowed the carriage up to the axle and piles of mud which stood, ground up by the action of the wheels, like walls' in the Harz.[4] The state of the roads was the ostensible reason (there were other obvious reasons) for the state regulations fixing the minimum number of horses to be hired by passengers travelling post. In Prussia for instance, even in the early nineteenth century, it was only a light carriage carrying one passenger and a single trunk that was allowed the minimum hire, two horses. For two people three horses were required, for three people four horses. For a heavier carriage with four passengers or more, the number of horses would be five, six, or even eight, if there was much luggage.[5] In Austria the regulations were less stringent, no doubt because of the better roads. Another indication regarding the state of the roads is the warning given by Nicolai, Reichard and others to strangers travelling

[1] *Guide des Voyageurs*, Weimar, 1793.

[2] *Reisen*, I, 117, 150.

[3] E.g. by Crabb Robinson in his letters (Edith Morley's edition, Oxford, 1929, p. 155).

[4] *Life in Germany*, p. 447.

[5] Reichard, 8th edition, 1817.

in their own carriage about the frequent changes in rut-gauge in the north. The ruts on the roads east of Hamburg for instance were wider than on those to the west. Either the track of the carriage wheels had to be adjustable, or one had to leave the road and drive over the fields. There were few stone bridges. In Bavaria and Austria bridges were usually of wood. On the Rhine below Basle, there were only floating bridges until the end of the eighteenth century. Small streams had usually still to be forded.

Though roads were poor, there were regular services of public conveyances, and post stations at intervals of two or three Meilen all over the country. The monopoly granted to the Thurn und Taxis family in 1615 had been greatly interfered with by the territorial princes since 1648. Many states now had their own services, but the Thurn und Taxis organisation still employed 20,000 people and, according to an estimate quoted by Reichard, made an annual profit of a million Thaler at the end of the eighteenth century. Until the end of the century few of the ordinary stage coaches were covered; they were great lumbering vehicles built to stand hard wear, much inferior, as Reichard admits, to the French and English coaches. Travelling post with one's own carriage, one could demand a speed of not less than a German Meile (about five miles) an hour on chaussées, but on roads classified as bad an hour and a half was allowed. Nicolai was very pleased when he did more than a Meile an hour on the good roads of the south. In the north of England twenty miles a day was a very good average, and that seems to have been about the usual distance covered in western Germany (5 Meilen or under). In the south, however, one could do three times that distance (15 or 18 Meilen, according to Reichard) in the latter part of the century.

The quickest way for younger men to travel was on horseback; the poorer travellers, wandering apprentices and most students had to be content to walk. Accommodation was primitive. There were good inns in the bigger towns, especially those with fairs (the Frankfort inns for instance are highly praised by English travellers), but in villages one had usually to be content with a 'Streu', a bed of clean straw spread on the floor of the public room. On the whole English inns seem to have been very much better in the eighteenth century than any but the best continental ones.

Travelling was not only slow and frequently dangerous, but expensive. Büsch reckoned in 1800 that it cost a business man travelling very modestly without a servant, and sharing a carriage with three companions, on the average about 1 Thaler 12 Groschen per Meile, roughly a shilling a mile, for all expenses (including tips and inn expenses). The post-chaise journey from Hamburg to Frankfort in 1800 cost Crabb Robinson £7. 8*s*., though he shared a carriage, first with three, then with four others.[1] After that experience he walked, although it was an almost unheard of thing for people of the better class to walk long distances for pleasure.

There had been a regular letter post all through the century, run by the Thurn und Taxis organisation or by individual states. To smaller places, if there was no 'fahrende Post' or mail there was a 'reitende Post' or messenger-service. Letters naturally travelled very slowly. They were usually sent by 'reitende Post' and paid for on delivery (though they could be prepaid). According to Reichard's tables it took a letter nine days to reach Frankfort-on-Main from Berlin (seven Meilen a day), four days to reach Munich or seven to reach Vienna from Frankfort (thirteen Meilen a day). This indicates incidentally the rates at which one could travel post. Small places made their own postal arrangements. The correspondence between Goethe in Weimar and Schiller in Jena was carried by Jungfer Wenzel, the Botenfrau, together with all kinds of parcels and garden produce.[2]

Waterways were in extensive use for the conveyance of

[1] *Crabb Robinson in Germany*, p. 178.

[2] See illustration in Könnecke's *Bilderatlas*.

goods and passengers. There were regular services of boats on the Rhine and Danube. One could sail from Ratisbon to Vienna for instance in three days, but the public boat was not well recommended. Wealthy travellers took a private boat for their party. David Hume, travelling with General St Clair in 1748, went from Ratisbon to Vienna 'in a large boat about eighty foot long, where we have three rooms, one for ourselves, a second for the servants and a third for our kitchen. 'Tis made entirely of fir boards and is pulled to pieces at Vienna. The wood is sold and the watermen return to Ratisbon on foot. We lie on shore every night'. Lady Mary Wortley Montagu had done the same in 1716. The journey up-stream on either river, pulled by horses, was intolerably slow for passengers. For heavy goods, water transport was the only available means. Big towns dependent on distant supplies or foreign trade were therefore only to be found on waterways or on the coast. All the navigable rivers were used, especially the Rhine, Danube, Elbe, Oder, Vistula and Main, and some canals had already been made. In Brandenburg, under the Great Elector, the upper Oder and the Spree, leading to the Havel and thus to the lower Elbe, had been connected by a canal. Under Frederick the Great the waterway from the Oder to the Elbe was greatly improved by the construction of the Plauer Canal and the Finow Canal, while the Vistula was linked to the Netze and Oder by the Bromberg Canal. Water transport was still greatly hampered by the existence of rapids and shallows, for the artificial 'regulation' of the rivers was hardly attempted before the nineteenth century, and, like the roads, the rivers were dotted with innumerable customs offices. Fourteen tolls had to be paid (many involving a long wait) between Magdeburg and Hamburg on the Elbe in 1800, thirty-three between Bamberg and Mainz on the Main, thirty-two on the Rhine between Strassburg and the Dutch frontier.

Poor as communications still were judged by nineteenth-century standards, they were good enough, especially by water, to make possible a great expansion of trade with distant towns and the export of a sufficient quantity of bulky goods to disturb the medieval 'town economy'. We have seen that in the Middle Ages there were a few towns standing out from the great mass of small market towns as centres of interregional or even international commerce, some of them owing their success mainly to trade brought by foreign merchants, others to pre-eminence in the production of some special kind of cloth or the like. This distinction was still maintained in eighteenth-century Germany, though it had grown less absolute than before, but the towns with wider relations were not always the same places which had been prominent in the Middle Ages. Through the shifting of trade routes, political changes, and variations in local enterprise over long periods, some of the old leaders had sunk to little more than local importance, and places insignificant or non-existent in the Middle Ages had taken their place. The leading towns of this later period may be further subdivided into those which were the capital of a small state, the place of residence of a prince and his court and administration, and those towns whose importance was not political but economic, the trading and industrial towns. The first class of towns has been described above, pp. 95 ff. Economically they were chiefly centres of consumption. They might have state-aided manufactures of some kind, but usually, as we have seen, these were on a small scale, concerned with luxuries and run at a loss, the products of a dilettante mercantilism. A second characteristic was that their fortunes, being dependent on the whims of a prince, were liable to sudden ups and downs. A state might be fused by inheritance with another state, or the prince might withdraw his court to another town in his state or found a new capital altogether (like Mannheim, Karlsruhe, Ludwigsburg). When that happened there would be a migration of craftsmen and servants from the old capital to the new. The old capital sometimes remained the centre of administration, but it might become simply a little market town again, as Durlach did when the capital of Baden was shifted to Karlsruhe.[1]

Of the older centres of trade, the northern towns steadily declined as the Hanse lost its monopoly of the Baltic and North Sea trade. The Hanse was officially dissolved in 1669, but it had lost all meaning long before this. England exported its own cloth and other products, through the Merchant Adventurers, from the time of Elizabeth, and the Dutch gained almost a monopoly of the Baltic trade during the seventeenth century, while the once profitable herring-fisheries of the Baltic passed to the North Sea. By the Peace of Westphalia the mouths of the great rivers (Rhine, Weser, Elbe and Oder) were left in foreign hands. The mouth of the Rhine was closed by the Dutch to German ships, and their closing of the Scheldt was legally confirmed. The main waterway of Germany, so important in the Middle Ages, came to be of merely local importance, except for the passive trade brought by the Dutch, for German shippers could not carry goods further than to Holland, and even on the Rhine itself were hampered by dozens of customs-stations.

The merchants of COLOGNE became agents of Dutch or English firms. Italian and Eastern goods no longer reached it through the south German towns, but through Amsterdam. Except for the commission trade and transport, it was of no importance in the eighteenth century. All visitors speak of its empty streets, its many beggars and monks. David Hume writes, for instance (in 1748): 'It is extremely decayed and is even falling to ruin. Nothing can strike one with more melancholy than its appearance, where there are marks of past opulence and grandeur, but such present waste and decay, as if it had lately escaped a pestilence or famine'. Like the southern towns it lost many opportunities by religious intolerance and narrow conservatism. Instead of welcoming Protestant refugees bringing new industries from Holland,

[1] For the effect on the population see Roller's admirable study *Die Einwohnerschaft der Stadt Durlach im achtzehnten Jahrhundert.*

as England and Prussia did, to their great gain, it put every difficulty in their way.

At the beginning of the century the mouths of the Weser and the Oder were under Swedish control. Although the Free Town of BREMEN remained independent, its trade was crippled by tolls, and its geographical situation was not favourable enough to attract foreigners, for the Weser tended to silt up and was not nearly such an important waterway as the Elbe. However, Bremen had survived the Thirty Years' War without serious loss, and continued in a state of quiet prosperity throughout the seventeenth and eighteenth centuries, though it was never a serious rival of Hamburg, the only Hanseatic town that made rapid progress in this period.

The Baltic ports, DANZIG, LÜBECK, KÖNIGSBERG and STETTIN, also could not compare with Hamburg during this period, but as ports they maintained a certain importance, though mostly through foreign initiative. Danzig was the great corn-exporting centre for Poland, on which it was politically dependent, and exchanged Polish natural products and those of the Vistula valley for English, Dutch and French industrial wares. Its main trade, with Holland, was carried on for the most part with the help of Dutch credit and enterprise. It had no important manufactures of its own, and its population was falling. With the rise of Prussia it lost a great deal of its trade to Königsberg and Stettin, thanks to the energetic mercantilist policy of the Prussian rulers. Both Königsberg and Stettin (when it became Prussian in 1720) grew steadily,[1] but were lacking in native capital and enterprise. In 1704 Königsberg had not a single sea-going ship of its own.[2] Lübeck, for many years the headquarters of the Hanse, had long lost its old pre-eminence, though it still contrived to maintain its independence in spite of the

[1] Königsberg 1688 *c.* 30,000, Stettin 1720 *c.* 6,000
,, 1780 60,000, ,, 1800 23,000.

[2] Kulischer, II, 243.

successive attacks of Sweden, Denmark and Russia. As it could count on no support from the Hanse or the Empire, its position was one of continual uncertainty, and the Danes could practically blockade the port for years at a time. Lübeck served as centre for the exchange of raw material from the Russian Baltic coast with western European industrial goods. Attempts to start calico and silk factories proved fruitless against the resistance of the gild spirit, here unusually strong.

The old towns of the south were in a similar state by the eighteenth century. In the sixteenth, as we saw, they were still wealthy and influential. Though the oriental trade via Venice became less important every year, spices coming now from Antwerp to Frankfort, the old-established firms of Augsburg and Nürnberg transferred their depots to Antwerp and were very successful there, both in the spice trade and later, increasingly, in finance. Some of them (the Welser of Augsburg for instance) even owned plantations in the Canaries and Spanish concessions in America for a time, many (the Fugger and Welser leading) owned mines in Tirol and other parts, even as far afield as Spain and South America, the Germans being recognised at that time as the leading mining experts. But the causes outlined above, the wholesale loss of capital, the eclipse of Venice, the rise of Holland and the ravages of the Thirty Years' War brought about the decline of the south German towns from about 1600. Another factor was, as with Cologne, the short-sighted conservatism and intolerance of the old towns, which deprived them of the new industries they might have fostered, put every obstacle in the way of Italian and Dutch refugees and drove the Huguenots to smaller towns like Ansbach, Bayreuth and Erlangen, as the Nürnberg Jews had already been driven in 1499 to Fürth, outside the walls of Nürnberg and beyond the control of its gilds.

NÜRNBERG remained a centre of commission trade and continued to produce its hardware, objects of applied art and maps. Like most of the south German towns it manufactured linen and cotton goods, but it was outstripped in the more important industries by smaller towns like Erlangen with their foreign colonies, and its population was steadily declining.[1] Externally it still looked quite prosperous. David Hume speaks of its air of industry and contentment, without splendour, and finds its people handsome, well clothed and well fed, though the old houses which we now admire seemed to him 'old-fashioned and of a grotesque figure'. This was in 1748. Nicolai uses much the same language about it some thirty years later. The old houses look to him like prisons. Quoting the famous dictum of Aeneas Sylvius in the fifteenth century, to the effect that the average Nürnberg citizen was better housed than the kings of Scotland, his comment is that the kings of Scotland must have lived in a very wretched style. He particularly disapproves of the absence of pumps and street-lighting, and of the oligarchical government. He praises the workmanship and ingenuity of its craftsmen, but finds the style of their wares too old-fashioned and ornate, compared with the simpler and more practical products of Birmingham and Sheffield. ERLANGEN on the other hand delights him with its hard practicality. The monotonous new two-storied houses where everyone was busily at work, evidently in domestic industries, the 'manufacture' of hats, stockings and gloves, the occupied air and brisk gait of people in the street, the three plain courses of the inn 'ordinary' are all contrasted with corresponding features in Bamberg, the capital of an ecclesiastical state. Even orphan children in Erlangen could earn 100 Gulden a year, Nicolai admiringly adds, by cotton-spinning. Ulm[2] still retained some of its trade in south German linen with Italy. AUGSBURG[3] was the most prosperous of these old towns,

[1] 1602, *c.* 40,000; 1806, 25,000 (Schmoller, *Deutsches Städtewesen*).

[2] Population *c.* 10,000 (Schmoller).

[3] Population sixteenth century *c.* 50,000; after Thirty Years' War 19,000; 1818, 29,800 (Schmoller).

though it had suffered severely through the rise of Holland, and the Thirty Years' War. Nicolai ascribes its superiority over Nürnberg in part to its more liberal government. It was above all a financial centre for all the neighbouring lands, particularly Austria, Bavaria, and parts of Switzerland and Italy. Its textile manufactures were considerable, especially its printed cottons. There was one mill where 350 people were employed, including many women and children. Augsburg's goldsmiths had still a high reputation, but the use of porcelain had reduced the demand for fine plate, their chief product in earlier days.

The gild tradition being strong in the older towns, they did not as a rule welcome the new large-scale industries, which were at this period almost all 'domestic industries'. The actual processes were carried out by cottagers in the country, but their work was organised by an entrepreneur in a neighbouring town. In general it may be said that up to the end of the eighteenth century and even well into the nineteenth, capitalism had only very modest beginnings to show in Germany. There were, however, industries in which 'Verleger', entrepreneurs, played an indispensable part. A Verleger was a man of some means, usually a merchant, who advanced money to a craftsman (the verb 'verlegen' could mean 'to advance money' even in Middle High German) in order that the craftsman might exercise his skill and produce saleable wares. He might lend him tools in return for a rent, in which case the craftsman could still buy his raw materials and sell the product himself, or he might supply the worker with tools and materials, pay him a fixed wage for his work and market the product, generally a more profitable procedure, and the one which gradually prevailed. The craftsman's dependence was naturally greatest, and occurred earliest, where tools or raw materials were elaborate and expensive, as in the printing trade, in connection with which the word Verleger is still used (in the sense of 'publisher'), or where the markets available were distant or scarce. At first, it will be remembered, craftsman and merchant were one person. It was only in the thirteenth century apparently that the word 'mercator' acquired its modern sense, in Italy. With the growth of a separate and powerful class of merchants, it often became necessary for the craftsman to secure the help of the merchant in selling his goods, and from this to the next stage of working under his control was only a step.

The chief German industries in which this early form of capitalism was common were, in addition to printing, such things as mining, the iron industry, textile manufactures and paper-making. With unified control, the productivity of an industry was greatly increased, especially where by the domestic system every possible source of labour in a district could be made use of. So with the linen industry of Silesia, the watch-making of the Black Forest, the toy-making of Thuringia. Most of these industries were carried on out of reach of the regulations of the towns, especially in the uplands of Silesia, Saxony, the Thuringian Forest, Westphalia, Württemberg, and also in Switzerland. In such districts, where owing to the unproductive land wages were low, the villagers welcomed the opportunity of earning money by work in their homes. Conditions were similar in many parts of England in the early days of the woollen industry. The 'clothiers' of those days were typical 'Verleger'.[1] It is the life of the German domestic weaver, at its worst, which Hauptmann depicts in *Die Weber*. Sometimes the manufacturers were combined into a sort of trust, as in the much-quoted company of clothmakers and dyers at Calw in Württemberg, founded in 1626, which lasted till the end of the eighteenth century, and at its best period employed 6000 persons. This was quite exceptionally large. Generally capital was lacking, and all businesses, except in the large towns under foreign influence, mentioned below, were on a small scale, though the aggregate of these small industries

[1] See Lipson, II, chap. 1.

might be considerable. South German and Silesian linen for instance was exported in large quantities.

It appears doubtful whether German enterprise would have effected the development to capitalistic methods until much later without the help of immigrants from already industrialised countries. Certainly the Protestant émigrés from France, Italy and Holland were the decisive factor in the spread of these methods, and helped to bring the Protestant parts of the country very much to the fore in economic matters. Brandenburg laid itself out to attract Protestant settlers from the time of the Great Elector, after the Revocation of the Edict of Nantes (1685). Through a number of edicts the country was thrown open to persecuted Protestants, and many privileges were conferred on them. Some were able to bring capital with them, others had to be helped by the state, which had great difficulty in raising the necessary funds and in finding markets for the goods produced. By 1740, as we saw, about one-quarter of the subjects of Frederick the Great are said to have consisted of immigrants or their descendants. In Berlin they were particularly to the fore. It would have been impossible to establish the new silk industry and the other minor industries, which the Prussian rulers fostered so assiduously, without their capital and technical skill, and these were the chief factors also in the rapid commercial advances made by Berlin in the seventeenth and eighteenth centuries.[1] They left a permanent trace on the intellectual and social life of the town, so that its clubs on the French model, the sociability, intelligence and political acuteness of the Berliner became a source of wonder to all visitors from other parts of Germany. It was no accident then that this capital became the focus of 'Aufklärung'. With Prussia one may contrast the south of Germany, where the Protestantism of the estates, and especially of the towns, was broken by the Catholic princes. First in Bavaria, then in Austria, the struggle

[1] For some details of the 'Industrial migration of peoples' which took place at this period see Kulischer, *op. cit.* II, 21 f.

led to a continual withdrawal of privileges from the towns, the emigration of many inhabitants and the gradual decay of their power in all domains, as compared with the more self-reliant and worldly-minded Protestant provinces. In the eighteenth century Bavaria had only thirty-nine towns, while Saxony had two hundred.[1] Beggars—and shrines—were the features that particularly struck the English traveller in south Germany, even in the early nineteenth century.[2]

The motives of the government in Prussia and other German states for encouraging manufactures were similar to those of the leading foreign powers in the mercantilist age, but in Prussia there was no power that could dispute the authority of the crown, and all measures were carried through more ruthlessly than in England, for example. The main problem of the government was how to support a large army in a country poor in natural resources. Frederick William I and Frederick the Great saw the solution in the fostering of industry and the taxation of its profits, encouraged in this by the example of Holland. Every method employed by the successful mercantilist nations was imitated. New industries were established, and it was sought to assure a safe demand for them by forbidding imports of the articles manufactured at home, and exports of the raw materials needed for them. To encourage the cloth industry, Frederick William I not only clothed his army in Brandenburg cloth, but required the citizens of Berlin to wear it exclusively, with more success than had attended English regulations of the same kind, which had begun a hundred years before this under James I, or those of Weimar, where another English precedent was copied, and it was ordained that the dead should be buried in home-spun woollen cloth.[3] His efforts were in general not

[1] Lamprecht, VIII, I.

[2] E.g. D. Hume, *Letters*, ed. Greig, I, 124, or W. Howitt, *Life in Germany*, 1842.

[3] Lipson, *Econ. Hist. of England*, III, 45; Hartung, *Das Grossherzogtum Sachsen*, 1775–1828, p. 93.

without effect; Russia in particular took large quantities of his cloth for her army. Silk spinning, dyeing, watch-making, and all the crafts practised by the immigrants were fostered in the same way.

One of the main advantages the newcomers enjoyed was that they were not made subject to the old gild regulations, becoming 'Freimeister' on the authority of the state. Repeated trouble with the Gesellen had, as we shall see, given the territories an excuse for attempts to suppress the gilds, and by an imperial law the Gesellen had been deprived of their right of association and handed over to the masters. The Empire did not, however, interfere with the masters, who also needed to be regulated in territorial interests. This reform was taken in hand by the individual states, led by Prussia from 1734. A great number of regulations were made settling the future of the gilds on the lines laid down in England under Elizabeth by the Statute of Apprentices (1563). The effect was to transfer the responsibilities of the gilds to the state and deprive them of their power, but to retain the gild forms to facilitate state control of industry. Local boundaries were broken down, and the restrictions concerning admission as a master, the 'Wanderjahre' of apprentices and other disputed points were much relaxed, to weaken the authority of the gilds. They were left little but the duty of supervising the quality of wares and workshop conditions. These regulations were imitated by most of the other German states in the course of the century.

Having broken what remained of the resistance of the gilds, the states proceeded to encourage the manufactures that suited their purposes, the chief of which was to raise revenue. They had not the capital necessary to take over the more important industries themselves, but gave concessions to manufacturers, bound up with regulations influenced by gild ideas. In general, each manufacture received a separate constitution, in which the interests of the workers too were considered. All the chief industries were in this way brought under state control. Efforts were made to adapt supply to demand, to ensure efficient technical working, to limit competition, and to set up organs for determining a fair rate of wages. It was only in Prussia that these measures could be carried through consistently and effectively, thanks to its elaborate civil service. The attempt was made everywhere, but not with Prussian energy, for in Prussia the official opinion was: 'Der Plebs geht von der alten Leier nicht ab, bis man ihn bei Nase und Armen zu seinem Vorteil schleppt'.

The manufacturer was not favoured at the expense of the country landowner and peasant, however, for if it was the duty of the town-dwellers to furnish revenue, particularly the excise levied at the town gates, the peasantry had to supply men for the army, and as the country squires were of the same class and tastes as the king himself, their interests could not be neglected. Accordingly, although the towns claimed the first call on the corn produced by the country, and would have had the Junkers only permitted to export what was over when their claims had been met, the Prussian kings in the eighteenth century allowed the nobles the right of freely exporting corn, as they desired, but in return restricted trade and industry to the towns. This latter concession to the towns was double-edged, for the excise, the chief source of revenue, could only be levied on town-made products, so that the concentration of all industry within the town walls was also in the interests of the government. It was possible, by keeping Poland economically a subject state, to combine the advantages of free export of corn with those of a stable and reasonable price for home consumers. The government, and only the government, could import Polish corn, and by doing so when it was cheap, it could lay in stores that were not only a reserve for the army, but could be released in years of bad harvests to bring down the price in the home market.

The smaller states too in many cases tried to make themselves economically self-sufficient, but their efforts were necessarily fruitless in view of their size and isolation. As we have seen (p. 38) many courts encouraged local industries, luxury trades for the most part, here a porcelain factory, there a silk or cloth factory, but they did so because of their French models, and many of their industries were as much of a caricature as their armies. They had to contend not only with foreign countries, but still more with other German states, especially Prussia and later Austria, which could take measures in the control of trade that did not remain mere paper threats. Prussia's policy for instance caused Leipzig and Hamburg very anxious times, however much it may have benefited them in the end. In general, though the subjects of these small states could not count on much direct assistance from their governments, they were comparatively free from interference, undisturbed in their 'Behaglichkeit' by a too rational and active ruler. Except for an occasional grandmotherly edict things were allowed to take their own course. The gilds retained greater freedom and power in these smaller states, and the whole view of life there was calmer, more philosophical, if more passive, than in the ambitious larger states. It was the view still typical of Germany taken as a whole, the view that is idealised in *Hermann und Dorothea*, traditional, modest, inclined to despise as upstarts the new manufacturers and merchants, though a little envious of their wealth.

Although the older towns were in decline and the new forms of domestic industry were cultivated above all in villages, there were a few towns which, owing mainly to their geographical position, had made considerable progress since the Middle Ages.

Dealings with foreign countries had to take place through certain centres, if only for the convenience of the foreigners themselves, and a number of towns on the borders of Germany or in other favoured positions were by these means able to avoid the fate of the great majority. Although this trade began by being almost entirely carried on by strangers, it provided many opportunities for the German inhabitants too. From these centres goods were carried all over the country by pedlars, whose part in distribution can hardly be appreciated by us now, with our immensely superior communications and shops in every village. They were looked upon by the old-fashioned Möser as an almost unmitigated evil. 'There are three times as many retailers (most of them pedlars) now', he says, 'as there were a hundred years ago, and only half as many craftsmen.' 'Not a year passes without at least ten Englishmen travelling in Germany for commercial purposes and canvassing for customers.' Ten sounds a small enough number, and indicates sufficiently how little the country depended on trade at all; but it was apparently large in comparison with the number of German traders. 'What is the Krämer (retailer)?' he asks. 'A man who only makes foreigners rich, whether they be friends or foes, and encourages luxury, tempting everyone with novelties, continually springing new fashions on us and making the craftsman's wares out of date. He is so proud too that honest handiwork is held to be contemptible, and every young man of parts must needs become a trader like himself.' Pedlars ought only to be permitted to sell goods from their country of origin, Möser says, and luxuries such as lace should not be allowed in at all. It is the same doctrine of self-sufficiency that we have met with in the medieval townsman and the later mercantilist alike.

Germany as a whole stood in the same relation of inferiority to countries like England and Holland as its own small towns did to the large centres, and the reasons for this relation were clearly perceived by contemporaries. We may sum them up with the invaluable Möser as follows:

(*a*) The successful masters in the large towns, having as many as thirty or forty Gesellen, had naturally introduced the principle of specialisation, with the result that in time their workmen, being only familiar with one subordinate process, could not become independent. The masters had the advantage of the services of very highly skilled assistants at the wages they cared to fix.

(*b*) For first-class work the help of painters, gilders, sculptors and so on was needed, and as they could not make a living in small towns they were not to be found there.

(*c*) The general level of taste was higher in large towns than in small, which therefore turned out old-fashioned work.

(*d*) There was an economy in working expenses when a single master could have forty men busy in one building, instead of twenty small masters having two men each.

(*e*) Many people could combine for the purchase of raw material in large towns.

(*f*) One particular kind of manufacture often needed the help of others, so that it was often impossible to start new industries in a small town because the supporting industries did not exist there.

(*g*) Only large concerns could afford to instal machinery, and use mechanical power.

(*h*) Talented men were attracted to the large towns, where they found a ready market for their inventions. It is worth noting that the use of machinery is not stressed by Möser. The fact that it comes so low down in his list is an interesting confirmation of the opinion of those economic historians who hold that centralised manufactures, carried on in factories by machinery, were rare, even at the end of the eighteenth century.[1] 'Fabrik' is used by Möser in the sense of 'manufacture', as the French word 'fabrique' was used in phrases like 'la fabrique des toiles'.

Of these newer centres of trade the most important was Germany's chief North Sea port, HAMBURG. Hamburg enjoyed a great advantage in possessing the best natural harbour on the German North Sea coast, for along the greater part of this coast the water is shallow, only deepening sufficiently for large ships in the estuaries, especially in that

[1] E.g. Kulischer, II, 148 ff.

of the Elbe. Hamburg was therefore marked out as the port for bringing the North German plain into touch with England, France and Holland. As an internal avenue of trade the Elbe was second only to the Rhine. Hamburg was the seaport of Berlin. In the best times of the Hanse it had not been so flourishing as Lübeck, for the Baltic trade was then far more valuable than that of the North Sea, but it had later an advantage over Lübeck and all the other Hanseatic ports in being the depôt chosen as the most convenient by the English trading company that proved the Hanse's most serious rival. As we have seen, the Hamburger were false enough to the Hanse to welcome the English 'Merchant Adventurers' in 1567, and though forced later to eject them, it was not long before their city became the main depôt of this important company, which had the monopoly of English trade with Germany. It was already the most important port on this coast except Antwerp, and had built an exchange in 1558, only four years after Antwerp itself. The fall of Antwerp in the Spanish wars greatly increased its trade, though from now it had a serious rival in Amsterdam. Its participation in the colonial trade, combined with its English connections, made it a commercial centre of international importance, an importance that was not diminished even by the Thirty Years' War, in spite of the damage done to its hinterland. A Dutch bank was founded there in 1619, and the growth of the town's fortunes is reflected in the fact that the tax yield was doubled during the course of the war. The town was spared an occupation, and its population was swelled by numerous refugees. Through its neutrality in the various wars between the sea powers it was often able to play the part of *tertius gaudens*, acquiring at times almost a position of monopoly. As its capital increased, it was able to enter into competition with England and Holland in manufactures. Its local trade with Holland was enormously increased by Dutch immigration during the Dutch Wars of Independence. Its population soon became international, for like Amsterdam and unlike Nürnberg or Ulm it was a refuge for exiles of all kinds, Jews and Protestants. Even in the eighteenth century only about 160 of the 2000 ships that arrived and sailed each year were owned by residents, the rest coming from abroad. It was therefore naturally open to foreign influences in all matters. It had the first coffee-house, the first 'Moralische Wochenschriften' in imitation of the *Spectator*, the first masonic lodge, and it was the home of democracy in Germany. Its importance for German civilisation was very great and its status among German towns from the end of the fifteenth until late in the eighteenth century was unique, in view of its size, prosperity and activity in economic, political and intellectual affairs.

Next in importance among the towns in German-speaking lands was the group which acted as intermediary between Germany and Italy and southern France, namely the SWISS TOWNS and STRASSBURG. Although these towns too ultimately owed their prosperity mainly to their favourable geographical situation on great ways of communication, 'passive' trade no longer predominated in them to such an extent as in the northern ports. Thanks in great measure to the skill and initiative of Protestant refugees from Italy and France they had developed by the eighteenth century important export industries, notably silk and woollen weaving. The prominent part played by Italian refugees in particular, with their expert knowledge of the new industrial technique and organisation that were known in Italy long before their adoption in other parts of Europe, can still clearly be traced by an examination of the names of Basle and Zürich patrician families. Starting in the sixteenth century, they successfully overcame Dutch competition in the seventeenth, being so little affected by the Thirty Years' War that their land seemed to 'Simplicissimus', for instance, an earthly paradise. 'The country seemed so strange to me compared with other parts of Germany that I felt I might have been in Brazil or China. I saw people going about their business in peace; the byres were full of cattle, the farmyards full of hens, geese and ducks; the roads were used by travellers in safety, the inns were full of people making merry.'[1]

The hold of the gild system was shaken here even in the seventeenth century, and manufactures on a domestic basis, with workers in the country, began to grow up, depending on export trade for their existence. The Rhine was the great channel of communication with Germany, the route for a flourishing trade with Strassburg and Frankfort. Silk was exported too to the towns of Bavaria, Austria and Hungary. The export trade was directed by central organisations in Zürich, Basle, St Gallen and Strassburg from as early as 1670, and large-scale industrial interests soon acquired the lead in social and political matters. The effects of the decay of craftsmanship that ensued are perhaps still to be seen in the extent to which foreign craftsmen outnumber native Swiss. A more welcome feature was the attention paid to education by those in authority, and the intellectual and artistic activity of the leisured classes. Even in the seventeenth century nearly half the population of Zürich could read and write, and quite half the children went to school. Basle was a centre of learning as well as of trade, for it had the means to support the ancient university founded there by the Humanist Pope Pius II.

The comparative prosperity of the towns so far discussed was due to their favourable geographical position, which led to their becoming centres of trade. The same considerations determined the importance of certain central German towns too during this period, towns which were for the most part insignificant for their own production, but which formed convenient trade centres owing to their position on natural lines of communication. There was first LEIPZIG. Before any roads had been made in Germany it was divided into two main areas of trade, one in the north and one in the south, connected only by the Rhine in the west. Central Germany

[1] Grimmelshausen, *Simplicissimus*, Bk. v, chap. 1.

was a neutral area. It became necessary to find a route through this region too when the colonisation of the east began, to allow of the exchange of western manufactures with eastern raw materials. Towns already existed in these parts on the main rivers, mostly on what geographers call the 'fall-line', where the hills meet the plain and goods brought from the plains by road or river had to be unloaded and distributed by pack-horse. The new cross-connections joined the most conveniently situated of these towns. The main road was the one through Frankfort-on-Main (the western gate), Eisenach and Erfurt to Leipzig and Halle, an old route of the Halle salt trade, following a series of troughs running east and west. The other skirted the Teutoburger Wald, passed between the Harz and the Thüringer Wald and north of the Erzgebirge and Sudeten to the Silesian colonies, divided into three stages by Cologne, Leipzig and Breslau, each in a fertile, thickly populated district. Leipzig was the meeting point of these two roads, and this alone would have made it the chief town in Central Germany except Frankfort, which was also the junction of two main lines of communication, by road and river. It was further helped by the rise of Hamburg and the necessity under which southern Germany found itself of turning its face to the north instead of to Italy, after the great change of world trade routes. The southern towns had to find a road to a northern port; owing to Dutch control and the innumerable tolls on the Rhine, Hamburg was favoured, and Leipzig was the most convenient half-way house between the sea and the southern centre Nürnberg, besides being the natural centre of concentration for goods from Saxony, Silesia and Poland.

No wonder then that for contemporaries Leipzig was as great a wonder as Hamburg. In this 'Klein Paris', as Goethe tells us in *Dichtung und Wahrheit*, one met at fair-time foreigners from all quarters, Polish Jews, Russians, even Greeks in their strange garb, as well as Englishmen and Dutchmen, for by this time its fair, held three times a year, had quite outstripped that of Frankfort, its great rival. There might be anything up to 7000 visiting merchants at fair-times, and the turnover might be in the neighbourhood of a million pounds.[1] In the fifteenth and early sixteenth centuries the town had acquired extensive privileges, reducing Halle and Erfurt to dependence. Its 'staple rights' held good for fifteen Meilen around and it attracted traders by guile and by force in order to cripple the trade by rival routes, such as that between Hof and Dresden. A textile industry was started by Dutch refugees, but on the whole Leipzig was far more important as a centre of trade than for its own industries. It was the market for the products of Saxony, the chief industrial province, with its widespread domestic industries, its porcelain at Meissen (Dresden china) and cotton at Chemnitz, and its trade grew with that of the northern ports, especially from the second half of the seventeenth century. Even in 1765 it produced the impression of a commercial city of recent growth. 'Leipzig evokes in the observer no memories of bygone times; its monuments speak of a new and recent epoch; a period of commercial activity, ease and wealth', as Goethe says. It had already blocks of flats like 'great castles, or even whole quarters of towns', and was extremely open to foreign influences, especially French, for its culture was more recent than that of Frankfort, which had long been in touch with the civilising West.

In virtue of its position FRANKFORT had long been an important market for goods, where Eastern wares were exchanged with south and west German industrial products. The importance of its fairs was increased by the destruction of its rival Antwerp, Frankfort's central situation making it particularly famous as a money-market. During the Thirty Years' War its position in this respect was much weakened owing to difficulties of communication and general uncertainty, and it lost much of its business to Amsterdam, to which it now had to play second fiddle till the nineteenth

[1] Figures from Kulischer, II, 255.

century. It lost its leadership in the book trade to Leipzig early in the seventeenth century for a number of reasons—the falling-off of the Italian trade since the Index of Pius IV (*c.* 1570), the strict censorship of the Imperial Book Commission, the high-handed behaviour of the Frankfort booksellers against foreigners, the increase in the number of German publications as against Latin, which reduced the number of books printed abroad. It had been possible of course to print Latin books anywhere, but German could only be printed well in Germany, and in those days, when publishers went to the fair in person, Leipzig was a better centre for the home trade. The tendency of the southern trade to avoid Frankfort and the Rhine in favour of Leipzig and Hamburg, and the competition of Basle, Nürnberg, and later the new town Mannheim, the distributing centre of the English and Dutch, all contributed towards Frankfort's decline, but its geographical position and old connections enabled it to retain more of its old glory than most of the south German Reichsstädte. It was tolerant of Protestant refugees and Jews—the Jews expelled from Nürnberg, Augsburg, Ulm, etc. congregated in the Frankfort ghetto. Besides patricians and officials there were manufacturers following in the wake of Western developments—Goethe describes for instance an oil-cloth factory owned and directed by a painter, in which large numbers of people were employed, but many of the refugees were driven to settle in Höchst, Offenbach, or Hanau to escape gild regulations. There were also already merchants and financiers (the Bethmanns and later the Rothschilds) with large fortunes, but on the whole Frankfort had to be content to rest on its laurels during this period, contriving by timely compromises, of which its constitution might be taken as a type, to avoid the fate of the smaller towns, but never energetic and venturesome enough to make any rapid progress.[1]

[1] See *Die Stadt Goethes*, ed. Voelcker, 1932, for a full account of Frankfort at this period.

Such a vegetative existence was by no means the fate of BERLIN in the seventeenth and eighteenth centuries. From the time of the Great Elector, its development was due to conscious effort on the part of the Prussian rulers, whose vigorous mercantilist policy gradually succeeded in remedying the defects of its natural position and tapping some of Leipzig's stream of trade. By the construction of the Friedrich-Wilhelm canal the Oder was connected with the Spree, and Berlin became the half-way house between Breslau and Hamburg by the water route. The Breslau merchants were encouraged by preferential tariffs to use the new route instead of the roads, sending their Silesian yarn and linen down the Oder and Elbe, and receiving in return colonial goods, fruit, wine and textiles for Poland, Russia and Austria. This was to the advantage of Breslau, which grew to be a considerable town, and still more to that of Berlin, where these goods had all to be transshipped, so that Berlin now acquired some of the advantages that Leipzig had enjoyed. Its river connections were now excellent, and they were further improved under Frederick the Great; its competition had been felt by Leipzig even before the end of the seventeenth century. Its population grew continuously: 1661—6500; 1721—over 60,000; *c.* 1760—120,000; 1777—140,000; 1795—150,000. It has been pointed out that only part of this increase was due to the growth of trade and industry. A large proportion was accounted for by the influx of French and Dutch immigrants, who were encouraged to come because of their industrial skill, and a still larger one by the growth of the Prussian army and the increasing political importance of Berlin. We have seen above that in 1783, out of a total population of 141,000, the garrison with their families made up 33,000, officials and their families about 14,000 and personal attendants on these and the court another 10,000, a total of 57,000 persons directly dependent on the will of the king.

Chapter III

MUNICIPAL GOVERNMENT AND THE STRUCTURE OF TOWN SOCIETY

We have seen that the towns may be classified according to the range and nature of their economic activities. Their political relationships are a further ground of differentiation, and one hardly less important for the general life of the town dwellers. According to their legal status in relation to the Empire and its component states they had been divided since the Middle Ages into Imperial or Free Towns and 'Landstädte', or towns under the control of a Landesfürst, a territorial ruler. A brief historical retrospect is necessary to explain the situation as it was in the eighteenth century.

The effect of the rise of absolute territorial states in Germany had been particularly disastrous on the towns, for most of the gains of the princes were made at their expense. There was no longer any superior authority to regulate the relations of town to territory; the struggle was decided by the strength of the opponents. The lords had, however, allies in the lesser nobles and country squires who had seats in provincial assemblies, where the Landstädte were also represented. Being of similar tastes, habits and extraction to the princes, it was natural that these landowners, each of whom exercised on his estate the same kind of patriarchal authority as the princes themselves claimed over the whole land, should need little inducement to take the princes' side rather than that of the bourgeois, the upstart shopkeepers whose intelligence and *esprit de corps* made them so dangerous, and whose towns attracted the poor but indispensable lower members of the feudal hierarchy, threatening the security of the whole system. But perhaps the main cause of the triumph of the territories was the desertion of important town forces to the enemy. As the territories became closer and stronger units, the towns lost their old organising power and sense of self-help, for their most intelligent members entered some prince's service and helped him to establish his authority at the expense of the towns that had reared them.

It was more difficult for a society consisting, as town society did now, of widely differentiated elements to form an organic whole than it had been in a simpler age. When the gilds demanded political authority in the towns proportionate to their numbers and importance, many of the wealthy old patrician families, which had always had much in common with the lesser nobility in their ways of life and general outlook, converted their fortunes into landed estates and deprived the towns of their capital and brains. They were often imitated in this by the most successful merchants, for they, like the craftsmen already spoken of, were not disposed to work any longer when they possessed a competence on which to retire and buy themselves a title and estate. Even where they did not do so, they generally no longer felt the interests of the town to be their own, and were ready to finance any prince, however hostile his intentions towards their fellow townsmen. Their loans and the great expansion of the currency due to the exploitation of the German, and later the American, mines brought about a revolution in prices, a fall in the value of money, which the masses attributed not merely to the Fugger and their kind, but to the bourgeoisie in general, so that they acquiesced in the policy of the princes, and looked upon robber knights as deliverers.

Thus even apart from the losses resulting from the Spanish bankruptcies and later from the ravages of the Thirty Years' War, there was not the same financial power at the disposal of the town authorities as in their prime. Many of those which had enjoyed the rights of toll and mintage lost them to the territorial lords, whose depreciation of the coinage impoverished them further. The princes exacted tolls of their own on roads, bridges and rivers, and prevented the towns from gaining any revenue from their own tolls by the provision that goods should pay duty only once within the territorial limits. The burden of taxation in the towns was, as we have seen, unevenly distributed, the rich and powerful paying least. The territorial finances, on the other hand, were rapidly improving, enabling the princes to buy the services of the mercenary troops that the towns had been the first to employ.

The old civic guards of volunteers had everywhere disappeared, for with money the towns had been able to pay for both men and material aids, strong walls and implements of war. They had thus been able for a time to maintain their rights against neighbouring nobles, but with the rise of the territories their own weapons were turned against them. The Lanzknechte went to the highest bidder, swelling the standing armies of the princes, while the invention of gunpowder and artillery made the old town walls almost useless. After the Thirty Years' War the trade of war became a territorial one, the princes alone having armies, which grew accordingly in size and efficiency, while the defences of the towns fell into decay. The difference between the Middle Ages and modern times in this respect may be seen by contrasting Machiavelli's description of the German Free Towns of his day, in the tenth chapter of the *Prince*, with Frederick the Great's comments on the passage in his *Anti-Machiavel*.

'The towns of Germany', says Machiavelli (he is referring to the larger 'free' towns), 'enjoy a high degree of freedom, although their territory is small; they obey the emperor when they so desire, and fear neither him nor any other powerful neighbour. For as they are all surrounded by strong walls and deep moats, possess an artillery suited to their needs and always keep their storehouses stocked with a year's provision of wood and foodstuffs, the investment of these towns is a long and difficult matter....They keep themselves always in training in the arts of war, and have many usages besides to prevent themselves from falling into decay.'

To this Frederick remarks:

> The picture presented to us by Machiavelli of the German Free Towns is quite different from their present state. One petard, or in default of that, one word of command from the emperor, would suffice to make him master of these towns. They are all badly fortified. Most of them have old walls with tall towers on them at intervals, and moats almost filled up with the earth that has fallen in. They have few soldiers and these badly disciplined; their officers are for the most part either obtained second-hand from German princes, or are old men no longer capable of service. A few Free Towns have fairly good artillery; but that would not be sufficient to enable them to oppose the emperor, and he takes every opportunity of making them conscious of their powerlessness.

Frederick is here alluding to those Reichsstädte which had at any rate maintained an outward show of independence, but even in these the same decay of the civic spirit had set in as in the other towns, a change clearly reflected in the oligarchical form of their government. The only towns that had changed their constitutions since the sixteenth century were Frankfort-on-Main and Hamburg. Although the Peace of Westphalia made them into sovereign states, the Free Towns had no real power in the Reichstag. Even in the middle of the sixteenth century they had only been heard after the other sections had come to an agreement. Their governments were thoroughly reactionary; the council consisted frequently of two bodies that relieved each other at intervals, and filled vacancies by co-option from the 'Ratsfähige Geschlechter'. There were in many towns hereditary posts, and even where this was not so, offices were chiefly valued for the pecuniary gain they involved, the reversion of some kind of office being a valuable form of legacy. The council had full power and no responsibilities. It would speak of 'its' citizens, and even assume a sort of divine right as sanction for its worst acts. The Hamburg[1]

[1] Hamburg, though it only became a Free Town in the eighteenth century *de jure*, had long been free *de facto*.

council for instance in 1602 addressed the assembly of citizens, supposed to share power with itself, in the following terms: 'Even if an authority is ungodly, tyrannical and avaricious, it does not become its subjects to rebel against it. They ought rather to recognise their fate as a punishment from the Almighty, which the subjects have brought upon themselves by their sins'.[1]

The paid officials who replaced the older voluntary ones, especially after the spread of Roman law, were often lawyers. Jurists assumed important functions in almost all towns, and were often members of the council as experts. In the Landstädte they, together with the council, were mere tools in the hands of the prince, who often appointed them and even nominated new members of the council when vacancies occurred. Independent town legislation was here a thing of the past, for every regulation had to be submitted to the central authority. Jurisdiction too had become a prerogative of the princes. There were no longer any town courts, with an appeal, if necessary, to their 'Oberhof', the court of the town that had served as model for their law. Roman law was everywhere recognised, and the only appeal was to the territorial supreme court.

That the management of the towns under these conditions was full of abuses was only to be expected. If the citizens appealed to the prince he had an excuse for sending commissaries to enquire into the matter, and really to replace the council entirely, so that democratic control was quite out of the question. There was no attraction in serving such a town for honour, when office-holders were responsible only in appearance and all real control was exercised from above. It became at last a common practice to pay the members of the council, which frequently consisted of superannuated state servants or invalided non-commissioned officers, for they were not even well paid. The mayor of Berlin for instance, who was in effect a minor state official, was paid 200 Thalers

[1] Preuss, *op. cit.* p. 147.

a year or less. Frederick William I said openly 'Mein Interesse ist, Bürgermeister zu setzen, die platt von mir dependieren'.[1]

The sovereign state had killed the spirit of autonomy, or at all events taken advantage of its decay, to substitute an authoritarian organisation, modelled on the disciplined armies of the time and receiving all orders from above, for the old decentralised self-government of independent groups. It is probable that this development was desirable in the interest of efficiency; a larger unit was necessary, and the towns were too much bound by tradition to recognise the fact. But that Prussia for instance went too far in the direction of centralisation, in the absence of any parliamentary corrective, is shown by the fact that Stein had to reverse the process in his 'Städteordnung' at the end of the eighteenth century.

The difference between Free and Territorial Towns was directly reflected in the structure of society in the towns, in municipal government and consequently in social life and ideals. It is a serious over-simplification to speak of a 'Bürger' without qualifying adjective, for citizens differed in different kinds of town and in the different social strata of any one town. Even in the medieval town, civic society was far from being a community of equals. There were harsh contrasts in plenty, with regard to social status and influence, wealth and manner of living. It is true that wealth was not the almost exclusive criterion of esteem that it has become to-day, but it was already a very important factor and was very unequally distributed. It has been calculated from tax-returns and so on that between one-fifth and two-fifths of the population in most medieval towns was quite without property. In Augsburg the proportion is said to have been two-thirds.[2] Usually more than half the total wealth was concentrated in the hands of some 4 or 5 per cent. of the

[1] Preuss, *op. cit.* p. 167.

[2] Kulischer, I, 176, where details are given.

population.[1] In every big town there were large numbers of crippled and blind beggars. Of course the ideal of individual equality was one that did not enter the heads of the citizens. 'Whereas the modern view is dynamic, and the struggle of whole classes to raise themselves not only in wealth and culture, but in political and social power, seems to us just as much a kind of moral duty as do the efforts of the individual to get on and if possible to rise into another class, the thought and feeling of the Middle Ages were static. Both the social orders in themselves and the bond between the individual and his order were looked upon as ordained by God.'[2] This instinctive acceptance of hereditary social orders was only slowly modified by the accumulation of wealth in the larger towns, and considerations of 'Stand' were, as we have seen, still very important in eighteenth-century Germany.

The sumptuary regulations which continued to be made (though no longer observed) well into the eighteenth century give us some idea of current opinion about the relative standing of various classes. In the last *Kleiderordnung* issued in Frankfort-on-Main, in 1731, five classes are distinguished. The first consists of the principal civic dignitaries (the Schultheiss, the Schöffen or Aldermen of the first bench, the town councillors of the second bench, the four syndics, etc.), the doctors (of law and medicine), and the members of noble families whose ancestors had taken part in the government of the town for at least a century. The second class consists of the councillors of the third bench (gild representatives), the most distinguished citizens, wholesale merchants and bankers with a capital of at least 20,000 Thalers. In the third class came notaries and advocates, artists and shopkeepers, and 'others of about the same standing'. In the fourth class we find 'die gemeinen schlechten Krämer'—small stall-holders and street-hawkers, shop assistants and craftsmen,

[1] J. Bühler, *Die Kultur des Mittelalters*, 1931, p. 124.
[2] *Ibid.*

and in the fifth class all the rest, labourers, coachmen, servants and the like.

This list reflects of course the reactionary town council's view of the social hierarchy, and would not have been accepted then by every one. It ranks the patricians of the town for instance higher than members of noble families from outside, of whom there were usually a number residing in the town. They are classed among the 'distinguished citizens' of class two, but would certainly consider themselves the superiors of any patrician. The wealthy merchants who were not in the council, again, would surely not hold themselves to be merely the equals of the gildsmen on the town council. But roughly speaking the list represents fairly enough the social order of precedence in a Free Town.

The patricians were amongst the wealthiest people in the town, but not all wealthy men were patricians. The patricians were 'the families with inherited wealth, organised as a caste' (v. Below). They liked to think that their ancestors had been the ruling class from time immemorial; they held themselves (as Goethe said to Eckermann) to be no whit inferior to the 'county families', the country nobility. Some few could trace their descent to the oldest town families, the early settlers who had fought for the town's rights with the town lord, or the lord's officials in the town, but though the governing class had tried from a very early date to close its ranks to newcomers, it had never succeeded in preventing the rise of new families to wealth and esteem, and had always gradually absorbed them. In Nürnberg itself the names in the various lists we have of patrician families at different dates are by no means always the same. 'A list of 1390 mentions 118 "ehrbare Familien", one of 1490, 112. Of these only 49 were named in the 1390 list. A list of 1511 mentions 92. Only 37 of the patrician families of 1390 are still amongst them.'[1] The patrician families usually formed

[1] v. Below, *Das ältere deutsche Städtewesen und Bürgertum*, p. 119.

themselves into a club or union to protect their rights, much as the craftsmen organised themselves in gilds. In eighteenth-century Frankfort for instance there were still two 'societies' of good families, the Limpurger and the Frauensteiner. The Limpurger claimed to be the older and more respectable, and looked upon the Frauensteiner as upstart traders, but it was a domestic quarrel and both alike held themselves to be equal to the nobility of the Reich. Their pride rested on a compound of inherited wealth, traditions of civic service, legal privileges and a high standard of living. As new members only sons of members were admitted, or full citizens who married into these families.[1]

In some towns old merchant families would predominate (in Hamburg and the ports), in others landowners and rentiers. In all towns, since the acceptance of Roman law, the class of university graduates in law had come, through their indispensability, to be considered amongst those of the first rank. Their right to this esteem was not undisputed. It was urged by the patricians that the status of a graduate was purely personal, confined to the man himself. He might be the son of a craftsman and his children might be 'Pöbel'.[2] There was not very much force in this last objection because it was only a man of considerable means who could afford to let his son study law. Poor boys usually had to be content with theology. The graduates (who had their own 'Kollegium' to defend their interests) were not lacking in arguments in their own defence. They appealed to old privileges, foreign example, and above all they urged that the claim of native ability was superior to that of inherited position. Legal training was a necessary qualification for most of the important civic offices and greatly increased a man's chances of being elected to the council. The 'doctors' enjoyed esteem accordingly as potential councillors. The university graduates,

[1] For details see article by Dr H. Voelcker in *Die Stadt Goethes*, pp. 97 ff.

[2] *Id.* p. 210.

amongst whom the lawyers stood in highest esteem, were so important in general in the development of German thought and literature, forming, as they came to do, virtually a new 'Stand' between the landowning nobility and the merchants and better craftsmen, that it will be necessary to devote a special chapter to them later.

The high standing enjoyed by the better merchants in Frankfort is easily explained by their importance in the city's economic life. We have seen earlier that though merchants had come to the fore in the bigger medieval towns, it was only in modern times that they were to be found in large numbers in any but a few towns. We have seen also that the distinction between merchant and shopkeeper was not rigid in the Middle Ages, and it had not become so even in the eighteenth century, any more than that between merchant and banker. The social standing of a trader naturally depended on the scope of his undertakings and consequent wealth. The social status of a master craftsman could still be high, especially where, as in Frankfort, the gilds had successfully claimed representation on the council. But generally speaking, in consequence of the falling off in the demand for gild products and the growth of capitalistic forms of industry in the country, it was not so high relatively as in the Middle Ages. Though gild forms were still observed, there was not the same proud spirit of independence among the masters as in earlier days. On the other hand, with the relaxation of gild regulations which, in spite of protests, proved inevitable, many craftsmen made considerable fortunes (one remembers Goethe's grandfather, the lady's tailor) and others became dealers and entrepreneurs. In the literature of the time, a master craftsman is usually represented as one of the lower middle class, a 'Kleinbürger', who works hard for a very modest living.

Below the master-craftsmen came, in addition to unskilled workers, the important class of those who were, at least in theory, serving their time in the expectation of becoming masters themselves, the apprentices and journeymen. A journeyman (Geselle) was an apprentice who had served his 'Lehrzeit', passed the journeyman's test and been solemnly promoted to the rank of 'Geselle' by his gild. He received a certificate to this effect, a 'Lehrbrief', which frequently contained good advice for his future conduct. Goethe made use of many of these details of course in his *Wilhelm Meister*. After his admission, the Geselle in the majority of gilds in Germany went on his wanderings for a period of years, as Wilhelm does. They might take him all over Germany and even into the neighbouring countries. The journeymen, then, were in the main a floating population of young unmarried men ('Junggesellen'), with few ties in the town. Many of them were naturally restless and irresponsible spirits, so that disputes between masters and journeymen were inevitable. Moreover, the rise of entrepreneurs and the growing exclusiveness of the masters within the gilds had led to an increasing disproportion in numbers between masters and journeymen. Many of the latter could no longer hope to attain independence; they might even suffer quite seriously from unemployment. The disproportion in numbers does not seem to have been very great in Germany in most trades until the nineteenth century, and the old patriarchal ways of life continued even in large towns, apprentices and journeymen still living and working in their master's house.[1] Yet it is clear from the unrest among them, which caused so much alarm in the seventeenth century and continued into the eighteenth, that the journeymen had become conscious of class interests of their own.

The separate organisations of journeymen deserve mention here, for they were hardly less important for their influence on life in the towns than the gilds of masters described in an earlier chapter. They combined some of the functions of a modern trade union with those of a labour exchange. From local fraternities with a function something like that

[1] Figures in Sombart, *op. cit.* II, 692.

of the Young Men's Christian Association, encouraged by town and Church, they had become unions for the defence of their members' rights as workers, joined in affiliations which covered the whole country. Each trade or group of trades had its 'Herberge' in every town, an inn where the members met for social intercourse and for the business of the association, which was conducted with many time-hallowed phrases and usages. The members enjoyed, in return for a fixed subscription, not only the privileges of local membership, but the certainty of a welcome from the allied organisations all over Germany. On coming to a town, the wandering journeyman would make his way to the Herberge of his craft, and here, if he had the necessary papers from his home-town and presented himself with the usual formula—at first a kind of shibboleth—he was received as a brother and helped to find employment by his fellow-craftsmen. If there were no vacancies, he received free quarters and was usually given a small sum of money from the common funds, to help him on his way to the next town. In any dispute with his master about wages or conditions of work the union would support him, if he seemed to them to be in the right, and to this end what we should now call the strike and the boycott were used by the journeymen with great determination.

It was a too class-conscious use of these weapons which evoked a series of measures passed by the Reichstag and culminating in an imperial law of 1731, by which the unions were deprived of their functions and every journeyman was compelled to carry a passport from his government on his wanderings. Led by Prussia, the territories very gradually proceeded to enforce these provisions, but many features of the old organisations survived, though under increasingly efficient state control. The journeymen continued to go on their wanderings, in some trades until late in the nineteenth century. The wandering handicraftsmen were still a prominent feature of German life for instance when Howitt visited Germany in 1840. 'One of the first things on your arrival in the country which strikes your eye', he says, 'is the number of young men on the roads with knapsacks on their backs, and stout sticks in their hands.' 'At each end of his knapsack peep the soles of a pair of boots; and he has often, moreover, attached to his knapsack, a pair of small wheels, by which, when his back is weary of it, he can trail it after him with his stick.' It was exactly in this way that Keller's *Drei gerechte Kammacher* were equipped. The journeymen were the first class of people, apparently, who were forced to go through the procedure, which now seems to foreigners so peculiarly German, of reporting to the police on arrival in a town and again on departure. 'It is amazing in the large cities the crowd of these Gesellen that you see at the police-office, bringing their passports, or fetching them away again.' This is not the only detail in Howitt's description of the Handwerksburschen which reminds us how much of the old way of life has survived into the present. The institution of Wanderschaft, affecting as it did the lives of so large a proportion of the inhabitants of the towns, was bound to leave its mark on German society even in the industrial age. The ordinary working man saw more of his own country than the same class in any other part of the world, as Howitt points out, and it was probably not merely fanciful of this writer to associate with the habit of Wanderschaft the 'nature-loving and poetic feeling which so universally distinguishes the German, even to the commonest class'. It is surely no accident that Germany, where wandering was compulsory for craftsmen so much longer than elsewhere, should have been the home of the Wandervögel and the Youth Movement, of school-journeys and youth-hostels. 'Wanderlust' had become part of the social inheritance, mainly through the century-old habits of the common people of the towns. For the same reason the Wanderlieder and the nature poetry, in which German literature is so rich, cannot be looked upon as the creation of Romantic intellectuals. They had their roots deep in popular habit and feeling.[1]

In every town the inhabitants formed nominally two, in reality in most towns three distinct groups in regard to their legal rights and duties as citizens. These legal survivals from the Middle Ages were still of some importance for purposes of taxation. In the Free Towns citizenship was still felt to be an honour, but in the other towns it seems to have been a privilege that was little esteemed. In towns like Frankfort and most of the Free Towns only the members of the 'Ratsfähige Familien' were really citizens in the fullest sense, enjoying an active share in the government. This seems to have been the normal state of things in the early days of the towns. In theory, however, the inhabitants of all towns were now either *Vollbürger*, citizens proper, or *Beisassen* (Hintersassen, Schutzbürger). The first were considered as full members of the city community, the second as 'associate members'. Only the citizens might own houses and land in the town area—though exceptions were made for noblemen and monasteries. Only citizens could be members of the council or civic officials. Only citizens could become master craftsmen or shopkeepers. The citizens still enjoyed privileges in the matter of tolls and dues and had rights in the city pastures and woods. It was not easy for strangers to become citizens, unless they married a citizen's daughter or widow, and they had to be men of some means. While sons of citizens became citizens themselves for a small fixed fee of a Gulden or so, a stranger paid 5 per cent. of his capital as entrance money, or 2½ per cent. if marrying a citizeness, in Frankfort. In Nürnberg he mortgaged his property to the town. If he did not wish to declare his means, he had to pay 750 Gulden and be assessed in the highest grade for taxation. In Nürnberg he had to be a Protestant. It was cheaper to become a *Beisasse*,

[1] For the organisations and customs of the journeymen see, e.g., E. Otto, *Das deutsche Handwerk*, 5. Aufl. 1920; art. 'Gewerbe' in the *Handwörterbuch der Staatswissenschaften*, IV; Howitt, *op. cit.* chap. 10.

but one's rights were then correspondingly reduced, and one lived in the town only on sufferance. A Beisasse could exercise a craft or carry on trade under certain restrictions, but he could not acquire a house or land in the town, or keep cattle. His entrance-fee was a few Gulden, varying according to means, but he paid taxes at double the normal rate for citizens.

Strangers staying in the town for more than a month or two and wishing to live in a private house needed in eighteenth-century Nürnberg or Frankfort, and no doubt elsewhere, a 'permit' granted for a year at a time, and they had to take the oath and pay taxes like the citizens and Beisassen. They were not allowed to carry on trade except at the fair, or to own land—but exceptions were made for people of standing.

Special conditions were imposed everywhere on Jews.[1] In some towns (Nürnberg, Augsburg and several other German towns) they were not allowed at all. In Nürnberg Jews from Fürth entering the town on business had to pay a toll and the regulations prescribed that they should be accompanied by an old woman appointed for the purpose, but in Nicolai's day they merely tipped her.[2] In Ulm only one Jew was tolerated.[3] The Jews from these towns had all been received, at the emperor's request, in Frankfort. In its Judengasse, which could only be entered or left by gates at either end that were shut at night, a number limited to 500 householders (usually about 3000 individuals) were accommodated, subject to strict regulations and the normal taxes. A newcomer had to possess 1000 Gulden in capital, pay considerable fees (over 70 Gulden in all), and his permit had to be renewed for a fee (12½ Gulden) every three years. The restrictions were however relaxed in the course of the century. Jews were for instance not prevented from having shops outside the ghetto.[4]

The foregoing with unimportant variations applies to the

[1] Details in Bergius, *Policey- und Cameral-Magazin*, v.

[2] Nicolai, *Reisen*, I, 310.

[3] *Id.* IX, 47.

[4] *Die Stadt Goethes*, pp. 63 f.

Free Towns in general. In the remaining towns, 'Landstädte' under the control of a territorial prince, there were Bürger and Schutzbürger, but a very large number of people were so-called 'gefreite Bürger'. In Durlach for instance these included all connected with the court, the nobility, all officials from the Bürgermeister down to the hangman, the purveyors by appointment to the court (Hofbäcker, etc.—this was the real value of the privilege), the personal servants of nobility and officials, all Lutheran ministers and their assistants even down to the organ-blower, school-teachers, doctors and apothecaries. Civic spirit had decayed so far that it was more honourable to be 'gefreit' than to be a full citizen. The wealthier and more esteemed inhabitants, the rich rentiers, artists, scholars, and later the factory owner and the chief men of his staff, were all Gefreite, and even the Bürgermeister, councillors and magistrates. The garrison were on the same footing. Officials, if natives and citizens, generally gave up their civic rights on appointment. In the Landstädte then, especially if they had any connection with a prince's court (Durlach as we have seen was originally a prince's seat), the medieval legal categories of citizens had lost much of their meaning. In Berlin, as was stated above, there were only 10,700 'Bürger' in 1755 out of a population of 150,000. Court, garrison, officials, and their dependents as well as the large foreign colony were all 'Gefreite'.

The second class, the 'citizens' proper, consisted therefore of shopkeepers, innkeepers, craftsmen and farmers. The great majority were craftsmen. They had much the same rights as the citizens of the Free Towns—the right to own land or exercise a craft in the town and to use the commons being the chief.

The third class, the 'Schutzbürger', included the agricultural labourers, small traders, pedlars, married journeymen, etc., all in fact who were not 'Gefreite' or 'Bürger', unless they escaped the notice of the authorities altogether, or like the new factory workers had been granted permission to live in the town on special terms.

There was not such a clear-cut distinction possible in any kind of eighteenth-century German town between municipal and state government as there is to-day, because the towns of the one class, the Free Towns, were states in themselves, while the territorial towns were controlled in all essentials by the central government of a territorial state. So Frankfort for instance had, as a republic, its 'Schultheiss' elected for life (originally an imperial official), whom one can look upon as a kind of president, and, as a municipality, it had its two Bürgermeister, elected for one year.

The council of a Free Town then was the government of a small republic. The town council enjoyed the same rights and prerogatives as a territorial prince, though under much stricter supervision by the imperial authority. Its delegates represented the town-republic in Reichstag and Kreistag, it directed 'foreign policy', made laws, levied tolls and taxes, and minted its own coinage like any sovereign prince. It was responsible for the administration of justice, and, since the Reformation, for the government of the established Church. As there was no strict separation of powers it was concerned both with legislation and in large measure with administration.

In such a town there was of course a regular system of Behörden, or departments of government, and a set of officials corresponding to the civil service of the states. No general description will serve for all towns, but taking Frankfort as a type of well-governed town the following departments may be distinguished.

The place of the *Regierung*, the superior judicial instance in a territorial state, was taken here by the senior bench of the council, the 'Schöffen', assisted by the four 'Syndics', trained jurists of distinction, under the 'Schultheiss'. In important matters an appeal was possible to one of the Reichsgerichte. The Bürgermeister, assisted by legal advisers, sat as a criminal court of first instance, and minor offences were investigated by the 'Oberstrichter', a kind of stipendiary magistrate. In serious suits, civil or criminal, recourse was often made to a university faculty of law for a final judgment.

For Church government and education Frankfort had its *Konsistorium*, with six lay and three ecclesiastical members. The *Treasury* was called *Rechneiamt*, and besides preparing a budget, taking charge of the town's income from every source and making all its payments, it administered all town property and exercised a considerable degree of control over industry and trade. It regulated weights and measures, fixed prices for bread, meat, cloth, issued licences to innkeepers and the numerous other persons who required them—barbers, brewers, smiths, bakers, café proprietors, etc., and farmed out the excise on meat, fish, salt, and several other dues to the highest bidder. As almost every function of the government had a financial aspect, the treasury tended to bring more and more affairs under its control every year. It absorbed the *Kriegszeugamt* and took over the recruiting and maintenance of the town's garrison of about 35 officers and 700 to 800 men. A special *Schatzungsamt* looked after the assessment of property and collection of direct taxes, and a *Rentenamt* the collection of the numerous indirect taxes, while five customs houses levied toll on goods coming into and passing out of the town.

In these various departments a large number of permanent officials were employed, in addition to the salaried Ratsherren who were delegated to supervise them. The number of officials was even greater in proportion in towns like Frankfort, where the ordinary citizen had asserted a measure of control, than in the territories, because there existed here a 'Bürgerkollegium' or citizens' committee, which besides deputing its members (at a small salary) to various departments for part-time service, maintained permanent 'Gegenschreiber' in all departments to keep a check on the official 'Schreiber' in all matters involving public expenditure. This meant a double system of accounts, but it put a stop to the financial mismanagement that was common in these Free Towns when the patricians had all their own way.[1]

In the Territorial Towns all essential affairs were controlled by officials appointed by the central government. The functions of the Steuerräte in the Prussian towns have been described above (p. 27). Here and elsewhere, even where the old forms of civic government were kept, they had lost almost all their meaning. No vestige of democratic control was allowed to survive. Mayor and councillors were as often as not nominees of the state, and any mismanagement of town affairs was used as the pretext for their replacement by commissioners. The gilds were brought under territorial control. The law of the territory was substituted for the old customary law of the town. Finance was managed in the interest of the territorial treasury, trade and industry being fostered mainly for the sake of the excise duties that could be levied on them.

[1] For Frankfort's Behörden see article by Dr O. Ruppersberg in *Die Stadt Goethes.*

Chapter IV

ARCHITECTURE OF THE TOWNS. PRIVATE LIFE, OUTLOOK AND EDUCATION OF THE TOWNSMAN

The function and history of the towns, as well as the social differences amongst their inhabitants, were more clearly expressed in their architecture in the eighteenth century than they are to-day. A town was, for instance, still clearly distinguishable from a village by the wall, with turrets and gates, which appeared to defend it, and at least made it impossible for anyone to enter or leave unobserved. Few old towns had spread beyond their medieval walls yet, though in some of course an outer ring had grown round the oldest city and had been walled in in its turn before gunpowder made walls useless. In or near the town there was often still to be seen the castle of the original lords of the town, or a monastery or cathedral might point to its origin, but even where its early history was not to be read in stone, there was a central market place flanked by civic buildings that told of the town's chief functions. The new towns on the other hand, built since the Middle Ages, were all creations of princes, and in their architecture they expressed, as we have seen, the aim of the prince to submit everything to his rational control. The town was architecturally an extension of the palace.

This baroque ideal, both of town planning and of architecture, was, as Dehio says, an aristocratic one. Comparatively few features of it could be adopted by the citizens of the older towns. The streets of these still continued to be narrow and crooked, even though houses were being continually altered or rebuilt as they decayed, for the life of the usual type of house, the 'Fachwerk' or half-timbered house, was at most about 250 years. The new capitals, and the 'new towns' built on to various older ones by a prince, usually for a colony of Dutch or French immigrants, could be and were carefully planned from the start. A street map of Berlin still reveals at a glance, in spite of many changes, how the new geometrical Friedrichstadt was added to the old walled town clustering round the Altmarkt. Similar 'new towns' were built in Dresden, Kassel, Bayreuth, Erlangen.

In all such places two types of house were to be found, the old-town and the new-town type. 'The old-town house has to adapt itself to a traditional site, or at best two old sites might be combined. The growing lack of ground space can only be met by increasing the number of storeys, in a direction therefore that runs counter to the artistic ideal of baroque architecture. The new towns on the other hand are given broad airy streets and the houses have a tendency to breadth rather than to height.'[1] In the old town, houses were much improved inside, but in external appearance the changes that were gradually made were not striking. From the sixteenth century the direction of the main roof ridge came to be parallel with the street, as in a palace, instead of being at right angles to it, but the gothic tradition was so strong that the 'Zwerchhäuser' or large projecting top storeys came to present a very similar appearance to the old triangular gable-end facing the street, and the horizontal line which was the aim of the change was again broken. Other fashionable improvements of the façade, all borrowed from palace architecture, were the substitution of symmetrically grouped and higher windows with flat frames for the many-mullioned small windows with leaded lights of bottle glass, and perhaps one more transparent 'peep-frame', the abolition of the oriel windows called 'Erker', and the introduction of pilasters, horizontal strips and an elaborate moulding round the windows to break up the flat surface into definite fields.[2]

[1] Dehio, *Geschichte der deutschen Kunst*, III, 315.

[2] *Ibid.* pp. 315 f. For examples from Frankfort see *Die Stadt Goethes*, pp. 22 ff., 318 ff.

The town authorities had for long issued and enforced building regulations, less from aesthetic considerations than out of regard for public safety (from fire), health and convenience. From 1719, for instance, the lower storey in new Frankfort houses had to be built of stone, only three storeys were allowed and not more than one storey was allowed to project, but we know from Goethe's description of the rebuilding of his father's house that regulations could be circumvented. The changes made by the Herr Rat were of the nature outlined above. The main aim was naturally increased convenience, light and space inside.

An old town like Frankfort, as we saw from Goethe's description quoted above, though it might have nothing 'architektonisch erhebend', had an unmistakable character of its own. That it was neither a prince's court nor a village, but the settlement of an independent community of craftsmen and merchants, was clear from the buildings this community had erected, the town hall and administrative offices, arsenal, mint, gildhalls, clothhall and so on, though civic pride was not so much in evidence now as earlier, and many indifferent old buildings still had to serve. In some towns the ravages of war were still evident, and in all of them there were tumbledown quarters hard by the modernised houses of the rich. It is evident from the statistics we possess that only a minority of houses were tenanted by one family. In Frankfort for instance the average number of occupants to the house was fifteen or sixteen. In Durlach there were often six to ten persons or even more living in a three-roomed flat.[1]

Though there were considerable differences between houses—in Frankfort for instance there were houses with four and houses with sixteen or more rooms—they were all roughly of the same type in the old town, poorer people living usually not in smaller houses but in sublet portions of large houses. Even in a small town like Durlach (in 1716) only about a quarter of the total number of houses had one

[1] See tables in Roller, *Durlach*, pp. 122 ff.

storey, and were meant for a single family. Most had two or three, with perhaps a shop or workshop and one little flat (consisting of kitchen, 'Stube' or living-room, and perhaps a bedroom) on the ground floor, and two similar flats on each of the other floors. A flat of the kind described was the general unit. If a family needed more space, it had to take two.[1] The commonest type of house had three storeys. The ground floor was built round a big *Flur* or hall, entered from the street by a wide door and leading to a courtyard behind, with outbuildings round it. The merchant would have his counting-house on the ground floor, and use cellars and outbuildings for storage of goods. The craftsman's workshop would also be on the ground level. If the houses were arcaded, as they often were, he would perhaps work under the arcade for light. One can still see such houses in Berne. The shop window of the craftsman and small shopkeeper had shutters folding horizontally, one from below forming a counter and one from above a 'pent-house' for shelter. Sometimes, as in the Hanseatic houses described in *Buddenbrooks*, vehicles could drive right through the *Flur* to the courtyard. The first storey in such a large house contained the reception rooms, and a bedroom or two round an upper hall, where the great chests stood with the family linen (enough to last for months without a washing day), and the top storey the remaining bedrooms. But the possible modifications were innumerable, because every house was built to suit its first owner's taste, often with rooms of differing heights, necessitating many dark stairs and corridors. There was an individual note about the meanest house for this reason, as it was all craftsman's work, but the elaborately carved and painted facades, the wrought-iron grilles, which we admire in pictures of old towns or in museums, were of course confined to the houses of the well-to-do.

Stone houses were by no means common even for the rich. The usual type was the Fachwerk or timber-framed house,

[1] Roller, *Durlach*, pp. 9 ff.

in which the spaces between the timber beams were filled in with brick or with wattle and daub. Thatched and often shingled roofs had been prohibited in the bigger towns for a long time, in Frankfort since the fifteenth century, but even so fires easily broke out and it was the chief duty of the watchman on the church tower and those patrolling the streets to give notice of any outbreak immediately. They had had tolerably efficient pumps since the seventeenth century, capable of throwing a jet eighty feet high.[1] Some towns had their fire station, in others the 'fire barrels' and so on were kept in the arcades of the Rathaus.

The most striking improvement that has been made since the eighteenth century, one that benefits all classes alike, is in public sanitation and water supply. Even the best houses were then lacking in what now seem elementary conveniences, particularly of a sanitary kind. It was only a palace that had a bath. There was sometimes a very rough and ready drainage system for certain houses, in Frankfort for instance for those that happened to lie over the 'Antauche', the tenth-century ditch of the oldest and now central part of the town, or one of a number of channels that had been cut to join it. It was, however, a doubtful privilege to own a 'Sitzgerechtigkeit' and have a sewer under one's kitchen. The alternative was a privy in the back court or in the top storey (the 'Stankgemach'!). Water had usually to be fetched from the public fountain, the 'Brunnen', in the street. All towns of any size had had to provide a water supply from outside, besides using any springs there might be in the town. Nicolai says that water was brought to Augsburg from springs at least one and a quarter Meilen away, stored in four reservoirs dating from the sixteenth and seventeenth centuries, and supplied in houses for a special payment. A somewhat similar system, he says, was to be found at Leipzig, Dresden, Nürnberg, Nymphenburg, Herrenhausen.[2] That

[1] Schultz, *Häusliches Leben der europäischen Völker*, p. 108.

[2] *Reisen*, VII, 80.

the quality of the water was often poor was inevitable from the dirty state of the streets. In towns the main streets were by now all paved, but it was often left to the citizens to dispose of their own refuse (in Frankfort for example till 1775). In Berlin criminals were employed as street cleansers, says Dr Moore. Nicolai speaks with admiration of the streets of Jena, where a brook had been diverted to flow through the middle of the streets and sweep all the rubbish into the Saale. In small towns the cattle and pigs still kept by citizens befouled the streets. It was not until 1681 that the citizens of Berlin had been prohibited from keeping pigs.

Another great inconvenience suffered by even the richest was the absence of good lighting at night, both in streets and houses, and the darkness of the houses by day. This latter defect was being remedied in the new houses, but all had still to be content with candles, usually home-made ones of tallow, oil lamps being useless except as night-lights until the flat wick and later the glass chimney were invented in the second half of the eighteenth century. There were no matches till 1820; flint and steel had to serve. In their public rooms the rich had of course great 'lustres' or candelabra with wax candles, for tallow candles were malodorous and required constant snuffing.

A good first impression of a German town is given by Howitt in his book published in 1842, when conditions had not altered very much since the eighteenth century:

As you proceed through the streets, you find around you gabled and picturesque white buildings, old squares and markets, with avenues of limes, or of dwarf acacias; people, many of them in the garb of centuries ago; and dreadful pavements. Coleridge has celebrated the six-and-thirty stenches of Cologne, and the invention of Cologne water to cover them; but a wide acquaintance with German towns leaves me the conviction that Cologne can boast no more queer odours than any other of the towns of the nation; for in most of them, as we shall have to show, every street, almost every house, and every hour, has its own appropriate, peculiar, and by no means enviable smell. The pavements, with a few exceptions, are of the most hobbly and excruciating kind. There appears no evidence of any special attention to them, or management of them. To pass through a German town or village in a carriage is one of the most rib-trying events in this life. But to walk through one is not much less hazardous. Russell, in his day, tells us, that to avoid being run over on the pavé by a barrow, you often step into the peril of getting your head split with an axe, or your arm torn off by a saw, from the people who are cutting up piles of firewood before the doors. This is pretty much the case yet. The pavés, where there are any, seem appropriated to every purpose but that of walking. There is a bit of pavement here, a bit there, or rather not a bit there. It looks as if the causeway were left entirely to the care, or want of care of the householders. Here is a bit of good pavement; in a few yards is a piece of the worst and most uneven pitching, evidently done ages ago. Here you go up a step, and there you go down one. If an Englishman, accustomed to his well-paved and well-regulated towns, were suddenly set down in a German town at night, he would speedily break his neck or his bones, put out an eye, or tear off a cheek. The towns, and that only on dark and moonless nights, are badly lit by lamps, hung, as in France, from a rope across the street. Here one twinkles, and at a vast and solitary distance glimmers another.... All manner of trap-doors leading down into cellars are in the pavés, and none of them very carefully levelled with the flagging or pebbles. Their covers often cock up their corners, faced with iron in such a way that you strike your toes most cruelly against them. All manner of flights of steps, from shops and houses, are set upon the pavement, are pushed out one-third of the width across them, and sometimes wholly across them, so that a man whom daylight and a few trips over them had not made aware of them would blunder headlong.... Then, every hundred yards, you are stopped by a great wood-heap, and its busy sawers and cleavers, or by a waggon or a carriage which is set on the trottoir to be out of the way![1]

The decoration and furnishings of the houses ranged from the most primitive to what seemed to the conservatives of those days a depraved degree of luxury. The walls of the

[1] W. Howitt, *The Rural and Domestic Life of Germany*, London, 1842.

better rooms in good houses had been panelled with wood in the Middle Ages, but panelling was no longer popular now because, though it made the rooms warm, it harboured vermin. Loose hangings hung on hooks were preferred, of woven stuff or preferably of leather and later of waxed cloth. People liked things that would last a lifetime, as Goethe says when describing the Wachstuchfabrik where these hangings were made in Frankfort,[1] and washable oilcloth hangings were preferred to wall-papers, though these were in common use, and had been obtainable since the seventeenth century, printed with patterns imitated from Chinese models. Poorer people had to be content with whitewashing their bare walls. Rugs and carpets were too expensive to be common even in good houses, but a kind of parquet floor laid with large square blocks was usual in the best rooms.[2] Ordinary folk were content (like Gretchen) with plain deal, well scrubbed and sanded.

Furniture was solid and plain; in the ordinary craftsman's house the furniture would be for the most part made of pine, painted green or nut-brown. There would be little beyond cupboards or chests for linen and clothes, a table, perhaps of oak, chairs and a box-bench, and a wooden bedstead or perhaps a simple form of four-poster. In better houses the old chests were being superseded by chests of drawers, a new invention, and deal by walnut. Canopied beds were carried to every degree of elaboration, and their curtains were still used.[3] Imported woods like mahogany, so fashionable in Georgian England, took a long time to reach the German middle class. The aristocracy had rococo and Chippendale furniture and German imitations of it, but in the ordinary 'Wohnstube' native oak, ash or alder were the rule. In pictures

[1] *Dichtung und Wahrheit*, I, bk. 4.

[2] See e.g. the illustrations in Chodowiecki's diary of his journey to Danzig (*D. Chodowieckis Künstlerfahrt nach Danzig im Jahre* 1773, edited by W. Franke, Leipzig and Berlin, n.d.).

[3] A full inventory of typical Frankfort houses, both of a craftsman and a merchant, is given in *Die Stadt Goethes*, pp. 338 ff.

and drawings the rooms in middle-class houses appear rather severe, furnished only with the bare essentials.

The typical middle-class house, unlike those of the nobility, indicated in general a desire for comfort, rather than display. Well-to-do citizens made use of their wealth for lavish hospitality, and often for collections of pictures, books and natural curiosities. The poor man would be content with prints from an itinerant print seller. In every town there were well-known private art collections which the well-informed traveller did not fail to visit. The ladies for their part collected fine linen and displayed their polished copper and pewter vessels and their glass in the kitchen and even in the living-room. Later in the century a new luxury, porcelain, tempted the collector. It came in with coffee and tea, those unhealthy luxuries that Möser and others never tired of condemning. Coarse earthenware had been available for a long time for dinner services and so on, but it had not displaced pewter.

In the matter of food and drink, too, the demands of the bourgeoisie were naturally simpler than those of the nobility. They kept to the traditional dishes, little influenced by French fashions. Crabb Robinson gives an Englishman's impressions of German cooking in 1800 at some length in his letters home.[1] He is particularly struck with the excellence of German soups, but deplores the absence of puddings, for which England of course had been famous since 'George in pudding-time came round'. He quotes as a typical good meal the 'ordinary' at his inn in Frankfort, at which for less than half-a-crown he was given soup, boiled meat, a dish of vegetables ('in which the Germans infinitely surpass us') with an entremets, and lastly roast beef and no doubt dessert, the whole washed down with a pint of Rhine wine.

The Germans had long had the reputation of being great trenchermen and heavy drinkers. The worst period, by all accounts, was round about the sixteenth century, but the eighteenth-century Bürger cannot have been more refined

[1] *Crabb Robinson in Germany.*

than the nobility, whose reputation was still, as we have seen, rather low. The regulations limiting expenditure at weddings and so forth indicate that the most was made of such occasions. How far the Augsburg citizen from whose diary the following extract is taken was typical it is no longer possible to say, but he seems to have had many companions of the same mind as himself. In the month of May 1715 he mentions eleven days on which he had extraordinary expenses for beer, wine and meals away from home. On 1st May he writes: 'To-day I was bled together with my wife, because the weather was so extraordinarily fine. After dinner we went to the "Froschlache" for a glass of wine and stayed till four. Then we took a walk round by the gate and supped. It was still light, and my wife complained of indigestion, so we drank another measure of wine at the "Weberhaus". Total for the day 1 g. 30 kr.' On 2nd May a visit to a coffee-house while his wife was entertaining her neighbours at home, was followed by a call at the 'Prince' inn, where he met several friends. After dinner his brother-in-law called for them in a coach and took them to the 'Jägerhaus'. Here there was a very different menu from the sausage or cut from the roast of the ordinary 'beer-house': fish, crayfish, capons, pike's liver, peacock's tongues (!), etc., and to drink there was Alsatian, Würzburg, Rhine, Mosel, Neckar and red Schaffhausen wine, and even Sherry and Madeira. After a modest beginning, he ended by spending nearly fourteen florins. Many fellow guests, he says, with more appetite than money, had to pawn a watch, a snuff-box, a silver-cornered prayer book, or even small articles of furniture which they had purposely brought with them, to the host. 'So Crispin said to his wife: Well Kate, if the pillow tastes so nice, what will the bolster taste like!' The excuse that is pleaded for this extravagance, and for other lesser ones on following days, is that when a man has been bled he must take care of himself. No wonder that on 10th May he had to borrow thirty-six florins from his gossip to pay the house rent. The landlord made a fuss about the late payment 'but people like him may well talk. They live on their interest and do not know how hard an honest man has to work to scrape a living together in these bad times'. However, in the afternoon he took his gossip a walk that led them to the Jägerhaus again. Naturally he had to treat such a good friend well, but this time he got off with an expense of four Gulden. In this way the short and simple annals continue. The climax came on Whit Monday, when after a walk followed by a game of skittles —and beer, in the morning, he went out again in the afternoon in spite of the pricks of his conscience, half persuading himself that a man needed a 'Bürgerlust' to refresh a body tired out with the week's work. He walked out to a neighbouring village, found friends there, played cards and when his wife and family followed him they supped lavishly and ended up with a dance. By this time they were all so merry that the only fit end was to smash the glasses on the wall, and this they did. Of course they had to pay for them, and all in all it cost him over twelve Gulden, half of which he had to borrow from friends.[1]

At the other end of the scale we have men like the bookseller to whom Fr. Perthes was apprenticed in 1787 in Leipzig, who worked from seven in the morning till eight at night, never played cards, never went to an inn, invited no guests and drank only water. On Sundays after church he would read the *Jena Literaturzeitung* and then take a walk round the town. Apart from this his only relaxation was an occasional trip in summer with his family to Entritzsch, where they drank a bottle of 'Gose', and an annual ten-mile drive with his apprentices.[2] His wife, however, drank. There must have been citizens very different from this Herr Böhme in 'Little

[1] Printed in E. Buchner, *Anno Dazumal*, I, 257. Source not stated. If it is an invention it is a contemporary one (perhaps from a 'moral weekly'?) and its details are such as would seem probable to the readers of the time.

[2] C. T. Perthes, *Friedrich Perthes Leben*, Hamburg and Gotha, 1848, p. 12.

Paris', but it was men like him who were building up the book trade. From the literature and letters of the time we see in fact that there were men of every type, then as at all times. They were no doubt more easy-going on the whole in the south and west than in the north, where we already find the ancestors of the severely rational business men of the nineteenth century. Among the craftsmen there was the same variety. We read of the sanctimonious hatmaker in Brunswick to whom young Moritz was apprenticed, who would preach sermons for hours about the wickedness of mankind, and warn his men that unless they worked faithfully in his service they would burn for ever in hell fire. His men could never work hard enough for him—at least once a week they worked all night—and he made a cross over the bread and butter when he went out.[1] Or we read again in *Dichtung und Wahrheit*[2] of the philosophical shoemaker with whom Goethe stayed in Dresden, a man after Goethe's own heart, 'whose endowment was sound common-sense, founded on a cheerful temperament and contentment with uniform traditional work'. What we hear of the simpler Bürger of Treves was probably true of most men of this class: 'They were modest, pious and quiet in their behaviour; both men and women were fond of their homes and took particular delight in their gardens, which they looked after themselves. They lived very simply and economically and dressed plainly. It was only a councillor or citizen of means whom you would see in a suit of fine cloth of self colour, with heavy silver buttons, carrying a stick with a heavy silver knob. Powdered hair was seldom worn by the citizen class. A silver watch or snuff-box was a great rarity, so were silver buckles; copper and steel ones were the usual wear for rich and poor.'[3]

In the matter of dress we have seen that the town authorities

[1] *Anton Reiser*, Erster Teil.

[2] II, 8.

[3] Graf Boos von Waldeck, describing Treves in the middle of the eighteenth century, quoted in Buchner, *Anno Dazumal*, I, 365.

attempted in vain to keep clear the distinctions between classes. It became more and more difficult to do so as the hold of tradition over men's minds grew weaker and the old methods of home or local production were modified by the increase of trade and production for export. The development had already begun which has continued ever since and has resulted in a levelling out of all differences in costume, so that what conservatives were then afraid of, that you would not be able to tell a lady from her maid, is now literally true. Until the eighteenth century the rate of change in fashions was very slow, especially for the middle class and peasantry. In the course of the century it became very rapid for the aristocracy, and hardly less so for the better-placed middle class. Only the craftsmen and still more the peasantry were left behind in pursuit of fashion, and it is in this way, as we saw earlier, that what we now know as 'peasant costumes' arose. They represent the fashion of long-past ages. A Frenchman who lived seven years in a small German town in the time of the Revolution said that the women there followed the fashions as well and as quickly as they could, but their best attempts were unsuccessful and slow. They resulted in a heterogeneous mixture of styles of different periods.[1] It was in some such way that the fashions of the nobility spread in time to other social classes. Individual towns still had their own style of dress—one hears of Strassburg, Augsburg, Nürnberg dresses. These differences persisted longest, of course, in the country, in some parts down to the present day. The higher social classes in the towns, however, soon lost their individual character, and were, as the phrase went, 'französisch gekleidet', though the Ratsherren usually had an official costume of black trimmed with lace in the old Spanish fashion, like the merchants painted by Vandyck, the details varying from town to town in accordance with old traditions. Thus certain marks of difference between the classes persisted all through the century, and one could

[1] Quoted in Spiess, *Die deutschen Bauerntrachten*, p. 30.

usually tell at a glance to what 'Stand' a man or woman belonged. There were still traditional differences of costume for special occasions too, for weddings and funerals, for instance. Married women always wore a bonnet out of doors, only unmarried girls going bareheaded.

The best clothes of the Frankfort craftsman, a cooper, mentioned above, and of his wife, were black or brown and of serviceable materials, made like everything else in the house to last for many years. The wife had a black dress of English cloth and a brown cloth skirt, a black camel-hair bodice, a black cotton cape and a crepe bonnet; the husband a black coat and cloak. But he possessed twenty-six linen shirts and his wife eighteen chemises, because the 'grosse Wäsche' came so seldom. So even the craftsmen and their wives were no longer content with homespun. People with more to spend chose more expensive foreign materials, silks and velvets and brocades. As the lower orders could not usually afford these stuffs, they came to be regarded as a badge of rank. A difficulty arose when the much cheaper printed cottons were produced. In many places they were at first prohibited altogether, both because of their levelling effect and because they did harm to the wool trade.

From illustrations such as those of Chodowiecki in his 'diary' and in contemporary plays and novels, as well as from documents such as the inventory quoted above, it seems that almost all people who worked in their houses, and even merchants in their counting-houses, usually wore some kind of dressing-gown while at work. Good clothes were expensive, much more expensive relatively than now because there was no mass production. Fathers of families, even if they were in easy circumstances like Goethe's father, liked to save expense by taking a man servant who understood tailoring. In country ministers' houses linen, spun and woven in the village, might be taken to a town to be printed with a pattern, after which the ladies made their own clothes from it. For men's clothes the cloth was bought in the town and a tailor came for a fortnight a year to do all the tailoring required.[1] Facts such as these explain why even the better middle class did not usually succeed in imitating at all closely the latest French fashions, the product of wealth and idleness. Yet even in the island of Rügen in the 70's, as Arndt tells us in his memoirs, just the same attempts at French ceremony and elegance were made in the house of a comfortable farmer or country parson as in that of a baron or an army major of good family, with results that were often grotesque. 'Slowly and solemnly, with ungraceful twists and curtseys the plump Frau Pastorin and Pächterin and their daughters approached each other, with swelling "Poches" round their hips, their hair, often false, piled three storeys high and thickly powdered, their feet forced in Chinese fashion into the tightest of high-heeled shoes, in which they tripped about most uncertainly.' The men were like a parody of Frederick the Great and his heroes.[2] For the first five or ten minutes everyone always attempted to speak High German instead of their homely dialect, and even to lard it with scraps of scarcely recognisable French.

It was easier for men to imitate English fashions than for ladies to dress in the French style. In practical England, as we saw, a more serviceable type of costume, made of good cloth and leather, had become usual for travelling and for the everyday wear of all but beaux, and this and military fashions (particularly the Prussian pig-tail) were the chief models for the dress of the more active classes. A long cloth coat (the ancestor of the modern tail-coat for evening wear) in a brighter colour than is now usual, short cloth vest and knee-breeches of stout cloth like corduroy, or leather, with high boots, or woollen stockings and shoes, were its chief features. The 'Werther' costume (blue coat, buff vest and breeches and brown high boots) was just a form of this dress, a

[1] A. Schmitthenner, *Das Tagebuch meines Urgrossvaters*, p. 47.

[2] E. M. Arndt, *Erinnerungen aus dem äusseren Leben* (1840); Reclam edition, p. 25 f.

common one even before Goethe's novel in northern Germany.[1] It would strike contemporaries not as picturesque, it should be noted, but as practical, the dress of a man who paid no heed to the fashions of polite society, and liked to walk out to his favourite village without fear of the weather.

Until the Revolution, wigs proved difficult to displace. They too were subject to the dictates of fashion. Round wigs went out of fashion in the 70's and bag-wigs were worn instead. Among other minor features it may be noted that it had become usual for the nobility alone to wear swords. Until the eighteenth century even craftsmen had frequently carried them when they were out of the apprenticeship stage, but in this more peaceful age the ordinary burgher was content with a walking-stick. In the second half of the century the umbrella, at first an object of ridicule, became more popular. It had been invented late in the seventeenth century. In cold and rainy weather women usually wore a long cloak with a hood that covered them from head to foot, while men put on a long 'highwayman's' cape, or a 'surtout', which had sleeves. The well-to-do made use of sedan chairs or, very rarely, of carriages, like the aristocracy.

It was the same with new ideas and habits of mind as with fashions in dress. Every class had traditions of its own, and the lower a class stood in the social scale, the more impervious it was to outside influences, because its contacts with other classes were fewer and its system of education and training more bound by convention. But the great body of townsmen had probably a good deal more in common with each other in outlook than at any subsequent period, and in discussing the psychology of the Bürger class these common features will be mentioned first.

As he was so seldom called upon to adapt himself to new situations, the average citizen was in the first place intensely

[1] Cf. *Dichtung und Wahrheit*, 3ter Teil, 12tes Buch. Jerusalem, from Brunswick, one of the 'models' for Werther, used to dress in this way.

conservative. There was something almost sacred for him in the established order of things, both in the practice of his particular craft or calling, and even in quite trivial matters of everyday life, so that his life was governed by petty rules and conventions to an extent which is now scarcely credible. A pedantic orderliness is an outstanding characteristic of almost all the good Bürger of that age. Goethe's father is in this respect entirely typical. His grandfather too, Goethe tells us, was as regular and punctilious in his gardening as in his official business. Every day for him was like its predecessor, so that Goethe associated with his way of life the idea of 'inviolable peace and endless duration'. Moritz tells us of lower middle-class families in which the same unchanging order was observed for scores of years, and many more instances could be quoted. No wonder that to Madame de Staël it seemed that 'Le plus vif désir des habitants de cette contrée paisible et féconde, c'est de continuer a exister comme ils existent'. In forms of address, compliments, congratulations, few variations were allowed on accepted models. There were days set apart at regular intervals for formal calls, even for family purgings and blood-lettings. Family celebrations, weddings, christenings, funerals, birthdays, and the recurring festivals of the year, Christmas, Mayday, Midsummerday, Martinmas, all had their established ritual, much of the poetic charm of which has survived to our own day. The many places that were half town, half village, would have their harvest or vintage festivals, 'Schützenfeste' were still common, and everywhere the gilds kept up much of their old ceremonial and pageantry. The old customs are frequently described in the writings of the time, they were illustrated by Ludwig Richter and others in the Romantic period, and they have now been systematically studied by the experts in Volkskunde.

Another characteristic commonly to be found in all classes of the towns and closely connected with this traditionalism was the love of slow painstaking work, the attitude of the old-fashioned craftsman. It was to be seen not only in those who worked with their hands, but in the learned men whose systematic collections of material in dictionaries and encyclopaedic works were already looked upon as a specifically German product. Goethe even finds in the Sisyphean labours of the jurists at Wetzlar 'that laudable industry of the Germans, which aims rather at the collection and arrangement of details than at results'.

Besides these historic traits of the middle class there were others, almost equally universal, which are less easily related to each other. There were survivals of the forthrightness and even coarseness of the peasant in many customs and many forms of speech. The old people ate and drank and said their say, and the young people made love, in a way which to sophisticated foreigners seemed at least naïve, and justified Goethe's line: 'Im Deutschen lügt man, wenn man höflich ist'. But there was also a strong sentimental strain in evidence, not peculiar of course to Germany at this time, but particularly pronounced there. This was perhaps most marked in the classes influenced by literature, though pietism had made it very widespread among the uneducated too. Occasions for emotional display were not avoided, as usually by the courtier, but sought after, tears were shed not only for sorrow, but for joy or gratitude, and the expression of friendship and admiration took extravagant forms. Yet, as often happens, these men of feeling were by no means unmoved by self-interest when it was a matter of arranging a marriage or gaining the favour of the influential. Marriages, as we see from almost any autobiography, were usually, in real life, affairs of good sense rather than of romantic love, certainly in the middle of the century and probably still at the end, and the court habits of dissimulation and flattery had spread to many sections of the middle class in their dealings with superiors.

The increasing refinement of the age had therefore its dark sides. The average citizen grew accustomed to taking his family to the 'coffee-gardens' that were now popular (the first cafés had been started in towns like Hamburg, Leipzig, Vienna very early in the century), instead of carousing with his fellows like the Augsburg citizen quoted above, but the feeling was widespread, especially after the Storm and Stress movement of the 70's, that the age was lacking in vigour and character. It is true that similar complaints had been made generations earlier by Moscherosch, Leibniz and Thomasius, who, like Lessing, had blamed French influence, with its emphasis on 'das Zärtliche und das Verliebte'. But Justus Möser and Goethe both ascribed this lethargy and ennui rather to the disproportion which they felt to exist between capacity and opportunity, in a Germany economically backward and politically in leading-strings. 'In such an atmosphere,' says Goethe, explaining the popularity of his *Werther*, 'tortured by unsatisfied passions, with no outward inducement to significant activities, with the sole prospect of persisting in a dull, spiritless, commonplace life, we became attached to the idea that we could at all events quit life at pleasure when we could no longer bear it.' The efforts of the great writers in the classical age were directed towards finding a new ideal for the middle class of their time, who were so lacking, as it seemed to them, in harmonious development of mind and body, in grace of bearing and personal dignity, and it is a strange comment on the period to discover that at one time Goethe, and not only Goethe, could imagine that the calling of an actor, in a world of make-believe, could afford an idealist like his *Wilhelm Meister* the opportunities of the good life which were denied to him as a merchant.[1]

In the middle-class home, to judge by the tone of letters and the frequency of the 'Haustyrann' in literature, the father was inclined to exact from his family the same deference that

[1] See 'Goethe's *Wilhelm Meister* as a picture and a criticism of society', by the present writer, in *Publications of the English Goethe Society*, IX, 1933.

he had to pay outside to his superiors. The discipline of the home seems to have been strict in all classes in the towns. 'Early to bed and early to rise', 'There is a place for everything', 'Speak when you're spoken to' and similar maxims were followed to the letter. Family prayers in the morning, in which servants or apprentices often joined, were usual even in families not ostentatiously pious. Personal relations between intimates were more formal, less spontaneous, than seems natural to us. It is hardly conceivable that the feelings of parents and children, brothers and sisters were really very different at bottom from what they are now, but they were certainly expressed in different forms, at least in the upper middle class. 'Sie' was used from child to parent, often between the parents themselves, and servants and apprentices might be addressed as 'Er'.

It hardly needs to be said that in such a society the place of woman was the kitchen and the nursery. The variety of tasks that fell to the lady of the house has been touched on above. All through the following century English visitors continue to express their astonishment at the contentment of the German Hausfrau with what seems to them such a restricted life. Howitt in 1842 speaks of their absorption in cooking and domestic management, their ceaseless sewing and knitting, their hoarding of linen and stockings. To a woman writer in *Fraser's Magazine* in 1875 the German married woman 'is simply an upper servant'. 'Of domesticities', she writes, 'there is enough and to spare, but of domestic life as we understand it, little or nothing. Beyond eating, drinking and sleeping under the same roof the sexes have little in common. The woman is a slave of the ring.' She speaks too of the devoted manner in which the young ladies of the house wait upon male visitors, and fetch and carry for their brothers. And Mrs Sidgwick in 1908 still has the impression that Germans think 'that woman was made for man, and that if she has board, lodging and raiment, according to the means of her menfolk, she has all she can possibly ask of life'. German women, she says, 'do not actually fall on their knees before their lords, but the tone of voice in which a woman of the old school speaks of *Die Herren* is enough to make a French, American or English-woman think there is something to be said for the modern revolt against men'. We may be sure that the lot of German women was no easier in the eighteenth century, though it probably never occurred to them, any more than to most of their sex later, to revolt against it, for individualism was a doctrine for men, but not for women. 'The husband who was willing to share a respected position and a sure income with the lady of his choice', says Freytag, 'was offering her in the view of that time a great deal; her gratitude had to take the form of ministering to the comfort of his hard, laborious days by unremitting faithful service.' The training of girls was naturally adapted to this end. In the classical words of Goethe in *Hermann und Dorothea*, it was for woman to learn in her early years to *serve* as nature meant her to do, to serve her brother and parents so that her life was a constant coming and going, a lifting and carrying, preparing and working for others. In such a school she would learn the unselfishness of which she would have so much need in married life, but she would also qualify herself for her future place of authority as mistress of a household. For a Martha of this type a literary education was of little use. It was enough if she could read and write and knew her catechism, and very few women, even wives of professional men, could write a good German letter or even spell correctly. But with the growth of circulating libraries the new novels found many readers among young ladies, too many for Goethe's taste, who, according to the second *Epistel*, would have had them all kept so busy in house and garden that they would want to read nothing but a cookery book. It is not surprising to learn that even in Howitt's day, household and social accomplishments were the sum of their instruction. There were exceptions, of course, but they were rare. The average middle-class girl was lucky if she received primary education. There were indeed few who shared the higher tuition received by their brothers, and girls' secondary schools were things of the future.

The bourgeoisie as a class prided itself on its virtue, its modesty, honesty and industry, as opposed to the loose living, the arrogance and the lack of principles of the aristocracy. These ideas must have been supported by age-old social tradition, by the discipline imposed for centuries by Church and gild, reinforced by the increased moral earnestness of Protestantism. The influence of the Pietist movement was very strong among all classes, and in many towns a little colony of Huguenots set a high standard of probity and moral zeal. The traditional virtues of the gildsman were, as we have seen, contentment and neighbourliness; their motto was 'Live, and let live'. These virtues would probably be most prominent now among the lower middle class. The more successful of the business community were more self-conscious in their industry. They did not merely work for their daily bread. Industry was for them a virtue in itself, like frugality and purity. Religion had become for the Aufklärung, in Goethe's words, 'trockene Moral'. It was concerned with the affairs of this world only and had allied itself half unconsciously with business ethics. The God-fearing man must know how to bear adversity, but he might legitimately hope for success in his enterprises because of his virtue. Not only might he aim at wealth, and not merely a sufficiency (as Luther and even seventeenth-century orthodoxy had enjoined); it was his duty, even when in possession of wealth, to work to maintain it. Sombart has made good use of Benjamin Franklin's famous autobiography as a document revealing the mind of the business man at this stage in economic development. Franklin's notions of an 'art of virtue', his belief that 'nothing was so likely to make a man's fortune as virtue', this marriage of virtue and worldly prosperity, was no doubt thoroughly characteristic of his time. It had come to believe, with the help of the English Deists, that virtue did not need a supernatural sanction but was justified of its fruits, even in a single lifetime. It even found a substitute for the confessional in self-examinations such as that which Franklin's autobiography made famous, in his story of the little notebook with its thirteen columns of virtues, 'temperance, silence, order, resolution, frugality, industry, sincerity, justice, moderation, cleanliness, tranquility, chastity, humility'. There must have been many thousands of aspiring young men in Germany who made similar resolutions to attain moral perfection, and worldly success as its reward. F. Perthes was one.[1] And there were German writers, such as Thomasius and his pupil C. A. Heumann, who propounded very similar rules to Franklin's, long before his time.

But in justice to Franklin it should be added that he possessed qualities of mind and feeling that are recorded not in this famous passage but between the lines of his autobiography and in his great public achievements. The natural wisdom of his mind enabled him to make good use of even the dry scraps of traditional morality, and the generosity of his temperament and his abounding public spirit made him a 'citizen' in a sense in which perhaps no German of that age deserved the name. Compared with him even the highest embodiments of German ideals, such as Lessing's *Nathan the Wise*, have something provincial and theoretical about them, while the citizen of reality displayed a submissiveness to authority very different from Franklin's 'humility', a late addition to his list, and a virtue which he was content with observing merely in appearance, by the avoidance of dogmatic statements of opinion. The average German business man was more like Werner in Goethe's *Wilhelm Meister*, who is eloquent in praise of order, frugality and industry but whose horizon does not extend beyond his own family. Of duties to town or state he has no conception. Freytag describes the

[1] *F. P.'s Leben*, pp. 28 ff.

middle-class Germans of the second half of the century admirably when he says:

> They had become men of honour and strict principle, they tried with a touching conscientiousness to hold things ignoble at a distance; but they were still too much lacking in the manly energy that grows by co-operation with many of like mind in handling great practical questions. The noblest of them ran the danger of becoming victims rather than heroes in political and social struggles. This trait is very noticeable even in literary creations. Almost all the characters freely invented by the greatest poets in their best works suffer from a lack of energy, of virile courage and political acumen; there is an elegiac trait even in the heroes of the drama, where it is least pardonable, from Galotti, Götz and Egmont to Wallenstein and Faust.

In the beau monde, as we have seen, a cynical disregard for the moral values was far from being uncommon. It might sometimes be necessary to present the appearance of virtue, but this was a means to an end. It was usually taken as axiomatic that all men are moved by self-interest. Beyond this, regard was paid to aesthetic rather than moral considerations. The last thing to be desired was self-conscious virtue. Of course there were many exceptions, and what has been said refers chiefly to the nobility of the larger courts, but it is certainly true to say that the average respectable citizen looked upon personal integrity and the domestic virtues as the nobleman looked upon honour and 'reputation'. In the domestic tragedies and the family novels of the last third of the century the contrast between the cynical aristocrat and the virtuous middle-class father of a family is a constant theme. Even if these works do not represent the whole truth, they evidently express what the middle-class public liked to believe.

In one of the most famous of these early 'problem plays', Grossmann's *Nicht mehr als sechs Schüsseln*, it is a high legal official who is the protagonist of the bourgeois party. The rising class of officials, although in many respects assimilated by the aristocracy, retained its middle-class outlook in matters of morality and gradually came to influence the standards of the aristocracy itself. In Durlach for instance, Roller tells us, it was only the new class of officials who took sexual aberrations seriously and insisted on the highest standards of conduct, especially for its daughters. Even in the first half of the century, there is little evidence of any moral lapses on their part in Durlach, still less in the second. The various mistresses of princes, who are mentioned there, all belonged either to the nobility or to the artisan class. But girls of the artisan class who had disgraced themselves easily found husbands of their own class. It was only in the nineteenth century, according to this informant, that the artisan class came to be as strict in this respect as the higher middle class. It seems clear from the gild regulations that even in the Middle Ages the gilds in their corporate capacity displayed an almost exaggerated moral sensitiveness (in their exclusion from the gilds of illegitimate children and so on). But when their best days were over the economic was perhaps stronger than the moral motive for the retention of these regulations, and the artisan class as a whole had fallen behind the educated middle class in ethical feeling as in general culture.

The several classes of Bürger naturally differed from each other as much in education as in outlook. After his home training, the son of a craftsman did not usually receive anything that can be called education until he was apprenticed to a trade. Very often he would be working from an early age, helping his parents perhaps in some 'domestic industry', winding yarn, carding wool, even spinning and weaving, knitting, lace-making and so on, or doing similar work in one of the new factories, if there happened to be one near. This was usually regarded as an excellent training in habits of industry. It was particularly good for orphans, so orphanage, prison, poor-house, if there was one, and madhouse were usually grouped together, perhaps in the same building, and as many of the inmates as possible were employed in spinning and weaving, stocking-making and the like. J. Kerner tells us[1] of a partly philanthropic cloth factory of this kind at Ludwigsburg, started by the duke of Württemberg, about the same time as his model academy 'Solitude', no doubt with equally good intentions. There are many parallels elsewhere in Germany and Switzerland (Nürnberg, Ratisbon, Frankfort, Pforzheim, Basle) as well as in England, Holland and France.[2] The example of Germany (Nürnberg), where every child, though but seven or eight years old, was put to work and enabled to earn its own livelihood, was held up in England as early as 1638.[3] At twelve or fourteen a boy was if possible apprenticed to a trade, and apprenticeship was still a form of social training, the apprentice living with his master. The master was expected not only to give technical training but to bring a boy up in the fear of God, and to look after his manners.[4] Anton Reiser was constantly being corrected by Herr Lobenstein the hat-maker, who not only edified him with long religious discourses but watched his table manners. The journeymen's unions too concerned themselves with the general behaviour of their members.

It is true that since the Protestant states had taken over the control of education from the Church, as they began to do in the sixteenth century, attendance had gradually been made compulsory in theory for all children in almost all states. Every parish had to provide a school, and the ministers of the church were made responsible by the Konsistorium for its inspection. Some small states (Weimar and Gotha for instance), in their desire for the purity of doctrine, were even more active in this matter than Prussia.[5] But the decrees

[1] *Das Bilderbuch aus meiner Knabenzeit.*

[2] See Kulischer, II, 149 ff., 188 ff.

[3] Lipson, II, 61.

[4] This was often expressly mentioned in the articles of apprenticeship, e.g. in 1787 for F. Perthes (*Leben*, pp. 8 ff.).

[5] See F. Paulsen, *Das deutsche Bildungswesen in seiner geschichtlichen Entwicklung*, I, 85 ff.

could not be enforced. Many children were put to work both in the towns, as we have seen, and of course in the country, helping in the fields and even in mining. The ministers who acted as inspectors could not improve matters, even if they took their duties seriously, while attendance was still so irregular, and while teachers received nothing but their small fees. Teachers were often men who were unfit for other work, or they combined teaching (as Jung Stilling did in his early days) with tailoring or some such sedentary occupation. In the towns one hears more of licensed private schools than of public schools, and they were as bad or worse. There were at some periods thirty or more of them in existence in Frankfort, some with 200 to 300 pupils. The teaching in all of them consisted of the catechism, reading and writing, and perhaps a little arithmetic and geography. There were no good school books and above all no training colleges for teachers. In town after town visited by Nicolai he speaks of the 'German' schools as bad.

The period of Aufklärung was deeply interested in education, but such of its energies as were not absorbed in theoretical discussion only influenced the better placed middle class. Goethe's father was typical, indefatigable as he was in his care for the education of his own children by himself and by private tutors according to a well-considered plan. Children of the better families were, as Goethe tells us, all privately educated. It was the golden age of the private tutor. There could be no uniformity when parents were the sole directors of their children's education, and tutors varied so enormously, but it is clear that class distinctions were intensified by this system. The end in view was usually a compromise between the educational ideals of the nobility outlined above, with their stress on preparation for the fashionable world, and the more solid but often pedantic teaching of the Latin schools. Modern as well as ancient languages were taught and dancing, fencing and so on were not neglected.

The town grammar schools ('Latin schools'), the product of the Reformation age and humanism, occupied themselves with the propagation of classical learning and sound religion, the chief stress being laid on accurate and if possible elegant latinity. Form was placed above content, at least until the reform of classical teaching in the universities, with which the name of Gesner is chiefly associated, spread to the schools. They were 'Gelehrtenschulen', intended for boys proceeding to the universities to be trained in the liberal professions, but they were used also by the sons of merchants, and even of some craftsmen, who intended to enter their fathers' business and left school half way through the course. There were usually scholarships for clever poor boys, and these 'Pauperes' were often distinguished by some external mark from the fee-paying 'Divites'—in Ulm for instance they wore black, while the rest wore blue. The majority of the pupils would be sons of officials, shopkeepers and successful craftsmen. For quite half of them some kind of Realschule would have been more suitable, but although a Realschule had been started in Berlin in 1747 and had been imitated in some other towns, this form of modern school did not become common until the business men of the towns became more vocal. Basedow, though a poor organiser and rather a crank, did much to awaken interest in a more realistic education through his short-lived *Philanthropinum* at Dessau (1774) and its textbook, the *Elementarwerk*. He laid more stress on modern languages, taught by a direct method, general knowledge and physical exercises than on gerund-grinding.

Education, it will be seen, would not be likely to modify seriously the general view of life current in the class from which the pupil came. It was intended of course to conserve it. The very great differences that existed between the various forms of education available for boys reflect differences just as great between the habits of mind of the various classes of citizens, even though at first glance they might seem to have so much in common. A large proportion of the population even in the towns was illiterate, and of the rest only a comparatively small number would be interested in the same works as a 'denkender Kopf von klassischem Geschmack'. It was only as literature became more realistic and less learned, in the second half of the century and particularly from the 70's, that a wide circle of readers could be counted on, and even then it still made its chief appeal to the academically trained professional men.

Chapter V

THE PROFESSIONAL CLASS

'Professional men' are a product of modern times. In the Middle Ages of course the Church had for centuries a monopoly of education and book-learning. Priests and monks exercised the chief functions that were later to fall to the professional man. They were the lawyers, public officials, doctors, professors and schoolmasters, and it was only within the Church that trained intelligence, unsupported by advantages of birth or worldly possessions, could find scope. We have seen in earlier chapters how, with the revival of Roman law in the Italian universities and the decline of the temporal power of the Church, laymen came to replace clerics in the councils of princes. The Renaissance and Reformation, and the strengthening of state authority that accompanied them, increased the demand for trained laymen beyond all precedent. The old universities ceased to be semi-monastic institutions almost wholly controlled by the Church. Secular learning became more and more important even in Catholic universities, and the intellectual element in the education both of clergy and laymen came to predominate more than ever in the many new Protestant foundations.

It was only with the development of humanistic studies that intellectual training became a source of social distinction. In Germany in the fifteenth century doctors of theology and of canon law were recognised as the equals of the lesser nobility in cathedral chapters, to which only men of good birth had hitherto been admitted. In England the doctorate of a university conferred a higher social status on laymen too. In France a regular 'noblesse de robe' grew up on this professional and cultural basis. In Germany, as elsewhere, the status of the educated layman rose as individuals distinguished themselves as scholars, doctors and servants of the state. With the continuous spread of absolutism, the university-trained Jurists became the leaders in this social rise of the educated middle-class, for although as we have seen the highest state offices were usually reserved for men of rank, the services of trained lawyers were indispensable in subordinate offices and particularly in the local Ämter, where the important function of jurisdiction was generally exercised by the Amtmann, so that his authority approached that of a local magnate. At a much slower rate medical graduates began to rise in social esteem. The Protestant clergy did not usually enjoy anything resembling the social consideration due to the officials of a prince, not at any rate until, in the second half of the eighteenth century, they came to be something very like state servants themselves. They were as a rule poorer in the goods of this world, but learning, intelligence and piety, as well as their important administrative functions in country districts, secured for many of them a high degree of respect.

As to the graduates of the Arts or Philosophical Faculty, one can hardly speak of them as an independent group in the eighteenth century at all. Students were matriculated as soon as they entered the university in one of the senior faculties of law, theology or medicine, and looked upon their course in arts merely as a preparation for their serious studies, a completion of their schooling. Men who had studied only arts and perhaps taken a master's degree might be compelled by circumstances to accept a post as teacher or tutor, but such a post was seldom considered to be more than a means of keeping body and soul together while the 'candidate' was waiting for a living in the Church. Of course a very large number of 'Kandidaten' never got beyond this stage, and there were some teaching posts, in the universities and the better schools, that satisfied normal ambitions at least as well as a Church living, but arts graduates as such had no obvious social function until the great expansion of secondary education took place in the nineteenth century. As 'scholars', however, possessing a knowledge of Latin, they felt themselves and were generally acknowledged to be socially superior to the ordinary shopkeeper or craftsman, though the court class might despise them as pedants. It is characteristic that in places where, as in Frankfort-on-Main, university graduates were organised and met to protect their common interests, the so-called 'Graduiertenkollegium' (founded in Frankfort in 1613 and still functioning in the eighteenth century) only included graduates of the legal and medical faculties. The Protestant ministers had an organisation of their own, but there was no society of graduates in arts.[1]

To understand the social position of the professional class we must take a glance at the state of higher education in eighteenth-century Germany.[2] Schools and universities had gone through many changes since the Middle Ages, but none of them had been so catastrophic as to eradicate entirely older traditions. After the attempted fusion of Renaissance and Reformation ideas of education by Melanchthon, the creator of Protestant higher education in Germany, the chief turning points had been the foundation of the university of Halle in 1694 and that of Göttingen in 1737. The general tendency had been to secularise education more and more, and to provide more and more fully for the needs of the social classes that successively took the lead in the world of affairs.

It was at the Renaissance that the interest in the things of this world, never suppressed of course even when the Church was most powerful, began to displace the scheme of values of scholasticism. Emancipation from the bonds of traditions that seemed outworn came to be men's ideal, an ideal encouraged by a more direct acquaintance with Greek civilisation, its spirit of free enquiry and its love of beauty. Study

[1] *Die Stadt Goethes*, p. 103.

[2] The standard work is F. Paulsen's excellent *Geschichte des gelehrten Unterrichts*, 2 vols. (1st ed. 1885, 2nd enlarged ed. 1896–7). A much briefer outline is the same author's *Das deutsche Bildungswesen in seiner geschichtlichen Entwicklung*, 4th ed. 1912.

of antiquity opened men's eyes again to the concrete world about them, to the practical problems of everyday life and the opportunities it offered to the individual of satisfying his natural desire for power and knowledge and happiness. These ideas, at first confined to an élite, had quietly permeated the German universities by about the year 1520 and brought about many changes in the curriculum. But in the next ten years their progress was abruptly arrested by the essentially popular and anti-intellectual movement initiated by Luther. Even the consciousness of having a common enemy, the old Church, could not keep such different natures as Erasmus and Luther in the same camp for long. Free enquiry and the love of beauty were incompatible with the insistence on faith and grace and a new orthodoxy. The first effects of the Reformation on education were entirely negative. In 1530 university studies in Germany were at their lowest ebb. But Luther was by no means blind to the necessity of secular learning and to the responsibilities of those who had swept away the educational system of the old Church. In vigorous pamphlets he reminded the new authorities in things spiritual, the princes and magistrates, of the crying necessity for good schools and universities, both for the needs of the Protestant Church and of civil society, and his humanist ally Melanchthon, 'preceptor Germaniae', organised a new educational system for him, wrote new textbooks, and as the trusted adviser of the Protestant princes devised regulations and provided teachers for innumerable new institutions.

It was essential to remind ourselves of the beginnings of Protestant higher education, because the Latin schools of Germany remained until nearly the end of the eighteenth century very much what Melanchthon had made them. Their curriculum still showed in the main the desire for a compromise that would satisfy both humanists and reformers, for its two poles were Latin and the Catechism. The aim was still that of J. Sturm, 'sapiens atque eloquens pietas'. That religion should be one of the chief subjects of instruction was a consequence of the new insistence on purity of doctrine. The need for Latin was equally obvious to that age, for Latin only slowly lost its position as the *lingua franca* of the learned. Until nearly the beginning of the eighteenth century there were more Latin books published in Germany every year than German ones, and Latin was still commonly used for university lectures even in the second half of the century. Every educated man had to understand Latin to acquaint himself with contemporary thought, and it was chiefly as a living language that Latin was taught, with the emphasis on 'Eloquence', the power to use Latin in speech and writing, not on the study of classical literature for its aesthetic and intellectual value.

Schools then as now became what their teachers made them, and this depended largely on the teacher's own training at the university. Reforms begun in the universities gradually made their influence felt in the schools. In the period under review, between Luther and Goethe, several such waves of reform can be traced by the historian of education, all of which left their traces on the practice of the eighteenth century. In the universities reformed by Melanchthon the Philosophical or Arts Faculty prepared the young student (not usually much older than fifteen when he came to the university) for study in the senior faculties of theology and law, in much the same way as the higher classes of a gymnasium now prepare boys for the university. The students followed a prescribed course of instruction in such subjects as Latin and Greek grammar, dialectics and rhetoric, the elements of mathematics, and prescribed Latin and Greek texts. Aristotelian philosophy was still an important feature in the later part of the course. After two or three semesters an intermediate examination (for the bachelor's degree) had to be passed, before the student could proceed to the two-year course for the master's degree. Written and oral practice in Latin (and to a much smaller extent in Greek) was given by means of 'imitations' of classical models, declamations and public disputations. It was not by any means every student who took the whole course and the master's degree before proceeding to the study of law or theology. 'Magister' still meant one qualified to teach arts subjects in a university, and few would seek this qualification. Specialised training in the appropriate higher faculty gradually came to be so indispensable for future Beamte and Pfarrer that a minimum of attendance on arts lectures was the rule. We hear in fact of many Protestant ministers who had only attended a university for a year or two in all.

Universities of this Reformation type were the new foundations Marburg (Hessen, 1527), Königsberg (Preussen, 1544), Jena (for Weimar, Jena, Eisenach, 1558), Helmstedt (Braunschweig-Wolfenbüttel, 1576), and the reformed older foundations Wittenberg (Sachsen), Tübingen (Württemberg), Leipzig (Sachsen), Frankfort-on-the-Oder (Brandenburg), Greifswald (Pommern), Rostock (Mecklenburg), Heidelberg (Pfalz). Every Protestant state of any importance had at least one university of its own, and universities now drew their students for the most part from the state in which they were situated and by which they were endowed.

The universities were fed by the town grammar schools and by the many new state schools (Fürstenschulen or Klosterschulen). The Fürstenschulen of Saxony (Pforta, Meissen and Grimma), founded by Moritz von Sachsen in 1543, sent a succession of able boys to the state universities Leipzig and Wittenberg. The Klosterschulen of Württemberg (founded 1559), feeding the Tübinger Stift with theologians, were no less famous. Brandenburg had its school at Joachimsthal (1607), Pommern at Stettin (1543) and even smaller states like Ansbach and Koburg followed suit. The aim of the founders of these schools was to provide future servants for the state in its Church and civil service. In many cases the whole training could be had free of cost in return for a promise to enter the state service. The state schools continued to lead until the nineteenth century. Those of Saxony turned out in the eighteenth century Lessing and Klopstock, those of Württemberg produced Hölderlin and Hegel, and they would have been able to claim Schiller if he had not been compelled by the prince to attend the newest state school of Württemberg, the 'Karlsschule', where everything but theology was taught. In the state schools, as in the grammar schools, founded and controlled by the town council, which existed in every town of any note, Latin was the main subject of instruction all through the period. Until late in the eighteenth century the entire stress was as we have seen on the practical command of the language. It was used as early as possible as the medium of instruction. Greek if taught at all was given far less attention. The only other important subject was religious instruction. The elements of rhetoric and dialectics, arithmetic and geometry, physics and cosmogony were thrown in, all taught in the medieval way. It will be seen that there was a very great deal in the school curriculum that had remained unchanged since the Middle Ages.

One can distinguish at least two subsequent waves of reform, each affecting the universities first and ebbing away in the Latin schools, that had left their mark on education by Goethe's day. The first was the modernism propagated by court circles, the demand for a realistic knowledge of the world of the day, for modern languages, geography and history, and above all for mathematics and the new sciences founded on it, all at the expense of Latin and religion in the timetable. We have seen above what was considered necessary for a gentleman in the age following the Thirty Years' War, and how these needs were met by the new Ritterakademien. These ideas first reached university circles through the foundation of the Prussian university of Halle in 1694.

It is significant that the new university was founded in a town in which the court of an archbishopric (Magdeburg) had resided, until the small state had fallen by inheritance to Brandenburg. In the buildings formerly used by the court there was housed first a Ritterakademie and then the university that grew out of it, and Thomasius, one of the two outstanding men among the professoriate, congratulated the students on having before them as models of good breeding the councillors of the old court. The French aristocratic culture of the day was what he wished his German students to emulate, that they might be men of the world and not dry pedants. He discarded academic dress and gave university lectures, for the first time in Germany, in the German language. His aim was to break down the barriers that existed between the learned and the ordinary society of their day, to make useful knowledge available to the widest possible circle. He appealed for complete freedom of research, freedom from the gild tradition in scholarship, 'which permitted no one to exercise the scholar's craft without paying dearly for a master's rights, unless he were a master's son or had married into a master's family', and freedom from persecution for unpopular opinions. He was supported in his opposition to medievalism by the theologian A. H. Francke, who was with Spener the leader of the Pietist movement. Francke too was of a practical turn of mind. He was not interested in niceties of dogma so much as in the raising of moral standards and the improvement of social institutions. With his missionary zeal and his talent for organisation he succeeded in making some of the dreams of Comenius a reality in the great complex of institutions that he built up in Halle, the Orphanage with its two schools, a Latin and a German one, the Paedagogium, a secondary school for paying pupils, and several appendages, such as a printing-press and a bookshop. In the long run, however, the rationalist and the sanctimonious elements in Halle were bound to separate out. They did so soon after Thomasius had been joined by Christian Wolff, the father of the Aufklärung in Germany, whose textbooks, based on the work of the seventeenth century, particularly that of Leibniz, soon entirely displaced those in the tradition of Melanchthon, and substituted their 'Vernünftige Gedanken' in every sphere for the appeal to authority. The persecution of Wolff and his disciples only served to advertise his views, with the result that in 1740, when Wolff returned in triumph to Halle, they prevailed in almost all the German universities and had given rise to a critical school of theology (under J. S. Baumgarten, followed by J. S. Semler) in Halle itself.

Halle stimulated the Prussian spirit of efficient practical organisation. 'All the important Prussian civil servants of the eighteenth century were trained at Halle, and that characteristic tendency towards the rational, useful and practical, which everywhere is revealed in Prussian legislation and administration, is only the application of doctrines imbibed at Halle.'[1] But this is only one current in the thought of the time, though the strongest. It is obvious that the influence of Halle was not likely to be good on humane letters. Thomasius and his successors were of course enthusiastic moderns. They did much to encourage the use of the German language. But they were little interested in either the ancients or the moderns as literature. They were practical men with no literary taste. Humanistic studies were badly neglected at Halle, the whole arts faculty being a mere appendage to the faculties of law and theology. If Halle's example was contagious, as we are told it was, it is difficult to see how the humanistic spirit could become so strong as it clearly was in the second half of the century. The explanation is to be sought in the conservatism of the schools and in the revival of humane letters initiated by the second new foundation, the university of Göttingen.

The schools continued to teach Latin and sound religion, little affected by any changes in the universities. The only change noticeable was that modern subjects began to creep into the curriculum, chiefly as extras, to attract, if possible, pupils from the higher classes of society. Progressive schools

[1] An anonymous historian quoted by Hettner, *Geschichte der deutschen Literatur im achtzehnten Jahrhundert*, I, i, chap. 2 (H. W. v. Raumer).

began in the first half of the eighteenth century to engage a mathematics master and sometimes a teacher of French. Latin continued to be the central subject, but time had to be found gradually for a little mathematics, history and geography, French and even German. Greek usually lost ground to French. But change was very slow. In the gymnasium at Frankfort-on-Main, for instance, room was not found for French until 1784.[1]

In the meantime the teaching of the classics was slowly being adapted in the universities to the needs of the age. The progress of modern science and philosophy had undermined their position. Men had come to look less and less to the ancient world, to what Thomasius for instance called 'Das Geschmiere des heidnischen Aristoteles', for information and guidance, and to use French or their mother tongue more and more in place of Latin. It seemed possible that the study of the classics would gradually die out altogether. That this did not happen was due partly to the schools and partly to the influence of a few university teachers, formerly schoolmasters themselves, who discovered reasons convincing even to the enlightened for studying the classics, but for studying them in a different way. The aim of the old school was, as we have seen, to teach their pupils to use Latin as they supposed a Roman used it, to produce the best possible imitations of surviving Latin models. The aim of the new humanism of J. M. Gesner of Göttingen and his pupils was to train the taste, judgment and intellect of their pupils by a study of classical masterpieces. They aimed at some such cultivation of the mind as is so persuasively advocated by Newman in his *Idea of a University*. The controversy between the defenders of Oxford and the utilitarian Edinburgh Reviewers, who, as Newman points out, were reviving old ideas of Locke,[2] reminds one strongly of the contrast between

[1] For a brief history of the Frankfort curriculum see *Die Stadt Goethes*, pp. 154 ff.

[2] *Idea of a University*, Discourse VII.

Göttingen and Halle. Newman was like Gesner in believing that 'a cultivated intellect, because it is a good in itself, brings with it a power and a grace to every work and occupation which it undertakes, and enables us to be more useful, and to a greater number'.

This change of aim necessitated a change of methods, the shifting of the stress from speaking and writing to reading and appreciating. Through his philological 'Seminar' (the first Seminar in a German university) and his immense influence with school authorities Gesner's views were disseminated far and wide. At the same time his former colleague at the Thomasschule in Leipzig, Ernesti, was working in the same direction there, first in the school and then in the university. Gesner was followed up in Göttingen by the great scholar Heyne (in Göttingen 1763–1812), the founder of classical archaeology. These teachers gave humane letters a new prestige. The literary study of the classics came to be looked upon as necessary for any cultivated man. At the same time advanced study and research in history and law, as well as in the mathematical sciences and medicine, were actively encouraged in Göttingen by the endowment of the only really satisfactory university library in Germany, together with scientific and medical laboratories and museums. Göttingen completed the process begun at Halle of bringing the universities into touch again with life and attracting the best minds of the day to their service. The success of these efforts is best measured by a comparison with France or England. In the second half of the eighteenth century the universities of Germany had taken the lead, not only in scholarship, philosophy and science but to some extent in public affairs, a lead they maintained in the nineteenth century, while the English and French universities only gradually approximated themselves to the German model.

It should not be supposed, however, that the German universities had retained the independence of free corporations. Their progress had been made possible by state support and involved a large measure of dependence on the state. The professors had become civil servants, appointed and liable to be dismissed in the same way as other officials. The government kept an eye on their various activities, regulating their salaries and dealing out praise and blame accordingly. The system of benevolent despotism made no exceptions in favour of the university. The government view of their function was almost purely utilitarian. They existed to train men for the civil service, the Church and the schools. The law faculty, drawing its students from the higher middle class and even from the nobility, and preparing them for the most influential and lucrative public posts, enjoyed much higher prestige than any other and set the tone for the whole university. Here court traditions were strong. The students wore swords and imitated as best they could the dress and manners of the courts until, after the Seven Years' War, the middle-class influence gradually asserted itself.

The further reforms initiated at Göttingen gradually penetrated to the Latin schools. The effect was to encourage the study of Greek for its cultural value, and of German, for self-expression, at the cost of Latin 'eloquence'. French continued to make progress, history, geography, mathematics and physics were given more attention. At the same time religious instruction was modified in the direction of 'natural' theology, with its stress on the moral aim of religion, the point of view of Lessing's *Nathan der Weise*. But these changes failed to attract to the schools the sons of the nobility or even those of the patricians of the towns and the richer merchants. These boys were still taught at home by private tutors, usually young theologians who were waiting for a call, men ranging in ability and cultivation from the standard of Kant, Fichte, Hölderlin, Hegel (all of whom, as well as many other intellectual leaders of Germany in the eighteenth and early nineteenth centuries, were private tutors in their day) to that of poor theologians who had left the university after a few months for lack of means.

In considering the professions opened up to young Germans in the eighteenth century by a higher education, the question of social origins cannot be neglected. Equality of opportunity was very far from being a reality. It was hardly even thought of as an ideal. The prospects of even an able boy depended very much on his father's position in life. For a poor boy there were almost insuperable obstacles to advancement in the higher professions.

At the universities (Paulsen says) we find two groups of students. There are young men who are preparing themselves by the study of law and 'political science' for office under the state. They are all drawn from the better classes of society. And there are others from families living in straitened circumstances or actual poverty, who are preparing themselves through the study of theology and school subjects for the Protestant Church and its appendage, school teaching and tutoring. When his academic studies are over the law student learns the practical details of his future work by assisting some Justiz- or Regierungskollegium. The theologian on the other hand looks out for a post as private tutor or as teacher at a Latin school, to maintain himself until the church living that is his ambition turns up. Apart from a few posts in large town and state schools no one remained a schoolmaster any longer than he was obliged to. Towards the end of the century however there are signs of a change, the change that has been completed in the nineteenth century: the teachers begin to separate off from the clergy as a special profession, and at the same time they gain in status and recognition.

Of the students in the clerical and scholastic group the great majority came from the lower middle class and peasantry. Hardly any came from the nobility or the families of higher civil servants, but an increasing proportion were the sons of Pfarrer themselves. Regular provision was made by some Protestant states, as we have seen, for the free education of candidates for the ministry in state schools and special theological colleges at the state university, but only the ablest boys could hope for such scholarships. At all universities there were many other theological students, most of them poor, enjoying no regular assistance. They struggled along on a small allowance from home, eked out by occasional free meals from charitable citizens and by what they could earn by coaching, school-teaching, proof-reading, clerical work and the like. They were particularly numerous at Leipzig, because, as a big town and the centre of the publishing trade, it offered more opportunities than most universities of part-time employment. Here many lived like Jean Paul's *Quintus Fixlein* and his three room-mates, whose principal material necessities, such as bed and overcoat, 'resembled so many Phoenixes, each being the sole one of its kind', though their good humour remained indestructible.

It was a lucky theologian who was able to find a post even as temporary assistant to a Pfarrer immediately on leaving the university. Almost all had to resign themselves to a period of private tutoring or schoolmastering before they could hope for a living. For 'Hofmeister' or private tutors conditions depended almost entirely on the kind of family with which they found employment. Their position was necessarily insecure. In general they were apparently treated as superior domestics. 'People who treat their children's tutor like a domestic servant should be ashamed of themselves', says Knigge, and he speaks of tutors in good families not daring to say a word at table and being made to feel their social inferiority to the children under their charge by friends and servants.[1] They were usually paid about fifty Thalers a year in addition to their board. Families desiring a tutor often asked a university professor to recommend one. In the first half of the eighteenth century Francke in Halle was the most popular adviser. Later it was Gellert in Leipzig, and after him C. F. Weisse, with his *Kinderfreund*, and J. J. Engel of Berlin.[2] A long list of famous men might be

[1] Knigge, *Umgang mit Menschen*, II, 10.

[2] See for this and further details Gustav Stephan, 'Hofmeister und Gouvernanten im achtzehnten Jahrhundert', *Zeitschrift für deutsche Kulturgeschichte*, N.F. I, 1891, and G. Steinhausen, 'Der Hofmeister', in his *Kulturstudien*, Berlin, 1893.

compiled who were tutors at least for a period. It would include Gellert, C. F. Weisse, Gleim, Götz, C. G. Heyne, Musäus, Hamann, Winckelmann, Boie, Voss, Lenz, L. Wagner, Jean Paul, Kant, Hölderlin, Fichte, Hegel and Schleiermacher. A tutor who was lucky might win the favour of a patron by good service in his family and be presented to a living, or he might be advanced to the post of secretary. Goethe's friend Behrisch for instance, who began as a tutor, displayed so much *savoir-vivre* that he ended by becoming a Hofrat.

The profession of schoolmaster in a Latin school was, as Paulsen states, not usually looked upon as an occupation for life, any more than tutoring. The status and conditions of life it afforded were such that it could only attract men from the lower middle class of the towns or from the peasantry. It was in the first place very badly paid. At the end of the century in Prussia a teacher's income ranged between 200 and 400 Thalers a year, little if any more than the average student required for his maintenance.[1] The greater part of it came from fees that he had to collect himself, and part often consisted of contributions in kind. For purposes of comparison it may be noted that village school teachers rarely received more than 100 Thalers, usually less than 40, while at the other end of the scale a university professor might receive up to 1200 Thalers, though the average salary would be well under half that sum. Almost every schoolmaster had to supplement his income by other work. Some (especially headmasters) were able to secure a few boarders, some might combine the office of schoolmaster with that of organist, some would earn a little by their pen. Their chief resource was the giving of private lessons. As we have seen, all the modern subjects were at first extras, but they were taught by the regular staff for special fees. The schools imitated here the practice of the universities, where it had become usual for a professor to treat the public lectures which he gave for his fixed salary

[1] Paulsen, II, 158 f.

rather perfunctorily, and to reserve his best teaching for private lectures, for which he received the fees himself. Even in the eighteenth century schoolmasters had often to join their pupils in the traditional 'Kurrende', hymn and carol-singing round the town at traditional times for alms, as well as to attend with them innumerable weddings and funerals. Schools were small, but they were nevertheless understaffed. A school rarely had more than three masters, called, in order of seniority, Rector, Conrector and Cantor. Schools were seldom if ever housed in specially constructed buildings. The accommodation ranged from the most primitive makeshift quarters to the gloomy old monastic building occupied by most state and town schools. No wonder that bitter complaints by schoolmasters were frequent. According to J. H. Voss, himself a schoolmaster, the schoolmaster ranked between the lowest of country ministers and the verger. In a prince's funeral procession Voss was asked to walk beside the valet.

The hardness of the schoolmaster's lot is less surprising when one remembers that university professors, especially those of the philosophical faculty, only slowly attained to the degree of social esteem that they enjoyed in the nineteenth century. The arts professors in particular usually came from the lower classes of society, for men with brains in other classes sought more highly respected and more lucrative callings. As study in the philosophical faculty had a preparatory character, the arts professors did not enjoy the same standing as the rest. They were glorified schoolmasters, who taught the elements of a fairly wide range of subjects for about as many hours a week as a schoolmaster teaches to-day. Being overworked and poor, and having had few opportunities of mixing in society, scholars usually lived the life of recluses. Amongst men of the world their vanity and pedantry were proverbial, and to judge by the fulsome dedications of their books, by the exaggerated value laid even by distinguished men like Gellert or Pütter on acquaintanceship with the great, and by the pictures of the typical professor drawn by Knigge and others, there were good grounds for the charge. The other side of the picture is to be seen in the heroic devotion to learning of a Heyne or a Winckelmann, and in the charming pictures of a scholar's happiness in his work and his family that we find in Semler's autobiography or the letters of Voss. Their world was admittedly not that of the 'man of the world', but it was just their willingness to devote their whole life to intellectual tasks, even at the cost of stunting themselves as men, that enabled the greatest of them to make the peculiar contribution of Germany to European culture. 'Amour de la retraite', to use Mme de Staël's phrase, was the characteristic feature of the life of Germany's scholars, philosophers and poets, as opposed to the 'esprit de conversation' of the French, and it was everywhere reflected in their work.[1]

It was only a few exceptionally able men who became university professors. The mass of the poorer students in the universities looked to the Protestant ministry as the goal of their ambition. By the eighteenth century a Pfarrer who had not studied for at least a year or two at a university was a rarity. In the early days of Lutheranism the reformers had had to improvise a ministry out of the available resources. Besides teachers and vergers, many printers, clothmakers and other craftsmen had been pressed into service, but in two hundred years of evolution the standard of culture of the average clergyman had risen to a fairly high level, and completely unsuitable appointments were not common. There was still, however, no satisfactory machinery to prevent mistakes. The power of nomination still remained in most parishes in the hands of an aristocratic and by no means always cultivated patron, who might be moved by one of

[1] The two books by Emil Reicke, *Der Lehrer in der deutschen Vergangenheit* and *Der Gelehrte in der deutschen Vergangenheit* (Monographien zur deutschen Kulturgeschichte) are popular and deal chiefly with the Middle Ages. They are largely dependent on Paulsen, *op. cit.*

a number of motives in making his selection, and who seldom consulted the congregation first. There was a theological examination, conducted by the consistory, which all candidates for orders had to pass. Sometimes, as in Prussia in the second half of the century, there were two, one to be taken after university study to qualify for the title of 'Kandidat' (which had previously been assumed by any who chose to use it), and one immediately preceding ordination to a particular parish. But no one was ever known to fail in these examinations. A candidate selected by a patron might be asked to present himself a second time if he proved utterly ignorant at the first attempt, but he was always successful in the end. A large proportion of the candidates were themselves sons of ministers. Not a few others, it seems, qualified for a vacancy by marrying the widow or a daughter of the previous incumbent, much as craftsmen married into a gild. Other strange conditions of appointment were sometimes imposed by patrons, while 'gifts' of money and discreditable intrigues were by no means unknown. A reference to them is admitted even into such an idyllic picture as Voss's *Luise*,[1] and Laukhard's autobiography is full of them.[2]

If the method of appointment did not tend to keep moral and intellectual standards high, the development of public opinion, under the influence of Pietism and rationalism successively, had done something to correct this defect, though neither movement had done much to earn for the clergy greater social esteem. The Pietist movement had shifted the stress from dogmatic teaching to care of souls, from preaching to pastoral visitations and prayer meetings, which brought the minister into closer touch with his parishioners. Rationalism had still further weakened the

[1] 'Ein ländlicher Pfarrer verbauert,
Haftet am Kloss und vergeht in Nichtigkeit oder Erwerbsucht,
Wenn nicht griechischer Geist ihn emporhebt aus der Entartung
Neueres Barbartums, *wo Verdienst ist käuflich und erblich.*'

Luise, 2te Idylle.

[2] Laukhard, *Leben und Schicksale*, I, chaps. 9 and 10.

hold of dogmatic religion. It had alienated the great mass of the educated laity from religion altogether, and made religion even for the nominally orthodox the handmaid of morality. As a class, therefore, the Protestant clergy, though their personal integrity was greater than ever, were not very highly respected in the latter part of the century. In spite of the vogue of Pietism in many courts, they were regarded by the majority of the court class with indifference or scorn, and by the cultivated as something of an anachronism.

Their standard of living was usually necessarily low, except in the towns, and here it was considerably below that of the official class. The average income of a country Pfarrer was only about fifty to seventy Thalers a year, his material comforts often fewer than those of a middling craftsman or peasant. He had always to eke out his income by gardening, bee-keeping, the cultivation of silkworms or regular farming. Part of his income was in the form of tithes. The Pfarrer's share of a crop might be laid out on the fieldpath and the whole of his family would have to help to carry it home. Most country Pfarrer would keep a cow or two and hens, so that though a minister's wife would buy very little in the way of food, she was always ready to entertain visitors, with the salt or smoked meat, poultry, eggs, vegetables and flour that she had at hand. She would make a thousand and one things at home that are now bought in shops, from preserved meats to soap and candles. Clothes too were nearly all made at home. The lady of the house and her daughters would spin their flax, weave it or have it woven in the village and perhaps send it to the nearest town to be printed with a pattern. There cloth could also be bought for the menfolk, and a tailor would be engaged for a week or a fortnight to help to make or repair the clothes of the family for the coming year. The few things that had to be bought would be provided by the annual fair in a neighbouring market-town.

In the Protestant states that followed the lead of Frederician Prussia the ministers of the Church came to be looked upon during the second half of the century as functionaries of the state. The absolute state had freed itself from every trace of theocracy and made a tool of the Church for its own secular purposes. This change gave Protestant ministers an assured place in society, but only with the sacrifice of much of their spiritual freedom. For the Aufklärung they were teachers of religion and instruments of social service. As religion was a useful prop for morality, it was in the interests of the state, even if it professed to concern itself solely with the temporal welfare of its subjects, to encourage it. At the same time the Pfarrer proved a very useful channel of communication between the government and the mass of the people. When newspapers were still rare and illiteracy widespread, to have a decree read from the pulpit was the most effective way of ensuring universal knowledge of it, and great use was made of this method of 'broadcasting' for purely secular affairs. Further, the Pfarrer, as perhaps the only educated man in the village, was called upon to perform all sorts of duties that now fall to state officials.

From the diary of a country minister in Baden, at the end of the eighteenth century,[1] we learn that he superintended the election of the village 'Vogt' and the appointment of midwives. With the 'Vogt' or village mayor he shared responsibility in all questions of administration. Not even the cleaning out of a brook or the repairing of a field-path happened without his knowledge. He was the confidential agent of the government in all sorts of matters. He was asked for reports about people in the village and about proposed changes involving government assistance or consent. The Pfarrer gave notice, for instance, as we learn from other sources, of epidemics, and of the death of persons on whose estate duties might be levied. He was the village registrar and statistician, who kept records not only of births, marriages and deaths but of the number of blind, halt, deaf and

[1] A. Schmitthenner, *Das Tagebuch meines Urgrossvaters*, Freiburg i. B. 1922 (3rd ed.).

dumb, of orphans, illegitimate children and homeless families. He conducted the census, drew up the list of recruits and had to be present when young men from his parish were called up for medical examination. In Prussia, we learn from other sources, the Pfarrer had to take care, if he valued his living, not to put any obstacles in the way of the king's recruiting officers. Our Baden informant was jointly responsible with the Vogt for poor relief. He was superintendent of the schools in the four villages in his parish and examined them all every quarter. He presided over the 'censura' or ecclesiastical court of the district, consisting of two elected representatives from each village and the mayors, the competence of which was very wide. It dealt with almost all offences except those against property and the person, and could not only reprimand offenders but sentence them to imprisonment in the village gaol. It was especially concerned of course with offences against morality. It will be evident that Herder sums up the position of the Pfarrer in his day truly when he says: 'A minister is only entitled to exist now, under state control and by authority of the prince, as a moral teacher, a farmer, a list-maker, a secret agent of police'.

With these secular duties in addition to his pastoral work, and perhaps the education of some of his children, even a country Pfarrer did not find that time hung heavy on his hands. In the towns there would no doubt be less administrative work and more visiting and preaching. That not all ministers were equally conscientious or well fitted for their task has already been noted. But if there were black sheep, especially in the country, who were almost as rude and ignorant as their peasant neighbours, and others who, like a familiar type in the Church of England, were more gentlemen-farmers than clergymen, there were hundreds of devout and learned men in Protestant parsonages and not a few of high literary cultivation. The part played by the clergy in literature was not, on the whole, very considerable in the eighteenth century. Herder is the only clergyman-author of the first rank; among authors of the second and third rank are Götz, Hermes, Miller, Lavater. It is interesting, however, as a partial index to the literary atmosphere of the Protestant parsonages, to note what a big part was played in the creation of an independent German literature by sons of Pfarrer, men like Lessing, Wieland, Claudius, Hölty, Miller, Boie, Bürger, Heinse, Lenz, Schubart. For all that it should be remembered that the pictures of Pfarrer painted by Voss in *Luise*, by Goethe in *Hermann und Dorothea*, or Jean Paul in *Jubelsenior* are much idealised.

Among professional men, doctors with a university qualification ranked high. They had usually had a good grounding in the classics, at any rate in Latin, at a grammar school, perhaps supplemented by a year or two in the philosophical faculty of a university, before entering on their professional training. Then three years of study in the medical faculty were necessary before they could obtain the medical doctorate of their university, the qualification usually required before a doctor could set up in practice in Germany. The doctor, or 'medicus purus', was still carefully distinguished from the surgeon, who till the end of the century, with few exceptions, was a man of little education who ranked no higher than a skilled artisan, trained as he was like a craftsman by apprenticeship in a gild. In Durlach, for instance, doctors and even apothecaries belonged to the 'exempted' class, but surgeons did not, any more than barbers, from whom they were often indistinguishable.[1] The two branches of the medical art were beginning to approach each other, but it was not until the second half of the nineteenth century that doctors in Germany were required to be competent in medicine, surgery and midwifery alike. In the eighteenth century they usually had at most a theoretical acquaintance with the last two branches and left the practice of them to the socially inferior barber-surgeon and midwife.

[1] Roller, *op. cit.* p. 407.

Medical teaching in the German universities varied very greatly in quality and quantity from place to place. At the beginning of the century few universities had more than two or three professors in their medical faculty. Each taught two or more subjects, usually in a purely theoretical way, with little or no practical anatomy or clinical work. By the end of the century, however, things had improved so much that the leading universities at least had medical faculties of specialists, provided with anatomy theatres, laboratories and clinical institutes. Vienna had nine medical chairs by 1780, Göttingen six by 1784. But figures are sometimes misleading. Würzburg for instance had five chairs according to the ordinances of 1749, but a student who went there in 1761 found that the professors received salaries of 200 to 300 Gulden and had had no pupils for several years. The number of students was small even at the bigger universities. At Göttingen it averaged 50 to 80 in all in the 'sixties and 'seventies, so that about a score would graduate each year. Jena in 1768 had 17, while Altdorf turned out an average of only two or three doctors a year throughout the century.[1] Comparing these numbers with those of the more famous medical schools abroad, we gain some idea of the relative standing of the German universities in medicine. Leyden, in the early years of the century, had about 300 medical students, and Edinburgh's average number in the second half of the century was 400.

The truth is that Germany had not yet attained the eminence in medicine which was to be hers in the nineteenth century. Holland led the way in medical science in the seventeenth and early eighteenth centuries, when Boerhaave (1668–1738), building on foundations well laid by his predecessors, attracted students from all Europe by his clinical skill, and though his pupils van Swieten (1700–72) and de Haën (1704–76) established a good medical school at Vienna, and Albrecht Haller, the poet-scientist, another pupil

[1] Puschmann, *Geschichte des medicinischen Unterrichts*, Leipzig, 1889, p. 325.

of his, as professor in Göttingen put physiology for the first time on a sound scientific basis and displayed immense learning in many fields, the German record of achievements during the century is inferior to that of France or England. Many Germans therefore studied medicine abroad, at Leyden, Utrecht, Paris or Strassburg. Surgery was particularly backward, the empirical skill of the surgeons being seldom backed by any theoretical knowledge. Academically trained surgeons like Heister of Altdorf (1683–1758) and A. G. Richter of Göttingen (1742–1812) were rare exceptions, and both had been trained abroad, whereas in France, largely through the foundation of the Académie de Chirurgie in Paris in 1743, the status of the best surgeons had been raised as high as that of good doctors and an equally thorough theoretical training had come to be demanded of them.

The opportunities for medical education being so unequal, and the reputation for honesty of some university faculties not being above reproach (they were often accused of selling degrees without examination), it was inevitable that the state authorities should insist on some form of supervision of doctors and surgeons. It was of course in Prussia that control was most effectively exercised, but most states made some attempt at it. By the Prussian 'Medizinaledikt' of 1725 medical graduates were submitted to a state test and obliged to attend lectures at the Royal Anatomical Theatre in Berlin before they could be recognised. Surgeons had to serve seven years' apprenticeship, gain experience in the field as 'Feldscher' or regimental surgeon, attend a 'course of operations' in the anatomical theatre and pass certain tests. They were not allowed to treat ordinary illnesses (which were the physician's province) except in small towns or in the country. There were so few large towns, however, that in practice the great majority of people had to be content with the services of a barber-surgeon.[1] Similar edicts were in

[1] For vivid pictures of a barber-surgeon's life and work see Meister Johann Dietz, *Lebensbeschreibung*, Munich, 1915.

force in most states and Free Towns. In Frankfort-on-Main for example control was exercised by the four 'Physicians' appointed and paid by the town council.

After their theoretical training young doctors might be called upon then to do some practical anatomy, the opportunity for which might not have been provided in the university—for it was only gradually that even the leading universities obtained proper dissecting rooms and a supply of material—but they were not yet compelled to seek clinical experience in a hospital or with an older doctor. Clinical teaching was usually scanty or non-existent in the universities, and only a few of them had satisfactory clinics by the end of the century. They were usually of course in small towns. Jung-Stilling, speaking from his own experience in the 'seventies, urges young doctors both to study surgery and to obtain experience under skilled guidance before setting up in practice. 'Where is there still more to be done', he says, 'than in the organisation of medical teaching and practice and state regulation of these matters?'[1]

The medical profession was by no means overcrowded in the eighteenth century. A well-qualified doctor, after the first difficult years, was assured of a comfortable living. In many states doctors were given a small official salary and their fees were often fixed, at any rate for certain poorer classes of patients. They generally settled in fair-sized towns or near some court, in a place, that is, where patients of the better middle class and the aristocracy were available. The barber-surgeon had usually to suffice for craftsmen and country folk. Even in the towns doctors proper kept strictly to their own sphere and assisted the surgeon or the midwife only with their not always highly respected theoretical advice. Though they were not numerous, most of the doctors one hears of seem to have led a very regular and unhurried existence. In Weimar, for instance, each doctor (there were four in this small town) had time enough to visit all the

[1] J. H. Jung-Stilling, *Lebensgeschichte* (Häusliches Leben).

families who had entrusted themselves to his care at least once a week, whether anyone was ill or not, and it was thought necessary for him solemnly to purge the whole family with rhubarb once a quarter.[1] In the bigger towns the medical men had their professional organisations, which often played an important part in civic affairs. There were many progressive and public-spirited men among them who took the lead in pressing for the provision of more hospitals (many towns had still only the hospitals originally founded by the Church), better opportunities for medical and surgical education, improvements in town drainage and water supply and the systematic training of midwives, a very urgent necessity. In all these things much progress was made in the course of the century, and this is of course one of the reasons for the unprecedented growth of the population in the following century.[2] In *Dichtung und Wahrheit* Goethe draws attention to the important influence they had in cultural affairs. 'Following the example of a foreigner, Tissot,' he says, 'the doctors too (like certain theologians) began eagerly to make their influence felt in general culture. Haller, Unzer, Zimmermann were great forces.' Many doctors began to write not merely for other members of the profession but for the general public, and helped in this way to raise the level of German prose writing, more perhaps than the lawyers and philosophers. As cultivated men they naturally played their part too as patrons of the new poetic literature, though in spite of Haller's example few were creative writers.

We come now to the professional men who as students had belonged to the most highly considered class, the Jurists. They came almost always from what were considered the higher ranks of society, the nobility and patricians and above all the better placed bourgeoisie, prosperous merchants and

[1] Karl von Lyncker, *Am Weimarischen Hofe*, Berlin, 1912, p. 35.

[2] For details about these improvements see e.g. Puschmann's *Handbuch der Geschichte der Medizin* (ed. Neuburger and Pagel), Jena, 1905, vol. III.

successful state and civic servants. Nearly all law students aimed at entering the service of some prince or Free Town. The growth of a professional civil service has been traced in earlier chapters. We have seen that the benevolent despotism which was the political ideal of those in authority in Germany necessitated an expansion of the bureaucracy far in excess of English developments. The multiplicity of authorities in itself made necessary a much larger number of officials in proportion to the total population than is required to-day under a more highly centralised system. Apart from three hundred independent 'territories' there were five times that number of semi-independent Grafschaften, Ritterschaften and so forth, each of which needed its staff of officials, although it might have taken a score of these units to make up a modern Prussian Regierungsbezirk. The Reichsritter needed a few officials to collect revenues, dispense justice and maintain order, the Reichsgraf, a stage higher, required a 'Privy Council', a Free Town had to have its Senate and a whole series of committees served by permanent officials, and a ruling Prince, finally, had the Council, Treasury, Department of Justice, Consistory and so forth described in earlier pages. According to figures given by Biedermann[1] there seem to have been about twice as many officials in proportion to the population in most German states in the later eighteenth century as there were a hundred years later, when there was still certainly no lack of them. It did not escape the notice of independent-minded contemporaries that there were often too many cooks. K. F. von Moser[2] tells of occasions when five treasury decrees were needed before a few slates could be repaired on a palace roof, and he draws a similar contrast in 1758 between the treasury methods in small German states and those in Sweden as modern critics of officialdom do between the procedure necessary before permission to build may be obtained in

[1] *Deutschland im 18ten Jahrhundert*, I, 100 ff.

[2] *Vom Herrn und Diener*, 1758, quoted by Biedermann, *loc. cit.*

Berlin (involving a delay of from two to twelve months and the authorisation of some twenty-six departments) and that in London (where it is usually only necessary to consult the District Surveyor).[1]

The official class was of course chiefly concentrated in the towns, but scattered over the country a very large number of trained jurists were to be found in the Ämter, the smallest administrative units of the states of that day. We have seen above what paid officials were usual in little capitals and in town-republics like Frankfort-on-Main. Many of the higher posts were reserved in the courts, as we have seen, for noblemen, though trained lawyers could never be dispensed with. In the Free Towns, though patricians by birth were favoured for paid offices, they had usually received a university education and spent some time in travel before accepting office, and the highest posts were often occupied by men who owed their rise to personal merit and knowledge rather than to any advantages of birth. Everywhere there were large numbers of minor officials of every degree of cultivation, from brilliant young men from the universities awaiting promotion, to copying clerks and men of no literary education at all in the town watch, the cleansing department and so forth.

Conditions of appointment varied very considerably. In the more progressive states and the larger towns officials were by the second half of the century almost all appointed for long periods or for life (of course with safeguards) at a fixed salary, but in many smaller states and towns their appointments were still for short periods and terminable at any time, and they depended for their living almost entirely on the fees they were allowed to demand from the public. It is obvious that such a system was open to grave abuse. Abuses were still frequent, both in the manner of appointment of officials (nepotism and the sale of offices), and in their conduct in office (corruption, laziness and inefficiency). It was only very gradually, first in Prussia then elsewhere,

[1] W. Hegemann, article in *Neue Rundschau* of Aug. 1931.

that a tradition of honourable service was established. That it grew so slowly was not the fault of the employed only, but also that of the employers. What could be expected for instance from officials who were treated as they were by the 'extravagant and impecunious petty lords' of the first half of the century, who according to K. H. von Lang 'always did their utmost to induce wealthy men to take charge of their affairs, in order that they might make use of them for their personal credit like court Jews, and when they were squeezed dry dismiss them'?[1] In such small states the officials were, as Biedermann says, little more than members of the prince's court and household staff. Their only hope of advancement for themselves and their sons was to ingratiate themselves personally with their master. Schiller's picture of this relationship in *Kabale und Liebe*, where the son of the Präsident (the Minister of Justice, and in this court the leading influence) is asked, in view of the approaching official marriage of the prince, to become the legal husband of the prince's mistress, is historically justified.

K. H. von Lang in his memoirs gives many instances of the entire lack of consideration with which petty rulers treated their officials, and we gain the same impression from the memoirs of J. C. Mannlich, from Knigge's chapter on 'Intercourse with the Great',[2] and from innumerable memoirs and biographies of the period. The private life of civil servants was constantly being interfered with by their ruler. They might have to build themselves houses in a particular quarter (as in the Friedrichsstadt in Berlin), to hunt with the prince whether they wished to or not, to attend court ceremonies at considerable expense, to send their children, against their will, to a state school (Schiller!). It was only in the town-republics and towards the end of the century in the larger states that officials, apart from their

[1] K. H. v. Lang, *op. cit.* p. 15.

[2] *Ibid.* pp. 15, 66, 131, etc.; J. C. Mannlich, *op. cit.* pp. 310, 356, etc.; Knigge, *Umgang mit Menschen*, Teil III, chap. 1.

definite duties, were allowed in their private life as much freedom as other citizens.

It goes without saying that security of tenure of office was an ideal seldom attained in practice. It was only under Frederick II in Prussia and Frederick Augustus III in Saxony that officials were given security of tenure provided that they duly performed their duties. In Prussia a spirit of military efficiency pervaded the civil service under Frederick William I. Centralised control was motivated, as we saw above, mainly by the desire to increase the military power of the state, and it was Frederick William I and not Frederick II who, according to his lights, was the first Prussian ruler to consider himself 'the first servant of the state'. But it was only under Frederick II that the spirit of service to an ideally conceived state permeated the general mass of officials, encouraged by Frederick's stern efficiency, his hardness with himself and others, and his strict control of his subordinates, together with the keen personal interest he took in their activities. In Austria even Joseph II compelled 2000 civil servants to retire with little or no pension, in the first two years of his reign, and in Bavaria, the civil service had no legal security even at the end of the century.[1]

If the status of the official class was somewhat indefinite, it is still less easy to make general statements about the payment they received for their services. Salaries varied over a wide range for different appointments and for different states, and even when nominally fixed they were subject to great fluctuations owing to the financial instability of the states. It was not uncommon for officials to receive no salary for years at a time.[2] This was one reason why the abolition of the old feudal practice, by which the prince's bailiffs were responsible for the administration of his estates and the collection of dues, as well as for dispensing justice, was resisted by the officials themselves; they had a first claim on

[1] Biedermann, *op. cit.* I, 88 f.

[2] Examples in Biedermann, *op. cit.* I, 83 ff.

the dues, fees and fines they collected. Their offices were sometimes so lucrative that great sums were paid into the exchequer by aspirants to them and the reversion was looked upon as a kind of pension for the holder's widow or children. This state of things continued in most parts of Germany till the second half of the century, in some until after the French Revolution.

A few examples of salaries may be given. A young man fresh from the university would usually, unless he had powerful connections, serve for a year or two for little or no salary, as Lang did in the Regierungskanzlei at Oettingen. After a year Lang was appointed Protokollist at a salary that amounted with extras to 200 Gulden a year (nominally £16. 13*s.* 4*d.*). A year and half later he became secretary with 240 Gulden (£20) and free firing. Ten years after leaving the university he was earning 1000 Gulden (£83) as Keeper of the Archives at Bayreuth. His highest salary was 4000 Gulden (£333), when after twenty-seven years service he became Archive Director and departmental chief in the Foreign Office at Munich. But this was in 1812, and Lang's was an unusually brilliant career. Körner, Schiller's Dresden friend, as a young man only earned 200 Thalers (£30) a year for the combined offices of Oberkonsistorialrat and Assessor on another board. Goethe in Weimar was given an allowance of 1200 Thalers (£180) on his appointment as Legationsrat. Finally his salary rose to 3100 Thalers. Of the civil officials in Frankfort-on-Main we are told that only the Schultheiss (with 1800 Gulden) and the Syndics (1600 Gulden) received over 1000 Gulden a year. The Ratsherren, however, who were not civic servants but members of the governing body, received high salaries (the Schöffen or Aldermen 1800 Gulden, the Second Benchers 1200, the Third Benchers 500). Only very responsible officials (Town Clerk, Council Clerk, Treasury Clerks, etc.) received over 400 Gulden. Officials of the second rank received 200 Gulden or less, and the rest mostly under 100 Gulden, though many had houses rent-free or received other perquisites. Towards the end of the century salaries were rising.[1] To find the equivalent purchasing value of these sums one should multiply by at least three. A useful standard of comparison is furnished by Schiller's estimate of the income required about 1790 by a single man to live decently in Jena or Rudolstadt. It was 400 Gulden. In Dresden 600 Gulden would have been required, he said, and in Weimar, though it was such a tiny capital, nearly as much. From Goethe's letters to his protégé Krafft[2] we see that it was possible to live very modestly on about half the sum Schiller mentions.

It is clear from the foregoing that the standard of living of state and civic servants as a class was by no means uniform. There were many at least as poor as an average artisan and there were others enjoying an income and social consideration resembling those of a nobleman. It was only very gradually that the brain workers were differentiated socially from manual workers. It has been proved for instance for the town of Durlach in the eighteenth century that at least half of the members of the official class or their children married, according to present-day ideas, beneath themselves. Daughters of officers and officials frequently married artisans, footmen, ostlers, factory workers and common soldiers. Young ministers, doctors, officers and officials often married ladies' maids, who might however themselves, especially in aristocratic households, be daughters of professional men of high standing. As the century advanced fewer 'misalliances' of this kind occurred. The officials and professional men were slowly cutting themselves off from the rest of the middle class. This happened partly as a consequence of their growing economic security, which allowed them to follow the accepted social models, the aristocracy, as regards the material comfort and the external forms of their life. The conflicts that might result in families drawn between the

[1] *Die Stadt Goethes*, p. 69.

[2] Goethe allowed him 100 Thalers (£15) a year.

traditional ideals of the bourgeoisie and those of the nobility are well depicted in the literature of the time, in works like Grossmann's *Nicht mehr als sechs Schüsseln* for instance. In this play we have the theme of Molière's *George Dandin* (the rich peasant marrying into the nobility) translated into terms of German life in Grossmann's time. Instead of a rich peasant we find a Hofrat of middle-class origin, and instead of his humiliation at the hands of his aristocratic in-laws we witness his triumph. Further causes contributing to the separation of this new class from the bourgeoisie were the legal privileges conferred on it in many instances, its sense of solidarity, through its particular responsibility, with the ruling class rather than with the mass of the ruled, and its growing taste for and need of literary culture and that social refinement to which a young man was introduced by a university education, and which he was encouraged to maintain by the nature of his duties in later life.

There is a certain resemblance between the rise of some elements of the middle class, through the possession of knowledge and skill, to higher social rank, and the rise of the 'ministeriales' for similar reasons in medieval times. But whereas the successful ministeriales made their offices, and the fiefs by which they were rewarded for their services, hereditary in their families, and converted themselves into a new Estate of Knights, the boundaries of the official and professional class of modern times have remained fluid. They were rewarded by money payment, enjoyed therefore far less security than their medieval counterparts, and additions were constantly being made to their number from the class to which they belonged. The result was that they retained many more of their inherited habits of living than the Knights. They were not simply absorbed by the existing upper class but formed a group which, though not very clearly delimited, still had a character of its own.

The older middle class had comparatively little artistic or literary culture, while its ideas of physical well-being were at best unsophisticated. It liked plain solid furniture, clothes that would wear for ever, an abundance of simple wholesome food and drink and its traditional homely customs and amusements. The influence of the courts and of rationalism had produced only superficial effects on its way of life. As was to be expected in a compact and hard-working society, it took questions of conduct far more seriously than intellectual or artistic matters. It was conservative and provincial in thought and taste, strict and a little pharisaical in its ethical views, as we have seen from certain gild regulations. The court classes on the other hand were far less moved by considerations of principle. They had a certain code of honour, but they were more self-seeking and opportunist than the middle class. Their consideration for others seldom extended beyond their own ranks. They had however more external polish and elegance, more feeling for style both in art and in the details of ordinary life, though in Germany, as we have seen, their forms were usually rather slavishly copied from France. In their wealth and leisure they had at least the prerequisites for a predominantly aesthetic approach to life, and speaking generally the beautiful did even in Germany mean more to them than the good or the true.

The new class of brain workers owed its position to its knowledge and intelligence. It tended necessarily to put the intellectual values first. But through its origin it retained much of the ethical rigour of the middle class, especially in regard to the relations of the sexes. It has been mentioned above that its views in this matter were in marked contrast with those of the average courtier, and that from the solid bourgeoisie and the educated middle class a stricter sexual morality, at least for women, gradually spread in the late eighteenth and early nineteenth century to the class above and the class below, the nobility and the working class. It was much the same with the other virtues which we still think of as typically 'middle class', honesty, industry, and sweet reasonableness. The educated middle class did not quickly lose its virtue then in its new life. It could not, however, resist the contagion of aristocratic ways of living. It felt the attraction of new luxuries, it imitated the nobility, at a certain remove, in dress, manners, food and drink and all kinds of externals. Many also acquired a taste now for forms of art that had come to be in Germany the preserve of the courts, painting for instance, the opera and literary drama. It is not surprising that the educated middle class responded more readily than any other section of society to the writers of the great age of German literature, such as Herder, Goethe and Schiller, with their ideal of 'Humanität', in which an attempt was made to reconcile the respective claims of morality, religion, art and philosophy to be the supreme value, and if any class can be said to have evoked this philosophy of life by its need of it, it was this educated section of the middle class.

PART IV

REACTIONS ON LITERATURE

Chapter I

THE PROFESSION OF LETTERS

It was only in the second half of the eighteenth century that it became possible for a German writer to take up literature as a whole-time profession, and even at the end of the century Germany had probably fewer professional authors than England. The number of authors of the first rank who were entirely dependent on the public was of course small in both countries. Nearly all the considerable writers either possessed private means or exercised some lucrative profession. In England there had been a period during which writers who devoted their whole time to letters and possessed few or no other resources could count on the support of aristocratic patrons. Patronage had not been unknown in the Elizabethan age. When the appreciation of literature had become fashionable again after the Restoration, patronage again occurred, but it was not until the reign of Queen Anne that it became widespread. It was to ministers of state like Somers and Montagu, Harley and St John that men like Locke, Congreve, Addison, Newton, Steele, Swift, Prior and others owed their advancement, and the fashion of patronage set by these ministers was followed by many great aristocrats. In England's Augustan Age, the patronage of literature, either as literature or as a political weapon, was a well-established custom.

Under George I the sinecures and pensions previously granted to literary men were needed for the management of

Parliament, but the practice of private patronage was kept up for some time longer. In the second quarter of the century, however, patrons began to play a smaller and smaller part because the reading public was growing, and by 1760 Goldsmith could write: 'At present, the few poets of England no longer depend on the great for subsistence; they have now no other patrons but the public, and the public, collectively considered, is a good and generous master'. Long before this Pope had been able to dispense with patrons. His first imitators in the profession of letters, in Johnson's early days, had often a hard struggle, but with the rise of the magazines in the 'thirties, the vogue of the novel and circulating library in the 'forties, there came to be such a sustained demand for the written word that writers able to hit the public taste could make good terms with publishers, and live in comfort, while some publishers and booksellers made fortunes. Goldsmith is said to have earned as much as £1800 in one year, Arthur Young to have made over £1100 in 1770 by journalism. By the beginning of the next century popular poets were receiving offers of thousands of pounds for verse tales. Scott held the record with £4000 for *The Lady of the Lake*. Byron received £2000 for the third canto of *Childe Harold* and comparable sums for other works. These were men of genius, but even authors like Southey and Galt were able to earn a very comfortable competence by steady work.[1]

The history of the profession of letters in eighteenth-century Germany is not such a record of worldly success. Patrons were few and far between, there was as yet a much smaller reading public and, most important of all, there were no effective copyright laws. Moreover, the idea that it was beneath the dignity of an author, especially of a poet, to take money for his writings, died hard. Before Klopstock's time,

[1] For an admirable study of conditions in England see the two books by A. S. Collins, *Authorship in the days of Johnson*, 1927, and *The Profession of Letters*, 1928, or the briefer account in F. A. Mumby's *Publishing and Bookselling*, 1930.

as Goethe tells us in *Dichtung und Wahrheit*, 'the book trade was chiefly concerned with important learned works, books in steady demand, for which a modest honorarium was paid. The production of poetical works was looked upon as something sacred, and it was considered almost simony to accept or bargain for payment for them'.[1] Goethe takes the relations between Gottsched and his publisher Breitkopf as typical for that age. They lived in the same house, on the friendliest terms, and what the one gained in fame the other made up for in profits. In the circumstances of those days, a young author could consider himself lucky if he found a publisher to print his work, as success, especially in 'belles lettres', was so difficult to prophesy. If he made a name for himself, he was usually by that time in some official position and independent of literary earnings.

The authors of the sixteenth and seventeenth centuries had been men of academic training, and all of them, even Philipp von Zesen, or such a rolling stone as Grimmelshausen, had aimed at a post in the service of some state or municipality. It was their writing in many cases that enabled them to attract the attention of those high personages who had the gift of such posts or sinecures and who became in this sense their patrons, much as the ministers of state did in England. It was customary for authors, or publishers, for example, of reprints and translations, to reward the services of patrons by fulsome dedications, though the services might not necessarily be of a financial nature. It was desirable to enjoy the protection of some authority in publishing any work that might cause its author or printer difficulties. But owing to the intellectual deficiencies of the German aristocracy, the high prestige of French literature in court circles, and the lack of a capital where the habit of patronage might spread by emulation, nothing resembling the patronage of native poetry so extensively practised by the English aristocracy occurred in Germany.

[1] *Dichtung und Wahrheit*, Teil III, 12. Buch.

There was accordingly no profession of letters worthy of the name in Germany in the first half of the eighteenth century. Goethe has given us the classical description of the social position of literary men at that time.

> German poets, being no longer members of a gild that could act as one man, enjoyed no advantages whatever in civil society. They had neither protection, social position nor esteem unless some other circumstance than their writing favoured them, and it was simply a matter of chance whether talent brought its owner honour or disgrace. A poor mortal, fully conscious of his mental powers, had to make his way in life as best he could and squander the gifts he had received from the muses in the struggle with the needs of the moment. The occasional poem, the first and most genuine of all *genres*, fell into such disrepute that the nation has not even yet attained to a conception of its high value, and a poet, even if he did not go the way of poor Günther, played a most melancholy rôle in the world, as a mere jester and parasite, so that both in the theatre and on the stage of life he was a personage whom anyone could treat just as he wished.
>
> If on the other hand the Muse visited men of standing, she conferred on them a glory that was reflected back on to its source. Urbane aristocrats like Hagedorn, worthy city fathers like Brockes, distinguished scholars like Haller were accounted among the first men of the nation, the peers of those highest in birth and social esteem. And those men were particularly admired who besides possessing this agreeable talent had proved their worth as active and reliable men of affairs. Uz, Rabener, Weisse accordingly enjoyed a quite peculiar esteem, because they combined qualities of such an opposing character that they are seldom found together.[1]

The first German poet who looked upon his writing as a serious and all-absorbing calling, and who compelled respect from his countrymen solely on his literary merits, was Klopstock. In a certain sense he was, like Pope in England, the first professional writer of his country. But he was not able, as Pope was, to make himself independent of private patrons because of the ready sale of his works among an

[1] *Dichtung und Wahrheit*, Teil II, 10. Buch.

admiring public. He required a Maecenas, and found one in the king of Denmark. The first author of any standing who maintained himself for a lengthy period by writing for the open market was Lessing, and he needed all his spirit and Spartan endurance to make a bare living.

The possibility of earning money by writing depended on three factors, the existence of a public willing and able to buy books, of publishers willing to accept and pay for them and of effective legal protection against literary piracy. The political disunity of Germany made it impossible in the eighteenth century for publishers to secure a copyright law that would apply to the whole Empire. The first work for which legal copyright in the whole of Germany was sanctioned by the Diet was the definitive edition of Goethe's works, begun in 1828. There was no uniform law for the whole of Germany before the foundation of the German Empire. The state censorship that existed in all the leading states after the Reformation, with the system of 'privileges', granted by individual states for particular books for a short period, afforded a certain amount of protection to publishers, as long as the demand for books was still slight. Moreover, the states and towns controlled all those printing establishments that were not subject to gild regulations, and in general only permitted the establishment of presses in the larger towns. But as soon as piracy became profitable these measures of control proved quite ineffective. From the biography of G. J. Göschen, who published the works of so many leading writers of the classical age, it is clear that pirates were the bane of a publisher's life. In many small states in the eighteenth century the pirating by local printers of editions protected in some other state was even officially tolerated, for the encouragement of home industries. Baden was a very bad offender in this respect. Göschen had infinite trouble with Schmieder of Karlsruhe, in spite of many protests to the Margrave of Baden. But Schmieder was only one of many. There were others in Vienna, Berlin, Hamburg and every large town, and 'privileges' obtained at considerable expense were almost useless. It was not until 1794 that the first step towards the suppression of literary piracy was taken by Prussia, by a provision in the 'Preussisches Landrecht', and it was over forty years before the provision was made effective and imitated by other leading states. The result was that unauthorised editions of any book that seemed likely to prove popular followed hard on the heels of the first impression. The only remedy open to the legitimate publisher was the issue of special cheap editions to undersell the pirates, a step that was often taken by Göschen, Cotta and others.

In this respect then conditions were infinitely less favourable to the professional writer in Germany than in England, where a copyright act had been passed by Parliament on the petition of the booksellers in 1710. The only grievances of the English booksellers were that the penalties were not severe enough and that they had not been granted rights in perpetuity, but only for a limited period. Copyright was secured for fourteen years, and was renewable if the author was still alive for a further period of fourteen years. The Act did not apply to Ireland and was not imitated by the Irish Parliament, so English writers of popular works had practically no sale in Ireland, where they were pirated immediately. A publisher was still liable to be undersold in England itself by Irish or foreign pirate printers, but on the whole he was sufficiently protected.

In view of the danger of piracy and the risk that is always involved in publishing 'belles lettres', the terms offered by German publishers, at any rate in the second half of the century, do not seem to have been unreasonable. Of course they varied considerably, according to the power and desire of both sides to make a bargain, and other special circumstances. First novels or plays naturally did not earn high fees, but authors with a name were able to command quite considerable sums for their copyright. A few examples may be given from the records of the more important publishing firms, and particularly from those of G. J. Göschen, who was more generous than most publishers and was treated by many of his most distinguished clients as a personal friend.

At the beginning of the century, authors seldom received more than a trifling sum in money from their publishers, partly, as explained in Goethe's words above, because they disdained and did not need such earnings, and partly because their writings were by no means popular in character. The relations between Gottsched and Breitkopf have been mentioned. Those between Gellert and his publisher Wendler are an even better example for the transition period, when publishers, but not writers, had realised the commercial possibilities of more popular writings. Wendler bought the complete rights of the *Fables*, 'perhaps the most popular book of the eighteenth century', for a ducat (less than three Thalers) a sheet, and made a fortune out of them. In 1787, twenty years after his retirement, the stock and copyright of Gellert's works were sold for 10,000 Thalers, and Wendler had long had the reputation of a philanthropist for the gifts he had been able to make to charitable causes. When Klopstock and Wieland published their first works, their honoraria were still very low. For the first books of the *Messias* (1749) Klopstock received three Thalers a sheet. For the very different *Komische Erzählungen* (1765) Wieland was remunerated at about the same rate. But by 1773 Klopstock was receiving twelve Thalers a sheet for his still unfinished epic, while Wieland, at the height of the literary boom, asked and received up to fifteen or sixteen Thalers a sheet from Reich for his extremely longwinded later works. From this publisher alone Wieland drew 6700 Thalers, enough to keep him and his family for ten years,[1] while the *Collected Works* published later by Göschen brought him in at least 7000

[1] Figures from Goldfriedrich, *Geschichte des deutschen Buchhandels*, Leipzig, 1909, III, 118 ff.

Thalers.[1] Even authors of the middling sort were being paid five to six and a half Thalers a sheet by Reich in the 70's, and translators two Thalers.

In the classical period proper, we may note that Schiller's total gain from the book edition of his second play *Fiesco*, published by Schwan of Mannheim, was ten Karolin (about ten guineas), as he complained in 1788, when a third edition was being brought out. For the first instalment of his *Thirty Years' War* for Göschen's *Damenkalender*, on the other hand, he was paid a year in advance 400 Thalers (over £60). At this rate Schiller hoped to make 1000 Thalers a year from his writings. Goethe received 15 Thalers a sheet for the *Collected Works* brought out by Göschen in the late 'eighties. For the eight volumes he received a lump sum of 2000 Thalers (£300). Much of this work had of course appeared already. For new work he received far higher payment. For his contributions to Schiller's *Horen* for instance he received from Cotta 40 Thalers (£6) a sheet. A. W. Schlegel received half that amount. The highest honorarium paid by Göschen seems to have been the 30 Thalers (£4. 10*s*) a sheet paid to F. A. Wolf for his edition of Homer, more than was paid to A. Müllner for the second edition of his very popular play *Die Schuld* (for which the honorarium was 26 Thalers a sheet, but the first edition had already brought the author 200 Thalers). Among the more popular novels of the time, Thümmel's *Reiseroman*, in ten slim volumes, earned for the author 5000 Thalers (£750) from Göschen, more than Goethe and Klopstock together received from him for his editions of their collected works.[2]

Compared with what could be earned in England by writers of no greater merit, these sums were very small. There too, of course, new writers or those who did not press their claims received little, but the established writer could make high demands. So though Goldsmith only made £60

[1] K. Buchner, *Wieland und G. J. Göschen*, Stuttgart, 1874.

[2] See Viscount Goschen, *Life of G. J. Goschen*, London, 1903.

out of the *Vicar of Wakefield*, Fielding's *Tom Jones* brought him £700, and *Amelia* £1000, while *Rasselas* had earned Johnson £125 even in 1749. A really successful play was worth about £150 by 1780. Works of learning were very well paid for. The sums received by Schiller tor his historical writings seem modest beside Robertson's £600 for *The History of Scotland*, and £4500 for *Charles V*, or Hume's £3400 earned from *The History of England* between 1754 and 1760, or Smollett's £2000 in 1758, and Henry's £3300 in the 'seventies, for similar works. Percy gained £300 from his *Reliques* in 1765, and Adam Smith £500 for the first edition alone of *The Wealth of Nations* in 1776. As to periodicals, the £6 a sheet paid by Cotta to Goethe for *Die Horen* may be compared with Constable's ten to twenty guineas for reviews later in *The Edinburgh Review*. The Jena *Allgemeine Literatur-Zeitung* paid only 15 Thalers a sheet (£2. 5*s*.) for reviews. The enormous sums earned by Byron, and above all by Scott, in the literary boom of the early nineteenth century, were beyond the wildest dreams of any German author. Scott could make over £10,000 a year on his novels alone. Goethe received about £22,500 in the course of his lifetime from Cotta. This sum, together with the £300 which Göschen had paid him for the first collected edition of his works, represented almost the whole of his literary earnings. So Scott earned more from literature in three years than Goethe in all his long life.

The chief cause for the disparity between the two countries in the matter of literary earnings was no doubt, as has already been suggested, the more effective monopoly conferred by the possession of copyright in England, combined with the greater public demand for books there. As to the size of the reading public in Germany, the following figures will give some idea. In Germany as in England there was a wider and steadier market for the 'household stuff of literature', Isaac D'Israeli's term for cookery books, 'useful knowledge for the million', and so forth, than for the higher flights of literature. One of the most profitable publications of the leading Leipzig bookseller, P. E. Reich, was Peplier's *French Grammar*, of which editions of 5000 copies continued to be printed until the nineteenth century.[1] Much the best seller that Göschen ever acquired was R. Z. Becker's *Noth- und Hülfsbuch*, a kind of 'Outline of Knowledge' for the countryman in 800 pages, sold for eightpence. Of this 30,000 copies were printed for the first edition in 1787—it took two years to print them. Eleven authorised and four unauthorised editions had appeared by 1791. By 1811, according to its author, a million copies of this work had been issued.[2] The public for whom works such as this were published was of course not interested in literature proper, but the figure gives some idea of the numbers of buyers who might be attracted by the popular 'Calendars' that the pedlars carried in their packs. In the country round about Zürich 2500 copies of a Calendar could be sold in a year by such pedlars.[3] Next in order of popularity came the Calendars for better educated people, like Göschen's *Historischer Kalender für Damen*, of the first issue of which 7000 copies were sold in 1789, a record sale. It was for this calendar that Schiller wrote his *Thirty Years' War*. Of books properly so called, it was very rarely that more than three or four thousand copies were sold. Of Goethe's *Works* (1787–90) Göschen printed an ordinary edition of 2000 and a cheap edition of 3000, but they sold very slowly. There were only 602 subscribers to the whole series, and after two years only 536 other copies of the first four volumes had been sold, together with two or three hundred copies each of single plays, etc.[4] Even a popular play like *Die Schuld* was only bought by some five thousand people.[5]

[1] Goldfriedrich, *op. cit.* III, 41.

[2] *Life of G. J. Goschen*, I, 94. This works out at 40,000 a year, a figure difficult to accept. Murray in England considered 5–10,000 a year for Mrs Rundell's *Domestic Cookery* a very high figure.

[3] Goldfriedrich, *op. cit.* II, 279.

[4] *Life of G. J. Goschen*, I, 165.

[5] *Ibid.* II, 420 (1st edition 2000, 2nd 3000).

This figure was however exceeded by Schiller's *Tell*, of which 7000 copies were sold in a few weeks. A second edition of 3000 was exhausted by the end of the year. Of *Wallenstein* 3500 copies had been sold in two months.[1]

Perhaps a better indication of the size of the reading public for good literature is the circulation of the literary magazines and reviews. The best of the reviews was the Jena *Allgemeine Literatur-Zeitung*, which, as Göschen wrote to Wieland,[2] was 'read by all classes in every city, in every little town, almost in every village' of Germany. Yet 2000 copies were sufficient. Göschen's explanation is that ten or twenty people read a borrowed copy of this and other periodicals and books to one who bought them. *Die Horen*, with its staff of all the talents, only approached this circulation with its first number, of which nearly 1800 copies were sold, twelve or more copies being ordered even in small towns. Wieland's *Teutscher Merkur*, a private venture, cannot have had a circulation of much more than a thousand.[3] In addition to these there were at any time from 1775 onwards usually some half-dozen reviews and up to a dozen literary magazines in existence, most of them short-lived and with a small circulation, often restricted to the neighbourhood of the place of production. There were *Gelehrte Anzeigen* for instance in most universities and many capitals and Free Towns. The best known were those of Leipzig, Göttingen and Frankfort, in addition to the review already mentioned. Two other reviews of importance were Nicolai's *Bibliothek der schönen Wissenschaften und freien Künste* (mostly concerned with art) and his *Allgemeine deutsche Bibliothek*. Among the more famous magazines of the last quarter of the century may be mentioned, in addition to the *Teutscher Merkur* (1773–1810) and Schiller's *Horen* (1795–7), the *Teutsche Chronik* of Schubart (1774–81), the

[1] J. H. Eckardt, *Schillers Verleger*, Börsenblatt, 1905.

[2] *Life of G. J. Goschen*, I, 305.

[3] *Ibid.* I, 98. About 800 copies were to be sold through Göschen, and 'a certain number' of subscribers were supplied by post.

Deutsches Museum of Boie (1776–91), the *Berliner Literarisches Wochenblatt* (1776–97), the *Berlinische Monatsschrift* (1783–1811), Schiller's *Thalia* (1785–91), Bertuch's *Journal des Luxus und der Moden* (1786–1826), Archenholtz's *Litteratur- und Völkerkunde* and *Minerva* (1782–1809), A. W. Schlegel's *Athenäum* (1798–1800), Goethe's *Propyläen* (1798–1800).[1] Few of these would have a circulation of more than a few hundred copies. Of the *Völkerkunde* for instance, Göschen says in 1785 that it is read everywhere, yet his sale is only 400 copies.

Apart from the learned and the literary periodicals there were further, from early in the eighteenth century, a large number of so-called 'Journals' modelled on the English *Tatler* and *Spectator*, containing essays of general interest on a wide range of subjects, usually rather didactic in tone. The avowed aim of their editors was to raise the moral and intellectual standards of the middle class by the dissemination of useful knowledge and the philosophy of 'Aufklärung'. They flourished wherever a large middle-class public could be reached. Of the 182 Moral Weeklies that appeared in Germany between 1713 and 1761, almost all short-lived and appealing only to a local public, more than one-third were published in either Hamburg or Leipzig, the chief commercial centres. The first appeared in Hamburg in 1713, and the most influential were the Hamburg *Patriot* (1724–6), edited by Brockes and his friends, which had 5000 subscribers, and Gottsched's two weeklies in Leipzig (1725–7). The interest taken in these productions was so great that they were frequently reprinted in collected form and of course often pirated. Their successors in the last third of the century were publications like Möser's *Patriotische Phantasien*, Claudius' *Wandsbecker Bote* and the Almanachs and Journals already mentioned. It was mainly for the supply of such ephemeral literature and of newspapers that the Reading

[1] For complete lists see R. F. Arnold, *Bücherkunde*, section I, 3 *b* and III, 10, and for a full historical account Goldfriedrich, *op. cit.* II, 55 ff.

Clubs, so popular from the 'eighties onwards, were started. With the circulating libraries that began to flourish at about the same date the habit of reading spread with ever-increasing rapidity, so that the old-fashioned began to complain of the 'reading madness' of the young generation and even Goethe deplored the effects of so much indiscriminate light reading:

> Zwar sind sie an das Beste nicht gewöhnt
> Allein, sie haben schrecklich viel gelesen.

or

> Und was das Allerschlimmste bleibt,
> Gar mancher kommt vom Lesen der Journale.
> (*Faust*, Vorspiel.)

'Formerly', says a provincial journalist in 1806, 'reading was the affair of the scholar and the truly cultivated man. Now it is a general habit, even of the lower classes, not only in the towns but in the country too.' Even soldiers of the town guard take out books from the circulating library, says another already in 1780. The well-read craftsmen mentioned by Goethe, Moritz and others do not seem to have been very rare exceptions, and one master-tailor in Hanau had a library of 3600 volumes.[1]

For comparison we may take again a few figures from England, where according to the successful bookseller Lackington, writing at the end of the eighteenth century, more than four times as many books were then being sold as were sold twenty years earlier. 'The poorer sort of farmers, and even the poor country people in general', he says, got their children to read novels to them now in the winter evenings instead of telling ghost stories.[2] Lackington sometimes stocked 6000 copies of one book. Of a poem like Roger's *Pleasures of Memory* 8000 copies were printed and sold between 1792 and 1800, and by 1816 a further 10,000. Long before this over 1200 copies of Gray's *Odes* had been sold

[1] Goldfriedrich, *op. cit.* III, 256.
[2] Collins, *Profession of Letters*, p. 83.

in a month (in 1757), and a really popular play like Cumberland's *West Indian* (1771) could be sold at the rate of 12,000 in a season.[1] As to periodicals, the circulation of the *Gentleman's Magazine* had reached 10,000 by 1739, and a few years later 15,000, though it had many rivals, for between 1731 and 1780 sixty magazines were started in London, ten in Scotland and eleven in Ireland.[2] The later reviews on a higher intellectual level also sold freely. The sale of the *Edinburgh* in its best days (about 1808) was 11,000 copies, and that of its rival the *Quarterly* had reached 12,000 by 1817. At the height of the Romantic movement record sales were achieved by Byron's and Scott's poems and Scott's novels. Of *The Lady of the Lake* 44,000 copies were sold before 1830; 10,000 copies of *The Corsair* were sold on the day of issue. When eight volumes of the 1829 collected edition of Scott's novels had appeared, the monthly sale had reached 35,000.

It will be clear that there were good reasons for the unremunerative nature of the profession of letters in Germany, apart from the publisher's desire for profit, but it was natural that at the time this last factor should be most stressed by writers. Several attempts were made by writers for whom literary earnings were important to secure a greater material return for their labours by cutting out the publisher. Ideas of this kind went back as far as Leibniz. In the eighteenth century it was Bode, soon joined for a time by Lessing, who first attempted to realise them in his *Buchhandlung der Gelehrten* in Hamburg (1767). This was to be a press and publishing house run in the interests of first-rate authors. It was hoped that copies of books published would be ordered direct from Hamburg and paid for in cash, instead of being sent to Leipzig and sold through the agency of the 'Kommissionäre' there, or exchanged for the products of some other publishing firm, still a common practice.

There might have been some hope for Bode's undertaking

[1] Collins, *Authorship in the Days of Johnson*, p. 255.
[2] *Ibid.* p. 240.

if there had been a sufficient number of retail booksellers in Germany for the distribution of his publications, but book production and distribution were still closely linked. A bookseller was usually a publisher and *vice versa*. The old system had been for the bookseller-publisher to go to the book-fair at Leipzig or Frankfort with a stock of his own publications and exchange them for the books of other firms. He would then have a varied stock of books to sell at home. The system was adapted to the chaotic state of the currency in Germany after the Thirty Years' War, but it naturally brought with it many disadvantages, and had to be modified to suit changing conditions in the eighteenth century. But although books were no longer exchanged unbound, regardless of quality, and booksellers were often allowed to stock books on the 'condition' that they should be returnable if unsold before the following fair ('Konditionsgeschäft'), Leipzig retained its hold on the book trade through its 'Kommissionäre' or wholesale booksellers, who acted as middlemen between the big publishers and the country booksellers. The country booksellers, having little capital, would not pay Bode cash when they could have books from Leipzig 'for sale or return'. This difficulty, combined with piracy, proved fatal to the Hamburg experiment and to a rather similar but better organised one begun at Dessau in 1781, with which Wieland and Bertuch were closely associated.

The idea had meanwhile been given much publicity by Klopstock, the most respected author of the day. He suggested the formation of a German Academy, which should undertake the publication of the best new books and provide for the material needs of the leading authors and scholars of the day. Klopstock's ideas were very much in the air, but his preliminary notice evoked a reply from the publishers and aroused great interest, so that his *Gelehrtenrepublik*, the book about the proposed academy for which he invited subscriptions, was sold without the help of the booksellers in large numbers all over the country. Two hundred and fifty admirers came forward to collect subscribers, and in all 3600 subscriptions were sent in. 6600 copies of the first part of the book were printed, an enormous edition for those days, but the second part never appeared because the first proved almost unreadable, with its description of the proposed hierarchy of the cultured, ranging from creative authors and scholars and their various 'gilds' down to the 'Volk' willing to buy their works, its tables of laws, expressed in language borrowed partly from the gilds and partly from the ancient 'bards', and its imaginary account of proceedings at the Diet of the Republic. But the astonishing success of Klopstock's appeal for subscriptions, the nearest German parallel to the success of Pope with his *Homer* (for which 6000 subscribed), encouraged other authors to imitate him. Bürger published his poems in this way, and Lessing his *Nathan*, of which the first edition of 2000 was fully subscribed. And many who did not appeal publicly for subscribers printed their first works at their own expense. In this case they usually lost heavily. Goethe, advised by Merck, brought out his *Götz* in this way and Schiller his *Räuber*, with 150 Gulden borrowed from friends, and both lost their money.[1]

Apart from the men of letters proper there were journalists and publicists, some of whom made a precarious living by writing. It is usual to make a distinction between periodicals and newspapers, but at this early date the distinction was not so clear as it is to-day, for newspapers did not necessarily appear daily or contain very much in the way of current news. The most influential publicist of the century, one might almost say the only man who deserved the name, was the Göttingen historian A. L. von Schlözer, whose *Briefwechsel meist historischen und politischen Inhalts* (1776–82) and *Staatsanzeigen* (1783–94), periodicals appearing about six

[1] For the history and organisation of the book trade and the relations between authors and publishers see, in addition to works cited, *Das Buchgewerbe und die Kultur*, Leipzig, 1907.

times a year, were read even by monarchs and exercised a considerable influence in minor political affairs. Even Maria Theresa is said to have urged her privy council to think twice about matters that Schlözer was likely to criticise. His organs were particularly effective in directing public attention to acts of petty tyranny on the part of minor rulers or their officials. Sometimes as many as 4000 copies of his *Staatsanzeigen* were sold. Schlözer was not however a professional journalist, or his influence would have been negligible, but a public-spirited and highly respected professor of history in the leading university of Germany. A further advantage he enjoyed was that as Göttingen was in the state of Hanover his writings were not nearly so strictly censored as they would have been in any other state. Most of his material was sent in by correspondents, often people of high standing, who desired to bring something before the public in this forum and received no material reward except perhaps a free copy or two.[1] The editors of the other leading periodicals were also almost all scholars, active or retired officials, or authors who had made a name with weightier writings. Justus Möser, Häberlin, L. von Göckingk, S. von Bibra, K. F. von Moser, Büsching, Wieland, Boie may be mentioned among the editors of this kind who at least occasionally commented on current affairs. In the south, however, there were two men, Schubart (*Deutsche Chronik*) and Weckherlin (*Das graue Ungeheuer* and two other periodicals), who lived dangerously as professional political journalists.

There were regular newspapers of a kind, it seems, in almost every considerable German town by the end of the seventeenth century. They had developed gradually here as elsewhere out of the written newsletters of the late Middle Ages, *pari passu* with the growth of trade and the improvement of communications. Weekly printed newspapers are proved to have existed from as early as 1609 in Germany. Then papers began to appear two or three times a week. The

[1] Biedermann, I, 120.

ancestor of the *Leipziger Zeitung* was the first daily (from 1660). The news in these papers was mainly political, and, because of the censor, fuller about foreign affairs than about events nearer home. About this time too there were opened in many German towns, following Paris and London, the first 'Offices of Intelligence' ('Adress-Comptoire') where local announcements of many kinds were to be read, corresponding roughly to the small advertisements of the modern newspaper (lost and found, sale and exchange, property for sale or to let, coach times, etc.), and these offices began to publish their own advertisers (*Anzeigen, Intelligenzblätter*). When these took in notices of town appointments, marriages, births and deaths and other items of local news they were beginning to resemble local newspapers. In the eighteenth century there were a score or so of local 'Advertisers', one or two newssheets in almost every little capital and a few better ones in Free Towns and the capitals of the larger states. In Berlin for instance there was the *Vossische Zeitung* (so styled from 1785, but with a history going back to the middle of the seventeenth century), and the *Haude-Spenersche Zeitung*, founded in 1740, as well as the official *Advertiser*. It was for the *Vossische* that Lessing was engaged to write reviews, as editor of the 'learned' section, soon after his arrival in Berlin. His cousin Mylius, who initiated him into journalism, may be taken as a type of the numerous second-rate literati of that day. For years he led a hand-to-mouth existence by editing a series of short-lived 'Moral Weeklies' and by writing odd articles for the papers of others.[1] The German newspapers produced by writers of this stamp cannot be said to have attained a high level. The best were to be found in the centres of commerce, Hamburg, Frankfort-on-Main and Leipzig. Readers interested in politics used the foreign papers, especially the Dutch ones, to supplement them, and in spite of prohibitions, written bulletins continued to circulate more intimate items of news

[1] See E. Schmidt, *Lessing*, I, 60 ff.

and gossip until late in the century. Even the printed papers consisted for the most part of a mass of ill-sifted 'faits divers'.[1]

The number of pens that were kept busy to produce this abundance of printed matter was of course large. Old-fashioned authors like Möser were constantly complaining about the excessive number of 'Gelehrten' and 'Schriftsteller'—'scholar' and 'writer' were then almost synonymous expressions. Knigge said that the title of scholar was as common in Germany as that of gentleman in England, and was applied to every wretched versifier, compiler, journalist, anecdote-hunter, translator, plagiarist and in fact to anyone who abused the incomprehensible indulgence of the public to publish whole volumes of nonsense or of things far better said before. Goethe and Schiller castigated such writers singly and in groups in their *Xenien*, in couplets such as the following:

Sachen, so gesucht werden.

Einen Bedienten wünscht man zu haben, der leserlich schreibet
Und orthographisch, jedoch nichts in Bell-Lettres getan.[2]

Various attempts were made by contemporaries to estimate the number of living German 'writers'. On the basis of these, Goldfriedrich states that in 1773 Germany had 3000 writers, and in 1787 already 6000, so that the number had doubled in the fourteen years between *Götz von Berlichingen* and *Egmont*. About the year 1780 it is said that there were 133 writers living in Leipzig, 77 in Dresden, 33 in Wittenberg, 21 in Budissin, and nearly 400 more scattered over some 200 towns and villages in Saxony alone.[3] Most of these must have been very small fry. Besides the authors who

[1] For a large number of representative extracts see the volumes of *Das Neueste von gestern*, edited by E. Buchner.

For a brief history of the newspaper see Goldfriedrich, *op. cit.* II, 39 ff.; K. Bücher in *Kultur der Gegenwart*, I, I, Leipzig, 1906; H. Diez, *Das Zeitungswesen*, 2nd ed. 1919; Biedermann, *op. cit.* vol. I.

[2] *Wanted.* Man-servant required who writes legibly and spells well, but has done nothing in belles lettres.

[3] Weiz, *Das gelehrte Sachsen*, 1780, quoted Goldfriedrich, III, 249.

figure in histories of literature, they would include dozens of forgotten novelists, dramatists and scholars and a much larger number of occasional contributors to newspapers and journals, translators, editors of school texts, reviewers, proof-readers and the like. But the figures indicate at least a very high degree of intellectual activity in a great variety of places. According to another estimate quoted by Goldfriedrich, this activity was most intense in Göttingen (with one writer to every hundred inhabitants) and Leipzig (with 1 to 170). Berlin (with 1 to 675) and Vienna (with 1 to 800), in spite of their political importance, are far behind the centres of learning and the book trade. Taking the most conservative estimates, the numbers of writers and of writings must at least have doubled in the last three decades of the century. In the early 'nineties, says the Bernese bookseller Heinzmann, there were some 300 novels, original or translated, appearing in German every year,[1] while Herr von Göckingk even in 1784 knew of some 217 newspapers and advertisers appearing in Germany and thought that if the smallest and most primitive were included, the number could be doubled.[2] Between 1740 (the year selected by contemporaries as the turning-point) and 1800, Germany had changed from a country so unproductive of native literature that every educated man had depended on foreign writings for his culture to a land of 'poets and thinkers', amongst whom the few known to history were the apex of a pyramid firmly based on a countless mass of pedants and scribblers. It had developed a classical literature, and also something very like an intellectual proletariat.

[1] Goldfriedrich, III, 274.

[2] Quoted in P. Kampffmeyer, *Geschichte der modernen Gesellschafts-klassen in Deutschland*, 3rd ed. Berlin, 1921, p. 338.

Chapter II

THE INFLUENCE OF POLITICAL, ECONOMIC AND SOCIAL FACTORS ON LITERATURE

In the earlier chapters an attempt has been made to analyse the political and economic structure of German society in the eighteenth century, and to describe the social inheritance, the habitual point of view and the standard of living of each of the great social classes. In this final chapter some indication will be offered of the importance of this material for the student of classical German literature and the German national character.

Social and political factors exercise at all times a pervasive influence on culture in general, an influence which is none the less important for being difficult to trace with any final certainty. The study of them is an unsatisfactory pursuit for the precise scholar, because the result can hardly be more than an essay, but this is unfortunately the case with many other branches of literary study and criticism. Their interest is usually in inverse proportion to the degree of accuracy that can be attained in the result. Social influences are no more intangible than the personality of an author or the literary value of a work, and perhaps no less worthy of study.

In this brief study we will focus our attention first on the political and then on the economic and social influences, remembering always that to isolate any one influence completely from all others is impossible. Let us enquire in the first place what features in German literature and intellectual life can best be understood as a consequence of 'Kleinstaaterei' and absolutism.

It is obvious that an association of jealous small states could not possess a single metropolis like London or Paris, where, in Goethe's words to Eckermann, 'the best minds of a great nation are assembled in one place, teaching and stimulating each other in daily intercourse, contention and rivalry, where the best products of nature and art from every corner of the earth are always there for them to see with their own eyes, where they are reminded whenever they cross a bridge or a square of a great past and where every street corner has seen history in the making'.[1] In his later years Goethe was for ever drawing unfavourable contrasts between his own country and France in this respect, and, though not blind to the dangers of over-centralisation, envying the French that high degree of general culture that gave even young writers, and men of no social standing like Béranger, the support of an intellectual and artistic tradition.

It is clear of course that in order to enjoy similar benefits it would have been necessary for Germany not only to have a capital, but also to have developed, like France, in a way that had made a capital a necessity, for the possession of a capital and of a unified tradition are to be regarded as different manifestations of one process rather than as cause and effect. It is true further that when a country once has a metropolis, a further concentration of intellectual life is bound to follow. This effect will be considered later, when French literature, as eminently 'social', will be contrasted with German. But the first and most general consequence of separatism, which in a sense includes all the others, is one which can hardly be denied. It is the lack of general culture, of a national style, that German weakness lamented by Goethe, Nietzsche and so many others down to the present day. It is remarkable, as has often been pointed out, that Germany succeeded, in the absence of such a national tradition and of political institutions to support it, in producing a literature that came to be looked upon as classical, though it was, in Freytag's phrase, 'the almost miraculous creation of a soul without a body'. But it seems probable that the writers of any 'classical age' have

[1] Eckermann, *Gespräche*, under May 3rd, 1827.

been leaders as well as led—for even in formulating views commonly held but necessarily vague a writer takes the lead, like the chairman of a committee—and that the German classics only differed from the French or the Greek in being rather further ahead of their age, though not so far removed from the ways of thinking of any of their countrymen that a later generation could not accept them as classics in the primary sense, namely as the best authors to be read in the classes of their schools. Whether on a large view of world literature they are to be considered classical in the more ambiguous sense that depends on the opposition of classical and romantic is a further question to which we shall return.

We must remember that in denying Germany 'general culture' Goethe was contrasting it with France. The Germans had in reality already a great deal in common, though less than their western neighbours. They were descended, if not from one race, at least from a small number of races fused by long generations of intermarriage. They had lived together for centuries on the same land. It is true that these geographical and blood ties fostered provincial rather than national loyalties at this stage, but the boundaries of these provinces were the result of dynastic, not of racial history, and a kind of clan feeling extended even then beyond them. On the other hand the geographical factors making for national unity were rather weaker than they would have been if the boundaries of the German-speaking lands as a whole had not been so vague and shifting. It was possible, though difficult in that stay-at-home age, to form a mental image of one's small state as a unit, but 'Germany' was far too amorphous to evoke in the minds of German patriots images such as those which the thought of 'England' called up in the mind of Shakespeare's John of Gaunt—

> This precious stone set in the silver sea,
> Which serves it in the office of a wall,
> Or as a moat defensive to a house,
> Against the envy of less happier lands.

Mr McDougall has pointed out how important such images are for the formation of what he calls a 'group mind'; for confirmation we have only to think of the use made of the magic word 'island' in English patriotic literature.

If common racial origins and geographical propinquity were important at least potentially, language was already a strong and steadily increasing force making for unity. It had been so at times in the Middle Ages, but if we compare the beginning of the seventeenth century with the middle of the eighteenth as regards the literary use of German, we find a remarkable development. In a graph showing the number of German books and the number of Latin books published each year during that period, the line for Latin is at first more than twice as high as that for German. Both lines drop suddenly for the period of the Thirty Years' War (1618–48), the Latin one much more steeply than the German, though it rises again about 1650, when there are again twice as many Latin books published as German. But from that point the lines gradually converge, they cross each other just after 1680, and then, though both have their ups and downs, the general tendency of the German line is steeply upwards, that of the Latin line slowly down, so that by the end of the 1760's, when Goethe's first book appeared, the relative position of 1610 was reversed, German standing now four times as high as Latin, though the total number of books published, Latin, German and French, was about the same as in 1610 (over 1500 volumes). The quantitative increase in the use of German for the communication of thought coincided naturally with the gradual unification and purification of the language, the emergence of a literary language which Germans were proud to own. Luther's bible and catechism, in daily use in home, church and school, gradually made the mass of the people acquainted with a standard book German distinct from their dialect, a standard that here as in other countries had been made both more necessary and more easily attainable by the invention of printing in the preceding century. Luther's work was continued by Opitz and his school, with the example of the Pléiade before their eyes, and through the efforts of the various 'Language Societies' their influence slowly began to permeate educated circles. It was a conscious attempt to improve the German language, and there was certainly national pride behind it, but it was a long time before scholars and courtiers could be persuaded that German could be made into as fit a vehicle of communication as Latin or French. Leibniz had still to confess that though a German boy spoke his own language at twelve, he had forgotten it by the time he was a student, to become a Frenchified courtier or a pedantic Latinist. But the vernacular was used more and more for serious purposes, and 'Meissner Deutsch' recognised as the best German by wider and wider circles.

Before the middle of the eighteenth century there was also already a fairly widespread desire for national originality in literary matters in Germany, even though patriotic feeling in the political sense hardly existed. This desire does not seem to have been common in the Middle Ages, when the originality of individual authors too was much less stressed than now, and one is tempted to assume that it arose in Germany mainly through the contagious influence of France. Certainly French taunts had a marked effect in stimulating it. When le père Bouhours had asserted that it was impossible for a German to be a *bel esprit*, Thomasius, the most progressive professor of his day (we have seen that he was the first to lecture in German, in 1687), had retorted that at least they were better scholars, because they had more patience. He admitted that the French had a livelier temperament, but thought that freedom from religious, social and political restrictions would soon do much to foster German originality. For fifty years after this the general opinion seemed to be that it did not much matter whether the works published in German were original or translations provided that they were good, though the ultimate aim in view was an original German literature. Gottsched's work for instance and that of his circle consisted mainly of translations and adaptations. But in 1740 Mauvillon, a French teacher in Brunswick, roused German writers from their complacency by challenging them in his *Lettres françaises et germaniques* to name a single German author who had any reputation abroad, or whose work did not consist almost entirely of translations. The effect of this and similar taunts was to make Germany conscious of its language and literature as a national possession, and eager for literary prestige, long before it was a nation in any other respect, and the fact that the word 'German' had a definite meaning and one charged with emotion, at least as applied to language and literature, was to prove very important for the political unification of Germany later. It would hardly be too much to say that the liberals of 1848 were still fighting for a Germany worthy of Goethe, Schiller and Kant.

It cannot therefore be said that there was nothing in the daily life of a German to remind him of kinship with a community that extended beyond the boundaries of his small state, but we easily realise how vague and inadequate these reminders were if we contrast them with the symbols of national unity consciously made use of in recent times. It is undeniable that, as even the cosmopolitan Goethe who wrote *Dichtung und Wahrheit* complained, German literature in the eighteenth century was sadly lacking in 'national subjects'. 'If we look closely, what German literature lacked was a subject, and a national one; there was never any lack of talents.' 'It was Frederick the Great and the Seven Years' War that first gave German literature a subject with a real greatness and living interest.'[1] Not that a 'national subject' is the only or even the most important factor required for great literature. Goethe was probably inclined to stress subject-matter too much at the period when he wrote

[1] *Dichtung und Wahrheit*, Bk. 7.

Dichtung und Wahrheit, and a study of some of the later German work on 'national' themes almost drives one to the view that they are the worst possible ones for poetry. But it does seem true that the greatest writing requires a subject of intrinsic dignity and human importance, and that patriotic subjects amongst others often have these qualities. Goethe's own *Faust*, *Paradise Lost*, *The Divine Comedy*, the *De rerum natura*—these all remind us that religious, moral, metaphysical ideas have also served as the foundation of masterpieces, but they indicate too that the lasting works of literature have been rooted in great systems of beliefs and emotions that far transcend the individual. One of these great complexes, piety, in the Roman sense of the affection and awe that men feel for the things that have made them, a watchful pride in the part still played by their country and a sense of responsibility shared with compatriots, was almost entirely lacking in Germany as a result of the conditions that had produced separatism, for the individual states were too small to inspire it except in a very limited degree.

It is well known that the word 'national' was almost meaningless for the average German citizen of those days. 'Vaterland' almost invariably meant one's own particular state; other parts of Germany were referred to as 'foreign parts' (Ausland). Woldemar Wenck[1] has collected a series of remarks by leading writers of that time which prove that hardly anyone thought of the German-speaking lands as one unit. The famous historian Schlözer of Göttingen, a man of exceptional public spirit, says that when, as a young man in St Petersburg, he looked at the boats going down the Neva to Germany, for the first and perhaps the last time in his life he thought of Germany as a single whole, even as a Fatherland. Wieland says that as a boy he had been told of his duty towards God and his neighbour, and, occasionally, to those set in authority over him, but never anything of the duty of being a patriotic German. 'German in the political sense was

[1] *Deutschland vor hundert Jahren*, Leipzig, 1887, vol. I, chap. IV.

then an unknown word.'[1] Lessing looked upon patriotism as a 'heroic failing from which he was glad to be free'. Goethe cried in his youth: 'Roman patriotism! Heaven preserve us from anything so monstrous'.[2] The young Schiller considered that patriotism was only for immature peoples. Later, when reading Müller's *History of Switzerland* with his wife, he could not agree that Winkelried was to be admired. It was only under the stress of the Napoleonic wars that he was moved to celebrate the patriotism of the Swiss in *Tell*, while Goethe, as is well known, held himself aloof from the national movement longer still.

It is possible indeed to point to a few writings like Klopstock's 'Bardic' poems and the imitations of them by the Göttingen poets, Thomas Abbt's *Vom Tode fürs Vaterland*, J. G. von Zimmermann's *Vom Nationalstolz*, Herder's youthful essays and his ode *An den Kaiser*, Goethe's essay on Strassburg Cathedral and his *Götz*, all of which show traces of national feeling, but these works were decidedly exceptional and in most of them the treatment of the theme is rather abstract and second-hand. It is not so much patriotism that they express as a longing for it. In Nicolai's *Sebaldus Nothanker*, the hero, when called upon to write an essay on 'Death for the Fatherland', is at a loss to know which fatherland to think of. Many more distinguished German writers seem to have been in rather a similar predicament. When writers do take up the theme of Germany as a whole, it is a cultural community they usually have in view rather than a political unit. A typical example is Herder's ode, *An den Kaiser* (Joseph II), written in 1778:

> O Kaiser! du von neunundneunzig Fürsten
> Und Ständen wie des Meeres Sand
> Das Oberhaupt, gib uns, wornach wir dürsten,
> Ein deutsches Vaterland,

[1] *Neuer Teutscher Merkur*, 1793.

[2] 'Über die Liebe des Vaterlandes' in *Frankfurter Gelehrte Anzeigen*, 1772.

Und Ein Gesetz und Eine schöne Sprache
Und redliche Religion:
Vollende deines Stammes schönste Sache
Auf deines Rudolfs Thron,

Dass Deutschlands Söhne sich wie Brüder lieben
Und deutsche Sitt' und Wissenschaft,
Von Thronen, ach, so lange schon vertrieben,
Mit unsrer Väter Kraft

Zurückekehren, dass die holden Zeiten,
Die Friederich von ferne sieht
Und nicht beförderte, sich um dich breiten
Und sei'n dein ewig Lied.

It was partly because literature was not deeply rooted in the national life that it drew so much of its matter from foreign sources, until as we have seen a desire for national originality began to arise, in advance of political patriotism. It is obvious that the free use of the intellectual and artistic capital of her neighbours was an advantage, even a necessity for Germany in her backward condition; these countries themselves had freely plundered superior civilisations in their own day as every 'young' literature must. Goethe in particular made no secret of his immense debt to France and England.[1] That the results of these borrowings were not always fortunate goes without saying; *Insel Felsenburg* and *Die schwedische Gräfin* have few of the merits of the work of Defoe and Richardson. But what is perhaps peculiar to Germany in this matter of imitation is that the habit became so deeply rooted that even national pride could not affect it much, and came in fact, by a natural compensation, to claim this very receptivity as a national virtue.

The difficulties that its political condition put in the way of the creation of a classical literature may be summed up in Goethe's words in the essay *Literarischer Sansculottismus* (1795). A classical 'national author' may be expected to appear, he

[1] See for details H. Loiseau, *Goethe et la France*, Paris, 1930, and J. Boyd, *Goethe's Knowledge of English Literature*, Oxford, 1932.

says, 'if the history of his nation furnishes him with a happy and significant system of great events and their consequences; if his fellow-countrymen show him examples of high thinking, deep feeling and bold and sustained action; if he himself, filled with the spirit of his nation, feels he has genius enough within him to share sympathetically both its past and present life'. To be truly impressive a book, like a speech, must have living experience behind it, and a national author of the first rank can only be thrown up by a nation. The German nation, narrowly confined geographically and politically disunited, cannot be expected to produce one, and, speaking just after the French Revolution, Goethe hesitates to wish for the upheaval that would be required in Germany to prepare the way for classical works. But his words indicate that it is by no means certain that he would have disapproved of the Nationalism of modern Germany if he could have lived to see it. He might have looked upon it as a necessary stage in the evolution of a truly classical German literature.

Continuing our survey of those characteristics of German literature, so far mainly negative, which we must associate with separatism, we note that besides being unnational, it was unsocial, and this almost inevitably because of the lack of big centres. Other factors of course in addition to the political one entered in here, the condition of trade and industry, communications, class distinctions and perhaps deep-seated racial traits. Literature was the work either of isolated ministers and officials in the country or of members of small groups in provincial towns. Mme de Staël, with great penetration and wit, drew a contrast in *De l'Allemagne*[1] (elaborating after her tour in Germany ideas she had sketched in *De la littérature considérée dans ses rapports avec les institutions sociales*),[2] between the 'esprit de conversation' which, spreading from the salons of Paris, had pervaded the whole of France, and the individualism which resulted from the solitary habits and the lack of lively social intercourse among

[1] London, 1810. [2] Paris, 1800.

the Germans. Her explanation of the difference may be too simple, but her description of the two types is admirable. A Frenchman tends, she thinks, to sacrifice the matter of his thought to the form, and the German the form to the matter. The French feel a social need to think like everyone else, much of their conversation consists of ready-made phrases, in short they draw on a reservoir common to all. The Germans value only bold independence of thought resulting from long solitary brooding. In France they study men and society, and their writings have a practical end in view. In Germany they study books, for life around them is too uneventful to occupy their attention, and the nature of the government prevents the thinkers from having any influence on the course of events. They are strong therefore in abstract speculation and lyrical poetry. But while admiring the solid merits of the Germans, she cannot help desiring for them some of the Frenchman's feeling for form, which she explains as the result of natural vivacity combined with the desire to please. A French thinker or writer feels that he is usurping the attention of his audience, for everyone else is eager to talk too. He must do everything to avoid boring them, he must be brief, clear, pointed, ingratiating, gay. A German on the other hand feels that he has a rightful claim to the hearer's time, for he does not speak unless he has something to say. But what he says must express his deepest thought, exhaustively and not necessarily with good humour. The Frenchman, in short, is too fully conscious of belonging to a society, and the German too little.

These ideas became a commonplace of French criticism. They were developed further by Taine, who traced the origin of classical French literature to the salons, and by Brunetière. Brunetière[1] emphasises strongly the essentially social character of French literature, the 'civilité', which seems to him to account for the excellence of French

[1] *Etudes critiques*, vol. 5, 'Sur le caractère essentiel de la litt. française', and elsewhere.

dramatists, letter-writers, 'moralistes' and orators, for their *genres* depend on the co-operation of a public. Lyricism is not a strong point, and to foreigners at least French writers often seem lacking in profundity, because they prefer subjects that interest men in general, and give themselves so much trouble to be clear. The German writer, on the other hand, is satisfied if he understands himself; if others have difficulty in understanding him he is all the more convinced of the depth of his thought.

In his conversations with Eckermann and others Goethe often discussed this question of the differences between French and German national character and its determining conditions, and on the whole he would have agreed with the French views quoted, but with a difference in emphasis. He too missed in the Germans the sociability and vivacity of the French, and he gave to Eckermann exactly the same explanation of the merits of French style as Mme de Staël's, that they never lost sight of their public. German style, he added, was spoiled by too much philosophic speculation.[1] But he saw too that conventions and traditions can have a deadening effect and must be constantly revised if they are not to produce in literature works like those French writings of the age of Voltaire which had repelled him in his youth as 'bejahrt und vornehm'. French writers seemed to him on the whole less serious, less idealistic and less open to new ideas than the German. German writers of his age, he says in effect, had both the strength and the weakness resulting from not writing for a clearly defined public in the hope of influencing its views. They lacked the tug from reality that even the most unworldly of French or English authors constantly experienced.

Literature then was unnational and unsocial, but it had positive qualities too. It was in the first place highly individualistic. If Germany had few literary traditions, it was at the same time comparatively free from the clogging effect

[1] Eckermann, 14th April, 1824.

of conventions. Originality was at a premium, and if taste was not critical, it was all the easier for young writers to find a hearing. The result was sometimes eccentricity, paradox, even nonsense, at other times profound and novel ideas and bold literary experiments. The natural fertility of the mind was given full scope in a society where men wrote to express themselves, revelled in hard work and were in no hurry for results. The pace of life was slow, 'time fell drop by drop' as Mme de Staël discovered, and there was one tradition at least well established by the learned compilers of preceding centuries, that of thoroughness. Schiller was speaking for all when he praised 'Beschäftigung, die nie ermattet'.

The strange opinions that sometimes resulted from their solitary brooding could generally be expressed with more freedom than in most countries, in spite of censors, partly because autocratic authority was so firmly established that writers rarely even imagined that their work could have any immediate effect in practice, and partly because an educated man who made himself unpopular in one state could nearly always find some small official or professional appointment in another. As Mirabeau pointed out, discussing the advantages and disadvantages of separatism in his *De la monarchie prussienne*, each state needed good professional men, and there were still so few of them that the services of the best were eagerly sought after. Fichte, speaking from experience, makes the same point that there were many refuges for outspoken writers in Germany: 'A truth that could not be uttered at one place, could at another...and so in spite of much one-sidedness and narrowness, a higher degree of freedom of enquiry and expression was possible in (eighteenth-century) Germany as a whole than in any other state before'.[1] The variety of conditions stimulated political and social criticism of a general kind, and so long as it was ostensibly directed against rival states, it could easily and safely be uttered. As for new views in theology, the

[1] *Reden an die deutsche Nation.*

other dangerous subject, so many shades of opinion were represented in high places that it went hard with a man who could not find some prince or other to lend him support.

Speculative freedom in the literature of thought was matched by lyrical sincerity in the literature of feeling when poets were no longer overawed by foreign models and had mastered their medium. That other influences counted here beside the lack of social interests is obvious. The most important, no doubt, was Protestantism, and especially Pietism. It cannot be an accident too that Germany had for so long excelled in music. But it remains true that the 'Gemüt' is best cultivated in solitude, not in a courtly or urban society where 'the proper study of mankind is man'. Nature poetry of the modern romantic type is one form of expression for this kind of feeling. Hence the contrast mentioned by Brunetière between French literature, strong in 'moralistes', and German, strong in purely lyrical and nature poets. The contrast is not unlike that which we find in English literature, here too associated with contrasting habits of life, between the school of Pope and the school of Wordsworth.

For the lonely spirits we have been describing life would have been intolerable without books. Their education had been bookish and their tastes continued to be so. It was a bookishness necessarily little modified by experience of the world of men. These omnivorous readers were moreover, as we have seen, very much the reverse of insular. The Germany of Goethe's age was open to every foreign idea, new or old, and interested itself in every accessible literature. The number and excellence of the translations it produced is a sufficient indication of the interest taken in foreign masterpieces, especially if we remember that the translators included Lessing, Wieland, Herder, Goethe, Schiller, Voss, the Schlegels and many others of the best minds of the day. This open-mindedness was the obverse of the lack of a national style. It is not surprising that catholicity, inclusiveness, became an ideal and that the outstanding characteristic of Goethe himself is, to use a phrase of an English critic, quoted by Goethe with approval in his maxims, his 'panoramic ability'. One of the merits of modern German literature is its atmosphere of 'Bildung', or broad intellectual culture. From Wieland to Thomas Mann, the German novelists, for instance, have owed much of their charm for the cultivated reader to the allusiveness and the aroma of learning of their style. It goes without saying that fine tact is necessary to prevent such culture from degenerating into pedantry.

The leading German classics were not only cosmopolitan in their culture; they were perhaps the nearest approach to the type of the 'good European' that we know of. Goethe's words to Eckermann, explaining why it had been impossible for him to write patriotic poetry during the War of Liberation, are the classical expression of his cosmopolitanism.

> How could I have written songs of hate without hating? And, between ourselves, I did not hate the French, although I thanked God when we were rid of them. And how could I, for whom the only thing that matters is whether people are civilised or barbarous, hate a nation which is amongst the most cultivated on earth and to which I owe so large a part of my own culture! National hatred is anyhow a peculiar thing. You will always find it strongest and most violent in the lowest stages of civilisation. But there is a stage at which it entirely disappears and at which one stands in a sense above the nations, and feels the good or evil fortune of a neighbouring nation as if it had happened to one's own. This stage was congenial to my nature, and I had been long confirmed in these views before I reached my sixtieth year.[1]

It is in a similar spirit that Kant sketched his plan for a League of Nations,[2] that Herder traced the development of 'Humanität', or that Schiller cried, in the song which Beethoven used as the text for his choral symphony,

> Seid umschlungen, Millionen!
> Diesen Kuss der ganzen Welt!

[1] Eckermann, 10th March 1830.

[2] In his *Universal History from a Cosmopolitan Point of View*.

For all these, as for Lessing, Klopstock and Hölderlin, it is the word 'humanity', not 'nation', that is invested with the fullest meaning. Yet they were certainly not 'intellectuals without roots anywhere', as writers with similar views were called in Nazi Germany. They expressed universal values in a definitely German idiom. While still striving to acquire this idiom, some of them had passed through a stage when to be German had been their highest aim, the stage at which Goethe wrote *Götz* or the essay on Strassburg Cathedral. It was not through lack of understanding for their own nation, but through the increased sympathy with other nations gained through a full knowledge of their own, that they were able to rise without self-deception to the conception of serving humanity. If opinions such as these were suspect in Germany later, it was because the development that Goethe half desired and half feared in 1795[1] had now taken place and Germany had become, or was in process of becoming, a nation, but one too anxious as yet about the maintenance of her individuality to be able to rise to Goethe's impartial appreciation of the eternal values, whatever national dress they might wear. It was easier for Goethe to hold such a view, the modern German writer might with justice urge, because he lived in a disunited Germany that was not tempted to take herself seriously as a political force in Europe, in an age moreover when, largely owing to the political circumstances, the ablest Germans were accustomed to devote their best energies to the creation or appreciation of literature and philosophy rather than to the pursuit of wealth or power.

Cosmopolitanism, it is clear, was attractive partly as an escape from the pettiness of political conditions at home. It was a Utopian ideal natural to men who had been allowed no political schooling and found little in 'fatherlands' like Württemberg or Weimar to satisfy their political idealism. The atmosphere of absolutism and rationalism in which they

[1] *Literarischer Sansculottismus*, quoted above, p. 299 f.

had grown to maturity, as well as their natural bent as poets towards contemplation rather than towards action, tended to make them more concerned with formulating distant ideals than with practical suggestions for immediate improvements. Goethe, it is true, had some experience of practical administration, but after the disappointment of his first hopes he came to look upon it chiefly as a means of self-discipline. Though he believed that every one should perform cheerfully the tasks that lay to his hand, he was far less interested in political and economic problems than in personal culture and the things of the mind, so that in the *Xenien* of Goethe and Schiller we find dicta such as these:

Das deutsche Reich

Deutschland? aber wo liegt es? Ich weiss das Land nicht zu finden.
Wo das gelehrte beginnt, hört das politische auf.

Deutscher Nationalcharakter

Zur Nation euch zu bilden, ihr hoffet es, Deutsche, vergebens;
Bildet, ihr könnt es, dafür freier zu Menschen euch aus.

The anti-naturalistic and essentially unpopular character of the two poets' work during the period of their friendship, their preference for Greek forms and non-German subjects, is also to be explained in part as a reaction against the narrowness and meanness of ordinary life in their own country. Compared with the God-like heroes whom Winckelmann had taught them to see in Greek art, or the passionate natures drawn 'on a colossal scale' by Shakespeare, how foolish the foppish courtiers and the timid philistines of their own 'ink-splashing century' looked to them! Believing that it was a poet's business, in Dilthey's words, 'to create a new world of art, in which the meaning of the real world is revealed', they could not be content, like Iffland and Kotzebue, to draw

Pfarrer, Kommerzienräte,
Fähndriche, Sekretärs oder Husarenmajors.

They preferred symbolic figures like Iphigenie, Tasso, Faust or Wallenstein, who might serve as the subject of a religious or philosophical art, which interpreted not merely the life of their own time, but the deepest problems of humanity at all times. Even apparently realistic works like *Wilhelm Meisters Lehrjahre* or *Hermann und Dorothea* were partly shaped in accordance with theories, whether of conduct or of art, which restricted their appeal. It was reserved for later writers to reveal the poetic qualities of that very narrowness against which Goethe revolted, and to prove that provincial life in its picturesque variety makes a more direct appeal to the imagination than the intellectually more satisfying abstractions of classicism. The infinite richness and diversity of German culture, exploited in the 'village story' and 'Heimatkunst', and evident centuries before this in folk tales and poetry, is of course even more clearly a product of separatism than the features of classical art discussed above, but it was only appreciated in the eighteenth century by a few exceptional spirits like Möser and Pestalozzi. The Romantic movement was soon to make good this omission.

It would be a great mistake to imagine that the whole German people in Goethe's age shared the views of their intellectual leaders. They were on the whole very tolerant of foreigners, but more from the incapacity to rise to the conception of anything larger than their small town or state than from a laudable large-mindedness. While the élite were cosmopolitan, the masses were frankly provincial. Their intellectual horizon is well indicated in the popular novels and drama of the day. Engel's *Lorenz Stark* and Iffland's plays give a far more faithful picture of the average middle-class German than the best works of the classics. We learn from them how seldom the thoughts of the inhabitants of Germany's many small towns strayed beyond the confines of their homes and their immediate surroundings. The political condition of the country was not the least of the factors that tended to restrict the interests of the citizen in this way to domestic or at most provincial affairs. He was intentionally kept in blinkers by the ruling class, and even the classical writers reacted to the French Revolution with a perhaps excessive cultural conservatism, as we see from Goethe's *Hermann und Dorothea* and *Episteln*, or from Schiller's *Lied von der Glocke*. Faust as one of the élite might cry, 'Wie ich beharre, bin ich Knecht', but the average man, Goethe seemed to say, would find true wisdom expressed in such lines as these:

> Aber wer fest auf dem Sinne beharrt, der bildet die Welt sich,
> Nicht dem Deutschen geziemt es, die fürchterliche Bewegung
> Fortzuleiten, und auch zu wanken hierhin und dorthin.
> Dies ist unser! so lass uns sagen und so es behaupten!

The average woman, needless to say, was to find her sphere of activity in the home:

> Dienen lerne das Weib beizeiten nach ihrer Bestimmung.

If a girl is given suitable tasks in the household, in the manner suggested in the second *Epistel* (1794), then

> Wünscht sie dann endlich zu lesen, so wählt sie gewisslich ein Kochbuch.

Though the early Romantic writers and their wives might find this view of society too complacently 'behaglich' and 'heiter', and parody it in such poems as A. W. Schlegel's

> Ehret die Frauen, sie stricken die Strümpfe
> Wollig und warm, zu durchwaten die Sümpfe,

their views in this matter were probably shared only by a small group of intellectuals, centred mainly in Berlin, and we may take the popularity of just those works of the classics that are in the narrowest sense 'bürgerlich' as a reliable index to general opinion.

The adjective 'bürgerlich' reminds us that it is not enough to consider the culture of the age of Goethe from the political point of view. Much light is thrown on its peculiarities by a study of the social structure of the country and its economic basis. Here our first question is: what was the relative share of the various social classes in the shaping of the new literature and the general philosophy of life expressed in it? Was any single class its main creator and supporter, as the Clerics were in the Old High German and the Knights in the Middle High German period? It has been seen above how the system of absolutism tended to preserve something like the medieval division of society into 'Stände', broad social groups whose individual members were linked by the performance of a similar function in the general life, a function to which they had usually been predestined by the social standing of their parents. It should therefore be easier to trace any particular influence each class may have had on culture than it would be for contemporary England, where class barriers had begun to break down much earlier than in Germany.

In the seventeenth century, to go no farther back, the dominating influence in literature had been, as in contemporary France, that of the aristocracy. Not that the nobility were usually themselves creators, as they had been in the age of chivalry. The Dukes of Brunswick (Heinrich Julius and Anton Ulrich) wrote themselves, Friedrich von Spee (a count) and Friedrich von Logau (a baron) were notable poets, and a few minor writers of good birth might be mentioned. But for the most part court circles were content to set the tone and encourage literary work by their patronage. The courts of Brunswick, Cassel, Stuttgart, Heidelberg, Vienna, Munich, Dresden were at one time or another literary centres, the Polish court, as Nadler has pointed out, exercised an important influence on the Silesian poets, the duke of Anhalt founded the 'Fruchtbringende Gesellschaft', the emperor himself frequently rewarded literary merit with a title (Opitz, Zesen, Rist, Birken).

At the courts of the rising territorial states literature, like the other arts, was forced to reflect the absolutist court ideal. The *genres* cultivated were the political novel, the 'roman à clef', the heroic novel, the pastoral, and characteristically aristocratic forms of stage performance like the opera, ballet, masquerade and the drama of the Silesians and the Jesuits. In the main the actual writers of these works were university-trained court officials and high civil servants, usually of good middle-class origins. This class was as yet too weak numerically and too dependent on the favour of the great to have interests and ideals of its own. It was usually content to trick out those of its patrons in forms that displayed its own bookish culture. The middle class had lost the naïve self-confidence of the age of the Reformation and was content to follow the lead of court circles in everything. The councillors and high officials of the towns, and the patricians generally, had no desire but to express the same tastes as the nobility of which they considered themselves a part. The majority of the leading authors were civic or state officials (like Opitz, Logau, Moscherosch, Gryphius, Lohenstein, Hofmannswaldau, Harsdörffer and even Grimmelshausen in his later years); the rest were also university men in other professions, clergymen, doctors or teachers in university or gymnasium. Zesen alone failed to find an anchorage. Among the actual creators of literature the middle class was just as strongly represented as at any time in the following century. The difference between the content and tone of their serious work, from which a realistic treatment of middle-class types was strictly excluded, and that of the later periods, would seem to have been very largely due to causes of a social and political nature, to that gradual social rise of the middle class described in earlier chapters.

The fact that it was the greater commercial centres like Hamburg and Zürich which first emancipated themselves from the influence of the courts is significant. In Hamburg, in the seventeenth century, as in Nürnberg and other big towns, the courts set the fashions in literature and the arts. It was the ambition of the patricians and rich merchants of Hamburg to equal the court towns in their own forms. They exchanged actors and operas with Brunswick, for instance, and their first theatre of note was an opera house, opened in 1678. It was only with the growth of English influence, resulting from the close commercial connection described above, that a literature more truly expressive of the middle class was able to arise. The example of the English middle class, already so fully aware of their own strength and importance, gradually roused the merchant class to a realisation of its own deepest needs and proved a stronger force than the prestige of the patricians with their aristocratic tastes. Opera, a court product, was from the first adapted to the requirements of a city audience, and given in German, not, as in the courts, in Italian. The only kind of opera that survived for long was a realistic comic opera; moreover many new forms of literature soon proved immeasurably more important. One of the chief aims of the writers in the 'moral weeklies', which now obtained such a vogue, was to encourage the self-respect of the middle class and to guide them to a culture of their own. Their establishment is the first clear sign of the coming age of 'Humanität'.

Leipzig was too much under the political and social influence of Dresden to follow this lead immediately, but Zürich, a strong city-republic, not overshadowed, like so many older German towns, by the power of any territorial prince, was free to go its own way. It was because the structure of their society was similar, as Nadler points out, that the Swiss towns and Hamburg repeatedly established cultural contacts with each other, and, one may add, with England. The famous quarrel of the Swiss and the Leipzig schools, on the other hand, was probably due in part to political and social differences, though of course many other factors entered in. Gottsched, in his laudable attempt to establish a literary German drama, could find no other model than the French plays performed for the delight of court circles in Dresden, a form of drama which was essentially the expression of an aristocratic minority, though at the same time he followed Hamburg's example with his moral weeklies for the bourgeoisie. There was an inconsistency in his position which paralleled that of the cultivated Leipziger in general, half citizen, half courtier, and in his attempt to make all Germany speak 'sächsisch' there was a despotic note which was naturally resented by the republican Bodmer. In Hamburg and Zürich, on the other hand, most of the best writers were public-spirited citizens with some sense of their dignity and responsibilities as such. It is noteworthy that they did not separate the pursuit of literature from that of the good life in the widest sense. Their chief literary societies (the 'Patriotische Gesellschaft' in Hamburg and, later, the 'Helvetische Gesellschaft' in Zürich) were also societies for the promotion of every kind of public-spirited effort. Not that these towns too did not produce authors like Hagedorn who were uncomfortably astride between the court and the middle-class ideal, but this was in the transition period at the beginning of the eighteenth century. Their more characteristic writers were whole-hearted 'Aufklärer' who, though their taste may not always have been impeccable, had usually the merit of sincerity.

In the first sixty or seventy years of the eighteenth century German literature gradually withdrew itself more and more from the courts, first, as we have seen, in the great centres of trade, and later almost everywhere. The few 'court poets' who survived, in places like Dresden, enjoyed no esteem outside their own circle, and patronage of German writers by German princes became rare. The Prussian court under Frederick William I had no use for poets at all, and, under Frederick the Great no use for German poets. The only considerable writer who enjoyed the patronage of a prince was Klopstock, and it was the king of Denmark who was his patron.

We have seen in the preceding chapter how the reading public gradually expanded and how with the absorption of new elements its tastes changed, becoming more and more markedly middle-class. The increased sale of books and periodicals transformed the book trade and made literature into a possible though not yet a lucrative profession. It was still for most writers a pursuit for leisure hours, but even when economically independent of their public, writers could not if they wished resist the influence of their ways of thinking. The drama and the novel, under pressure from the middle class, inevitably became didactic and realistic. With the advance of science based on experience and reason the attitude of the instructed classes towards revealed religion and established institutions became more and more critical, and it was no longer possible to prevent this scepticism from trickling slowly down to the general reading public. Very timidly at first, especially in Germany, the middle class began to claim the right to order its life for itself in the light of reason, at least in those activities which concerned it most closely, its manner of making a living and its family life.

More than one generation's work was necessary in Germany to persuade the mass of the public which could read to turn to other books than the Bible and catechism, and the chap-books and calendars sold at fairs or by pedlars, as well as to enable the writers to discover by experiment a way of writing which would appeal to this new public. Between 1700 and 1750 much of this preparatory work had been accomplished, and a large number of writers, the 'niedere Aufklärer' as they are now ungraciously called, who filled the columns of the moral weeklies and newspapers, had learnt to write not for a gild of fellow scholars but for people who had no further equipment than common sense and the ability to read printed everyday German. This literature was hardly what is usually called literature at all. It was written for use rather than for delight, it provided enlightenment in a palatable form.

The new *genres* most favoured by the middle-class public were the domestic drama and the family novel, both distinguished from the older drama and romance not so much by their themes as by the general philosophy, the system of values which they implied. The serious drama of the French classical writers and their imitators had treated of princes and heroes whose will knew no restrictions except those imposed by fate, men without obligations to any society, for whom their lands and subjects were material that they might fashion according to their personal desires. In these figures, though they might be taken from classical history or myth, the feelings of a ruling caste could be fittingly expressed. In the domestic drama on the other hand, even when its figures (as in Lessing's *Miss Sara Sampson*) were not strictly of the middle class, the point of view was always that of this class, especially in questions of morality. It was not at all surprising that the Hamburg public listened to the enlightened merchant Mr Thoroughgood, in *George Barnwell*, with delighted approbation, whereas the Viennese nobility found him intolerably prosy.

Naturally the new forms had to be considerably adapted to suit the peculiar conditions that prevailed in German society. There was a rising middle class in Germany as in England, so that the fundamental social condition for the acceptance of these *genres* was present, but the German middle class differed, as we have seen, from the English in many particulars. It is characteristic, for instance, that in *Miss Sara Sampson*, the first German imitation of *George Barnwell*, the conflict is one between private individuals, not between society, or a particular class, and an errant member of it, and that even this family tragedy had to be displayed against an English background if it was to have sufficient dignity to be taken seriously. Lessing evidently felt that a German family in its natural setting was still only a fit subject for comedy. It is interesting again to note that the first German domestic tragedies in a purely German setting realistically treated were those of F. L. Schröder, produced for a Hamburg public. Here too, though the Hamburg citizen takes himself seriously, he is not shown in any conflicts that affect more than the immediate interests of his family; he has no public spirit or patriotism, and no sense of independence and of pride in his calling like Thoroughgood. The first figure in the domestic drama who really stands on his own feet is Major von Tellheim in *Minna von Barnhelm*, and to explain his manliness Lessing has to make him a Prussian officer and a nobleman, though, as Eloesser rightly says, he is not really a Prussian and at bottom not a soldier either. 'Military service is for him a passing phase, an education to manliness, such as the author perhaps desired for the peace-loving, mean-spirited bourgeoisie in general.'[1]

An interesting confirmation of this interpretation may be found in a very sensible essay by Christian Garve, the 'Popularphilosoph', entitled: *Über die Maxime Rochefoucaults: Das bürgerliche Air verliert sich zuweilen bei der Armee, niemals am Hofe.*[2] In this essay Garve analyses the character of the middle class in a way which frequently reminds one of certain late passages in *Wilhelm Meister*, passages perhaps influenced by this book. 'Embarrassment in intercourse with people of higher rank' seems to him the most characteristic feature of middle-class manners, and he considers that it is in the army that an easy self-confidence and personal dignity can best be acquired by one whose birth gives him no standing at court. Much of the so-called militarism of Germany in more recent times, in the sense of the belief in the moral benefits resulting from military training, probably proceeds from considerations not unlike those of Garve. But in its passivity and externality Garve's ideal falls far short of Goethe's. Wilhelm Meister progresses in the end beyond the stage at which the easy bearing of a gentleman (and of a good actor!) excites his admiration, and is turned into a good and active citizen,[3] whereas even Tellheim's ultimate aim was 'cultiver son jardin', to lead an idyllic life in some little haven

[1] A. Eloesser, *Das bürgerliche Drama*, Berlin, 1898, p. 93.

[2] C. Garve, *Versuche*, 1. Teil, Breslau, 1792.

[3] See the present writer's essay: 'Goethe's *Wilhelm Meister* as a picture and a criticism of society', in *Publications of the English Goethe Society*, 1933.

apart. This was in fact the ideal of the average good citizen in Lessing's time. *Emilia Galotti* gives us a similar impression of the age. It is, in Lessing's phrase, 'eine von allem Staatsinteresse befreite Virginia', true to its time in its presentation of a despotic but good-natured and charming prince and his unambitious subjects, whose one desire is, not to reform the world, but to be left in peace.

The second-rate writers of Lessing's time display the sentimental optimism characteristic of the Age of Enlightenment even more plainly. They shut their eyes to the evils of society and see only 'Wie wir's denn zuletzt so herrlich weit gebracht'. They treat social problems, such as that of the relation of the nobility to the other classes, much as Lessing treats the problem of religious differences in *Nathan der Weise*. Here the real difficulty of toleration is obscured because the representatives of the conflicting religions are made to appear so conciliatory and so like each other. So in the sentimental plays of the Aufklärung nobleman and bourgeois are represented as brother-classes, equally dear to the 'Landesvater' whom they both revere.

The young writers of the Storm and Stress period in the 'seventies were usually products of the same social stratum as their older colleagues, but they were, to use a modern phrase, much more class-conscious and consequently sound much more revolutionary. Steeped as they all were in the writings of the French critics of society, particularly Rousseau, they frequently present the conflict between classes, and almost always take sides for the middle class. They are far from objective in their pictures of contemporary society, painting their own class as unhappy but virtuous and the nobility as corrupt and arrogant favourites of fortune. They see defects in the middle class, narrowness of outlook, servility to superiors in some, boorish incivility in others, but they explain them as due to unfavourable social conditions.[1]

[1] See the well-documented study by Clara Stockmeyer, *Soziale Probleme im Drama des Sturmes und Dranges*, Frankfort, 1922.

The general tendency of their writings might be described as liberal. It is not the economic situation of the middle class—still less that of the peasant or the poorer town worker—which arouses their indignation, but their lack of equality with the nobility in social standing and legal privileges. The prince himself is never directly criticised, even in the boldest of Sturm und Drang plays, Schiller's *Kabale und Liebe*. It is always his advisers and agents who are to blame. There is never any incitement to political revolt. These writers hope rather by an appeal to the heart to secure recognition for the solid merit of their class, an extension of its rights and the outward respect due to its inner worth. They are interested chiefly in the section of the middle class to which they themselves belong, more or less cultivated and prosperous circles in the towns, and are usually indifferent to and ignorant of the life of the countryman and of the poorer townsman.

The passionate interest which the theatre at that time evoked cannot be explained as purely aesthetic in origin. The stage had come to be looked upon, in that age of waning faith, as a kind of substitute for the pulpit. In the earlier domestic dramas questions of private morality had been the subject of stage homilies. In this later phase a wider circle of interests was discussed and the topics ranged beyond those treated in moral weeklies to those of the so-called political journals. Being the work of young men, full of foreign theories but very ignorant of the world, the new plays made little appeal to court circles or to the more settled bourgeoisie, but the ordinary citizen found pleasure in them, says a contemporary, because, being excluded from court circles, he had no taste, and no sense for intimate relationships.[1] It was the contempt these writers felt for the Frenchified culture of the German aristocracy, rather than political nationalism, that lay behind their hostility to French forms of art, and particularly of the drama. In their criticism of the 'decorum', the 'squeamishness', the 'pursuit of external form' of the

[1] K. Risbeck, *Briefe eines reisenden Franzosen*, I, 71.

French dramatists they were repeating with more emphasis objections already raised by consciously middle-class French writers like Diderot and Mercier. It was class-feeling, far more than national feeling, that was expressed in these outbursts, so that it was not altogether unfitting that Schiller should be made a French 'citoyen' for his early revolutionary plays.

It is not surprising either that there was an open feud between several of the younger writers and Wieland, who had become more and more of a courtier in his outlook ever since his return from Switzerland and his friendship with the Stadion circle. Nothing could have been less revolutionary than his epicurean philosophy. Not that Wieland was without readers among the middle class. He was, on the contrary, almost a best seller. He appealed to people of taste through his wit and grace of style, to court circles through his urbanity and refined sensuality, to the cultivated middle class through his learning and sweet reasonableness, and perhaps not least through the aroma of social distinction that his books carried with them. But he was naturally anathema to the sworn enemies of the rococo. What could the author of *Luise* have in common with the author of *Musarion*? The young puritans of the 'Hain' solemnly burnt Wieland's works as those of a corrupter of youth, and the young Goethe wrote a skit against him.

But these generous young revolutionaries soon found that without more backing in society than they possessed they could only point to social evils and not do anything effective to remedy them. Theirs was from the first a theoretical protest, expressed with the exaggeration common in men whose words do not need to be followed by action. Their best works, like *Götz*, begin on a note of protest and end on one of resignation, and in their weaker works, as in the popular plays of Iffland made later on the same recipe, they are careful to lay the blame for the abuses of the time not on the princes but on their heartless ministers, not on the squires but on their bailiffs.

Most of the Stürmer und Dränger therefore soon made their peace with the courts. Before Schiller, the youngest of them, produced his *Räuber* and *Kabale und Liebe* in the early 'eighties, Goethe and Herder were established in high office at Weimar, Lenz had attempted to follow Goethe's example, and Klinger had begun the career at the Russian court which was to prove so brilliant. Just as Goethe and Schiller returned to verse and a form closely resembling the analytic construction of the French classical dramatists in most of the plays of their maturity, so also they came to perceive the value of many of the social conventions they had dismissed so impatiently in their youth. In *Tasso* Goethe praises just those qualities of reverence for tradition, restraint of impulse and respect for external forms which the companions of his youth, and he himself in some degree, had rejected as unnatural. The naïve individualism of the young middle-class 'geniuses' has given way to the considerateness and tact of the courtier. 'Erlaubt ist, was sich ziemt', not 'Erlaubt ist, was gefällt', is to be the motto even for an acknowledged genius. The ethical ideal put forward here and in all the great works of the 'nineties is 'Humanität', an ideal not discoverable by any man from his inner consciousness, or from the traditions of his class alone, but through intercourse with those by whom the culture gradually achieved by the best in each succeeding age had been inherited.

German classical literature then was the work of authors who were not restricted by circumstances to a narrow range of subjects, but could expatiate freely over the whole of nature and history, in an eclectic style influenced by innumerable foreign models. This literature was neither national in sentiment nor expressive of the outlook of any particular class of society. Cosmopolitanism and 'Humanität' were its ideals. Considered from the point of view of economic and social history, it was essentially the work of free artists, such as could only arise when the possibility existed of writing for a heterogeneous public, without much need of patronage or much fear of persecution. In earlier ages, a writer had not easily secured a hearing for himself as such. It has been pointed out how frequently writers in the *Spectator*, the *Tatler*, and their German counterparts, assumed some mask, such as that of a lady or gentleman of quality, instead of writing under their own names. It was not until late in the eighteenth century that the custom of making the hero of a novel an artist established itself. The first example was the half-merchant, half-artist Wilhelm Meister. Then with the Romantics the artist became almost the rule as hero, not only because of the technical advantage the author so gained, of being able to introduce his own verses and reflections and to draw more freely on his own experience, but because the artist embodied now the personal ideal of the educated middle class in Germany, the ideal of culture.[1]

In this culture of Weimar the broad stream of the humanist literary tradition was united with German currents from both the middle class and the courts. If, on the one hand, the great middle-class writers were influenced by the ideas of court circles, upholding as they did the accepted code of ethics and manners, the prevailing monarchical system of government and the division of society into 'estates' with relatively constant duties and privileges, the court itself was increasingly affected by ideas and habits which had their origin in the middle class. The irresponsible extravagant despots of the type of Augustus the Strong of Saxony were succeeded by princes more and more dominated by the ideas of duty, order and economy. In small courts like Weimar, owing to their modest resources, the forms of social intercourse, too, came increasingly to resemble those of the better middle class. There was nothing unique in this development. A similar fusion of middle-class and courtly ideals had already taken place, for instance, in French classical literature, to which

[1] See L. L. Schücking, *Die Soziologie der literarischen Geschmacksbildung*, 2nd ed. Leipzig and Berlin, 1931, p. 28.

German classicism owed so much. The really new feature about French classicism, as M. Berthelot[1] has pointed out, was the part played in it by bourgeois common sense. This is where it differed from the Italian and Spanish cultural tradition in which it was grounded.

C'est la formation de cette bourgeoisie organisatrice qui a le plus contribué à donner sa physionomie propre au siècle de Louis XIV. La bourgeoisie à ce moment s'appuie sur un ordre politique pré-existant, c'est à dire sur la monarchie militaire et administrative qui, seule, lui à permis de se constituer: son bon sens s'applique à la conservation et à la justification d'un certain ordre social et d'un ordre moral qui lui paraît lié avec la stabilité de cet ordre social.

The weakness of Weimar classicism, when compared with that of the age of Louis XIV, was that it did not proceed from so complete a synthesis. It was much less firmly rooted in the life of its time, more purely literary and derivative. This German classicism did not leave firmly established a cultural ideal fit to serve as the starting-point for the efforts of many succeeding generations, as French classicism had done. It owed its survival in the nineteenth century rather to the fact that it was made the basis of higher education than to its real fitness to express the deepest aspirations of the German people. Several phases of German life which were already in evidence and have since proved extremely important are scarcely to be traced in German classical literature. There is first all that is connoted by the phrase 'the Prussian spirit'. There is the spirit of capitalistic enterprise in commerce and industry. And there is that complex of tradition and sentiment proceeding from the old-time village which is now summed up in the vague conception of 'Volkstum'. The Germany of poets and thinkers was only one of several co-existing Germanies. There is therefore nothing surprising in the fact that large sections of the German people have often found themselves unable to accept the ideals of the Weimar classics,

[1] R. Berthelot, *La Sagesse de Shakespeare et de Goethe*, chap. III.

or if they remained unconscious of this essential incompatibility, paid Weimar only lip-service, neglecting in practice the humanistic teaching they had received at school.

The peculiar feature about German classicism is that it is not, like the earlier classical movements in other literatures, 'the product of a nation and a generation which has consciously achieved a definite advance, moral, political, intellectual, and is filled with the belief that its view of life is more natural, human, universal and wise than that from which it has escaped'. It is only in a very limited measure the expression of 'a body of common sentiments and thoughts which the artist shares with his audience, thoughts and views which have for his generation the validity of universal truths'.[1] Only a very small élite shared the view of life taken by the German classics. The figures in the last chapter show how limited the demand for their writings was in their own time. On the stage their plays aroused even less interest. The theatre at Mannheim, for instance, the first 'national' or repertory theatre of real importance, in the 27 years from 1781 to 1808 produced 37 plays of Iffland on 476 evenings, and 115 plays of Kotzebue on 1728 evenings. In the same period Schiller's *Räuber*, which had made the fame of Mannheim, was acted only 15 times, *Kabale und Liebe* only seven times, *Fiesko* and *Don Karlos* only three times each. Similarly at Dresden, between 1789 and 1813, out of a total of 1471 performances, Iffland and Kotzebue took up 477, about one-third, while Lessing, Goethe and Schiller together were acted only on 58 evenings.[2] Even in Weimar itself, under Goethe's management, the repertoire in the first seven years hardly differed at all from what was usual elsewhere. The opening performance in 1791 was of Iffland's *Jäger*, and the taste of the public continued to be met, with very few

[1] Quotations from H. J. C. Grierson's masterly essay on 'Classical and Romantic' in *The Background of English Literature*, London, 1925.

[2] M. Martersteig, *Das deutsche Theater im 19. Jahrhundert*, 2nd ed. Leipzig, 1924, p. 132.

experiments, until Schiller returned to the theatre in 1798 (*Wallensteins Lager*). From now till his death, Schiller provided the theatre with a good play every year, and the French classics and Shakespeare were occasionally attempted in his adaptations. Even Goethe's completed *Iphigenie* was at last staged (1802). *Tasso* was not acted till 1807, however, and *Faust*, part I, till 1829, in both cases rather against the author's wishes. In between the few literary plays, the only ones which are now remembered, the usual concessions were still made to middle-class taste. It is clear then, as Georg Brandes pointed out long ago, that Goethe and Schiller 'did not find a public in existence that understood them, still less a nation that could provide them with subjects and, as it were, commission work from them'. Their classicism was rather in the main a means of escape from their narrow world to that ancient Greece which they imagined as so free, so full of a noble simplicity and serene grandeur. For Mr Santayana, therefore, 'Goethe was never so romantic as when he was classical. His distichs are like theatrical gestures; he feels the sweep of his toga as he rounds them off'.[1]

But German classicism did not merely look backwards to the past. It was not always content to hold the world at a distance. It hoped to save the world through art. This is the sense of Schiller's *Briefe über aesthetische Erziehung* and of his philosophical poems, and probably a similar idea underlies the second part of *Faust*. Faust's vision of ideal beauty in Helen is a necessary step towards his realisation of the true aim of life, active co-operation with others for the good of the community as a whole. 'Classicism', says Strich, 'has usually been the product of corporate feeling, but German classicism looked upon it as its mission to call this corporate feeling into existence through art.'

This is not the place for us to consider how much Weimar contributed in actual fact to the creation of a unified Germany. On a superficial view the poets might seem through

[1] *Three Philosophical Poets*, Harvard, 1910, p. 176.

their horror of any state interference with the liberty of the individual to have been partly responsible for the failure of the German states to offer any effective resistance to Napoleon. Goethe's remarks about internationalism, quoted above, were his reply to the often expressed reproach that he had not put his pen at the service of his country. Wilhelm von Humboldt, the friend of Schiller, voiced the ideas of the classical age in that essay on the *Sphere and Duties of Government*[1] which was the chief inspiration of Mill's *Essay on Liberty*. 'The grand, leading principle, towards which every argument unfolded in these pages directly converges, is the absolute and essential importance of human development in its richest diversity'—it is this sentence from Humboldt which Mill quotes as a motto for his own essay, and he agrees that it is the state's business simply to guard the lives and property of its subjects. As Heinrich von Treitschke sees the matter, however, this meant that 'the admirers of classical antiquity preached flight from the state, the very antithesis of Greek virtue'.

Yet Treitschke himself defends the poets' attitude.

> They guarded the most individual possession of our people, the holy flame of idealism, and we owe it to them, above all, that there was still a Germany, when the German Empire had vanished, that the Germans in the hour of suffering and humiliation were still able to believe in themselves, in the abiding value of the German spirit. It was from the complete development of free personality that our political freedom and the independence of the German state proceeded....This active humanism was not really either effeminate or hostile to the state. It had simply not yet understood the nature of the state, and only needed the schooling of experience to develop all the virtues of the good citizen and the hero

—as is seen by the example of Humboldt himself. Hegel's gloomy saying, therefore, that it is only in the dusk that the

[1] *Ideen zu einem Versuch, die Grenzen der Wirksamkeit des Staats zu bestimmen*, 1792.

owl of Minerva begins her flight, was true of Greece, according to Treitschke, but not of Germany. 'Our classical literature was not the dying note of an old culture but the promising first phase of something new.'[1]

Though there is much truth in this, it is clear that the abundant new growth in the nineteenth century in both the political and the economic spheres was rooted in other soils than that of Weimar. Potsdam and Berlin on the one hand and the rising commercial towns like Hamburg and Leipzig on the other were the real growing points of Germany's power and wealth, while the innumerable small courts became less and less important even culturally, as first philosophy and then natural science celebrated their triumphs in the universities. Here, as at the beginning of our study, the essential ambiguity of the word Germany must be insisted upon. For some it means Goethe, Schiller, Kant, for others Haydn, Mozart, Beethoven, but their Germany, the Germany of poets and thinkers and musicians, was only one of several co-existing Germanies, in fact it did not exist at all as we know it from their work, for what we know is a world constructed by these artists, a 'world of aesthetic semblance'. They never ceased to complain of the harshness of the reality that surrounded them. It will not do, therefore, when modern Germany offends her neighbours in the field of politics or trade, to appeal against her to that older, better Germany that we imagine. What we conjure up is in the main a poet's dream; so far as it corresponded to any features of reality, these were but a fraction of the whole.

It is, however, true that whereas in Goethe's age the best minds of the nation were absorbed in poetry and philosophy, and a new poem was an event to be interpreted and admired in long letters and criticisms, the energies of the nineteenth and twentieth centuries have been directed far more towards the acquisition and control of material things. In this swing towards materialism Germany was following her western

[1] *Deutsche Geschichte*, Teil I.

neighbours, influenced like them by the needs of a rapidly expanding population and the corresponding development of technique and organisation. The realists (in Schiller's sense) triumphed over the idealists, but there was nothing unprecedented in this struggle between the spiritual and the material, and there is no reason to believe that it will ever end. How familiar Schiller was with the realist even in his idealistic age may be seen from his *Wallenstein*. Some words he puts into the mouth of his hero, anticipating as they do so much of the mind of nineteenth-century Germany, may serve as an epilogue to this study:

> Was die Göttlichen uns senden
> Von oben, sind nur allgemeine Güter;
> Ihr Licht erfreut, doch macht es keinen reich,
> In ihrem Staat erringt sich kein Besitz.
> Den Edelstein, das allgeschätzte Gold
> Muss man den falschen Mächten abgewinnen,
> Die unterm Tage schlimmgeartet hausen.
> Nicht ohne Opfer macht man sie geneigt,
> Und keiner lebet, der aus ihrem Dienst
> Die Seele hätte rein zurückgezogen.

Appendix I

GERMAN MONEY AND ITS VALUE WEIGHTS AND MEASURES

(The following notes are intended as a brief practical guide for the English reader. Fuller information will be found in Muret-Sanders' German-English Dictionary, second half, and in many older works of reference, such as those by Bergius and Reichard given in the bibliography.)

COINAGE

The commonest terms used for the expression of money values are: Thaler, Gulden, Groschen, Kreuzer. Thaler and Groschen were commonest in the north, Gulden and Kreuzer in the south, but in all states the four values stood in the following fixed relation to each other:

16	(Gute) Groschen	or	60	Kreuzer	made one	Gulden.
24	,,	,,	90	,,	,,	Reichsthaler.
32	,,	,,	120	,,	,,	Speziesthaler (Konventionsthaler).

A Gulden was therefore half a Speziesthaler, or two-thirds of a Reichsthaler. The Guter Groschen was divided into 12 Pfennige (while the Mariengroschen, less commonly used, was worth only 8 Pfennige), the Kreuzer into 4 Pfennige. Of the one kind of Pfennig there were therefore 192 to the Gulden, of the other 240.

Owing to the multiplicity of mints, the value of the Gulden and Thaler could and did vary considerably from state to state and at different times. There were five standards in common use for the minting of silver coins in the later eighteenth century, as well as some half dozen minor ones.

(1) In Braunschweig-Lüneburg the "Leipziger Münzfuss" of 1690 was still followed, giving 18 Gulden to the Cologne mark of fine silver. (This "mark" is of course a weight, not a coin.) The value of this Gulden in pre-war Reichsmark would be 2.338.

(2) In Lübeck, Hamburg, Bremen and Mecklenburg they observed the "Lübecker Kurantfuss", of 34 Kurantmark to the

Cologne mark of silver, established in 1726. A Thaler was equivalent to 3 Kurantmark, but values were more commonly expressed in marks. The value of a Gulden (two such marks) on this basis would be 1.857 Reichsmark.

(3) In Brandenburg-Prussia from 1750 the Prussian Kurantfuss of 21 Gulden (or 14 Thaler) to the Cologne mark was observed. A Gulden on this standard would be worth 2 Reichsmark.

(4) In Austria, Saxony, Braunschweig-Wolfenbüttel and most of Lower Germany the "Konventionsfuss" of 20 Gulden to the Cologne mark was the standard. The convention had been arrived at in 1753, in one of the numerous efforts to reduce the chaos of the German coinage. A Gulden of this type would be worth 2.105 Reichsmark.

(5) In 1754 Bavaria, one of the parties to the original convention, withdrew and depreciated its Gulden to 24 to the Cologne mark. It was followed by the Swabian and Franconian circles, the Palatinate, Frankfort-on-Main, and the territories on the Rhine and Main generally. This "South German" or "Rhenish" Gulden would be worth 1.754 Reichsmark.

The principal gold coins in circulation were:

Souverain d'or (Austrian),	worth	9	Reichsthaler,	or	13½	Gulden*
Carolin (Bavaria and elsewhere)	,,	6	,,	,,	9	,,
Pistole (also called *Louis d'or*, or named after the ruler, as *Friedrich d'or*, *August d'or*)	,,	5	,,	,,	7½	,,
Max d'or (Bavarian)	,,	4⅙	,,	,,	6¼	,,
Ducat (general)	,,	3	,,	,,	4½	,,

* 20-Gulden standard, No. 4 above.

Coins representing multiples and fractions of these, especially of the Ducat, were also issued, and some French and Dutch gold coins were in circulation, at recognised values.

For rough conversion into English money, the Speziesthaler, Reichsthaler and Gulden (except the Rhenish Gulden, No. 5 above) may usually be taken as equivalent to four, three and two shillings respectively. No simple rule can be given for arriving at the equivalent in purchasing power in present-day money, because some things were relatively cheaper than now, and some as dear or dearer. The factor for foodstuffs might be something like three, four or five, while for clothes and imported luxuries it might be one or even a fraction of one. The following specimen prices, etc. will give some idea of the purchasing power of money in the second half of the eighteenth century:

Typical commodity prices (taking the Gulden as equivalent to two shillings).

The price of beef, veal, lamb, pork in Frankfort-on-Main in February 1801 was 3¾*d.* to 4¾*d.* a pound. It had changed little since 1750, when an average price had been 3*d.*

Common ("black") bread at the same time and place cost 1*d.* a pound. (The price of bread was of course subject to variations according to the harvest and the price of grain.) Eggs were 1*d.* each at their dearest, and nearly 3 a penny at their cheapest. Fresh butter cost about 4*d.* a pound in summer, but up to 1*s.* in winter. (Careful householders laid in a supply in summer for salting.)

Luxuries like coffee, tea and sugar were dear, and their prices varied considerably according to trade conditions. In mid-century, coffee cost 1*s.* 6*d.* a pound and sugar 1*s.* In 1779 Herr Rat Goethe paid only 1*s.* a pound for coffee, and 1*s.* for sugar. For tea (usually bought by the quarter pound) he paid anything from 4*s.* to 8*s.* a pound.

Clothing was also expensive. A good scarlet dress for Goethe's mother in 1758 cost nearly £10, one for his sister in 1770 £3. 17*s.*, a suit for himself £3. 10*s.* to £5. An ell of English cloth cost about 10*s.* in Silesia in 1756, and the best silk stockings for men over 10*s.* a pair.

Wages and salaries.

An unskilled labourer earned 6*d.* or 7*d.* a day or less, a master mason or carpenter round about 1*s.* a day (less in winter). A spinner made about 2*s.* to 2*s.* 6*d.* a week on piece-work, but a factory worker in a favoured industry, or a skilled workman in particular demand, could earn up to 16*s.* a week.

A good cook or man-servant could be had even in the second half of the century for 30*s.* a year, wages varying according to experience from 24*s.* to 60*s.* Goethe's father paid his cook £2. 8*s.* a year, his man-servant a little more, his house-maids £2 and 30*s.* respectively. A private tutor was paid anything from £3 to £8 a year. All these had of course board in addition. For a servant like a coachman who did not live in, the board allowance was about 3*s*. a week.

An average annual allowance for a student was £50 (though many had far less). A teacher in a Prussian Latin school received between £30 and £60, a university professor £60 to £180 and fees. A young jurist as a subordinate official earned £20 or £30 a year. He was considered to have attained a good position if he eventually earned over £100. Goethe as minister received at first £180, finally £460 a year.

Living expenses.

Two modest furnished rooms could be had for from 8*s*. to 12*s*. a month. Schiller could dine in Jena for 3*d*. a day, and Crabb Robinson paid 5*s*. a week for dinner at the best inn there. To board with a private family cost him (in 1801) from 36 to 50 guineas a year. Schiller estimated that a single man of his class could live in Jena on £40 a year, in Dresden or Weimar on £60.*

WEIGHTS AND MEASURES

These varied as much from place to place as the coinage. A few examples may be given.

The pound (Pfund), of 32 Loth, was in the north 3 to 5 per cent., in the south (Munich and Vienna), 22 per cent. heavier than the English pound.

The chief measure of length for cloth was the ell (Elle), made up of two feet (Fuss) or 24 inches (Zoll). A Berlin foot was roughly an English foot, but a Viennese one was longer, a Hamburg one shorter. Some places had even different ells for different materials.

A German mile (Meile) varied between something over 9 kilometres and something under 7. The "common mile" was a geographical mile, one-fifteenth of a degree, about 4·6 English statute miles. A "Quadratmeile" was therefore about 21¼ English square miles.*

* Chief sources: *Crabb Robinson in Germany*; *Die Stadt Goethes*; Schiller, *Briefe*; J. H. L. Bergius, *Policey- und Cameralmagazin* and *Neues Policey- und Cameralmagazin*, Frankfort-on-Main, 1767–1780; Reichard, *Guide des Voyageurs en Europe*; Biedermann, *op. cit.* I.

Appendix II

STATISTICAL SURVEY OF GERMANY BEFORE THE NAPOLEONIC WARS*

A. ELECTORAL STATES

1. AUSTRIA within the Reich (Austrian Circle and Swabian possessions, Bohemia, and Burgundian Circle), 3534 Q.M.; 9,126,404 inhabitants.

   AUSTRIAN TERRITORY outside the Reich (Hungary, Illyria, Transylvania, Bukovina, East and West Galicia, Lombardy), 8105 Q.M.; 14,051,000 inhabitants.

   Towns with 20,000 inhabitants and over: Vienna (226,000), Milan (119,000), Brussels (80,000), Prague (75,000), Antwerp (60,000), Ofen and Pest (35,000), Graz, Trieste (30,000), Dobreczyn (25,000), Laibach, Lemberg (20,000).

2. PRUSSIA within the Reich, 1646 Q.M.; 2,756,600 inhabitants.

   PRUSSIAN TERRITORY outside the Reich (Kingdom of Prussia, Polish acquisitions, New Silesia, Neufchâtel), 3685 Q.M.; 4,890,000 inhabitants.

   Towns with 20,000 and over: Berlin (143,000), Warsaw (67,000), Königsberg (60,000), Breslau (57,600), Danzig (36,000), Potsdam (26,700), Magdeburg (26,300), Halle (20,000).

3. BAVARIA with the PALATINATE (KURPFALZ), 1028 Q.M., 2,204,700 inhabitants.

   Towns: Munich (50,000), Mannheim (23,000). Of the rest, only Düsseldorf (18,000), Elberfeld (14,000) and Heidelberg (11,000) had a population of over 10,000.

4. SAXONY, 708 Q.M.; 2,104,320 inhabitants.

   Towns: Dresden (50,000), Leipzig (33,000). Four more towns had a population of 10,000 or slightly over, Naumburg, Zittau, Chemnitz, Freiberg.

* Summarised and rearranged from Reichard, *Der Passagier auf der Reise in Deutschland*, 2nd ed. Weimar, 1803.

5. BRUNSWICK with LÜNEBURG, 514 Q.M.; 787,200 inhabitants.
Town: Hanover (15,500). No other town had 10,000 inhabitants.
6. MAINZ (KUR-MAINZ), 171 Q.M.; 224,734 inhabitants.
Town: Mainz (30,000).
7. TREVES (KUR-TRIER), 110 Q.M.; 280,000 inhabitants.
8. COLOGNE (KUR-KÖLN), 130 Q.M.; 198,000 inhabitants.

B. SPIRITUAL MEMBERS OF THE COLLEGE OF PRINCES

(*Area in Q.M. in brackets.*)

Archbishopric of Salzburg (180), *Bishoprics* of Münster (230), Liège (105), Würzburg (90), Trient (70), Bamberg (65), Osnabrück (56), Paderborn (55), Augsburg (54), Hildesheim (54), Fulda (37), Speyer (28), Eichstädt (22), Basel (20), Brixen (17), Passau (15), Strassburg (13), Freisingen (13), Regensburg (6), Constance (5), Worms (5), Lübeck (1). *Order* of Hoch- und Deutschmeister (6). *Prince-abbots' lands* of Kempten (16), Berchtesgaden (10), Corvey (6), Ellwangen (5). Estimated total population of these spiritual lands: over two and a quarter millions.

C. LAY PRINCES

1. OLD DYNASTIES.

MECKLENBURG-SCHWERIN, 240 Q.M.; 240,000 inhabitants. (Schwerin, 10,000.)
MECKLENBURG-STRELITZ, 60 Q.M.; 60,000 inhabitants.
HESSEN-CASSEL, 156 Q.M.; 434,499 inhabitants. (Cassel, 18,560; Hanau, 11,000.)
HESSEN-DARMSTADT, 104 Q.M.; 655,685 inhabitants. (Darmstadt, 9500; Pirmasens, 9000.)
HESSEN-HOMBURG, 2 Q.M.; 7000 inhabitants.
HOLSTEIN, 175 Q.M.; 320,000 inhabitants. (Altona, 20,000.)
WÜRTTEMBERG, 150 Q.M.; 608,667 inhabitants. (Stuttgart, 18,000.)

SACHSEN-WEIMAR und EISENACH, 36 Q.M.; 106,400 inhabitants. (Weimar, 7500.)

SACHSEN-GOTHA und ALTENBURG, 55 Q.M.; 165,000 inhabitants. (Gotha, 11,430.)

SACHSEN-COBURG-SAALFELD, 18 Q.M.; 56,953 inhabitants.

SACHSEN-MEININGEN, 16 Q.M.; 51,000 inhabitants.

SACHSEN-HILDBURGHAUSEN, 11 Q.M.; 31,800 inhabitants.

BRAUNSCHWEIG-WOLFENBÜTTEL, 94 Q.M.; 166,340 inhabitants. (Brunswick, 26,000.)

SCHWEDISCH- oder VORPOMMERN, 70 Q.M.; 104,748 inhabitants. (Stralsund, 11,000.)

BADEN, 64 Q.M.; 194,118 inhabitants. (Carlsruhe, 9000.)

ANHALT-DESSAU, 20 Q.M.; 37,700 inhabitants.

ANHALT-BERNBURG, 16 Q.M.; 30,000 inhabitants.

ANHALT-CÖTHEN, 16 Q.M.; 30,000 inhabitants.

OLDENBURG, 45 Q.M.; 95,000 inhabitants.

ARENBERG, 55½ Q.M.; 42,000 inhabitants.

2. NEW DYNASTIES.

Seventeen are mentioned, ranging from Nassau-Oranien-Diez, with 48 Q.M. and 97,000 inhabitants, to Lichtenstein, with 3 Q.M. and 6000 inhabitants. Total area of these principalities, about 200 Q.M.; population about 560,000.

D. IMPERIAL COUNTS (REICHSGRAFEN)

1. Wetterauisches Grafencollegium; thirty-one members, with about 125 Q.M. of land in all.
2. Schwäbisches Grafencollegium; thirteen members, with about 95 Q.M.
3. Fränkisches Grafencollegium; twenty-one members, with about 90 Q.M.
4. Westphälisches Grafencollegium; thirty members. (Total area unascertainable.)

E. REICHSSTIFTER

1. Twenty-seven Swabian Prelates.
2. Fifteen Prelates of the Rhine, with territory ranging from 6 Q.M. to ¾ Q.M.

F. FREE TOWNS (REICHSSTÄDTE)

1. RHEINISCHE BANK (fourteen towns). (*Population, in thousands, in brackets.*)

   Hamburg (150), Cologne, Frankfort-on-Main (50), Lübeck (42), Bremen (40), Aix-la-Chapelle (27), Mühlhausen (13), Nordhausen (10), Goslar (9), Wetzlar (8), Dortmund, Worms (6), Speyer (5), Friedberg (3).

2. SCHWÄBISCHE BANK (thirty-six towns). (*Population, in thousands, in brackets.*)

   Nürnberg (70 in republic, 30 in town), Ulm (37), Augsburg (36), Rothenburg (26), Ratisbon (Regensburg) (21), Schwäbisch-Hall (16), Rottweil, Schwäbisch-Gmünd (14), Esslingen, Memmingen (11), Heilbronn, Reutlingen (10), Biberach (9), Nördlingen (7), Kaufbeuren (6·8), Dinkelsbühl (6·5), Überlingen (6·3), Lindau, Weissenburg (6); and the following, in order of size, with less than 5000: Windsheim, Ravensburg, Schweinfurt, Kempten, Zell-am-Hammersbach, Wangen, Gengenbach, Offenburg, Giengen, Pfullendorf, Weil, Wimpfen, Leutkirchen, Bopfingen, Buchhorn, Isny, Buchau (1).

BIBLIOGRAPHY

A. CONTEMPORARY WRITERS

(NOTE: The imaginative works and letters of the classical writers have not been included in the bibliography.)

(Anon.) *Introduction to the knowledge of Germany*. London, 1789.

E. M. ARNDT, *Erinnerungen aus dem äusseren Leben*, 1st ed. 1840. (Reprint Reclam.)

Dr C. F. BAHRDT, *Geschichte seines Lebens*, 1st ed. Berlin, 1790–1. (Selection edited F. Hasselberg, Berlin, 1922.)

J. B. BASEDOW, *Elementarwerk*, 3 vols., Kupferstiche von Chodowiecki, 1774. (Reprint Leipzig, 1909.)

J. H. L. BERGIUS, *Policey- und Cameralmagazin*. Frankfort, 1767–74.

J. H. L. BERGIUS, *Neues Policey- und Cameralmagazin*. Leipzig, 1775–80.

ULRICH BRÄKER, *Der arme Mann in Tockenburg*, 1st ed. Zürich, 1789. (Reprint Reclam.)

A. F. BÜSCHING, *Beyträge zur Lebensgeschichte denkwürdiger Personen, insonderheit gelehrter Männer*. Halle, 1783–6.

A. F. BÜSCHING, *A new system of geography* (trans. by P. Murdoch). London, 1762.

D. Chodowieckis Künstlerfahrt nach Danzig 1773, ed. W. Franke. Leipzig and Berlin, n.d., Verlag Grethlein.

HENRY CRABB ROBINSON, *Diary, reminiscences and correspondence*, ed. T. Sadler, 3 vols. London, 1869.

Crabb Robinson in Germany, ed. E. Morley. Oxford, 1929.

Meister JOHANN DIETZ, *Lebensbeschreibung* (printed Munich, 1915, 'Schicksal und Abenteuer', XI).

C. W. v. DOHM, *Denkwürdigkeiten meiner Zeit*. Lemgo and Hamburg, 1819.

C. ESTE, *A journey in the year* 1793 *through Flanders, Brabant, and Germany to Switzerland*. London, 1795.

J. G. FICHTE, *Reden an die deutsche Nation*. 1808. (Reprint in 'Deutsche Bibliothek'.)

G. FORSTER, *Ansichten vom Niederrhein*. 1791–4. (Reprint Reclam.)

FRIEDRICH II, *Anti-Machiavel*. London and The Hague, 1740. (Reprint in 'Deutsche Bibliothek'.)

CHR. GARVE, *Versuche*, 5 Teile. Breslau, 1792.

CHR. GARVE, *Vermischte Aufsätze*, 2 vols. Breslau, 1796.

J. W. v. GOETHE, *Dichtung und Wahrheit*. 1811–33.

A. B. GRANVILLE, *St Petersburgh, a journal of travels to and from that capital*, 2 vols. London, 1828.

W. H. v. HOHBERG, *Georgica curiosa oder adeliches Landleben*, 2 vols. Nürnberg, 1687.

W. HOWITT, *The rural and domestic life of Germany*. London, 1842.

DAVID HUME, *Letters*, ed. J. Y. T. Greig. Vol. I. Oxford, 1932.

W. JACOB, F.R.S., *A view of the agriculture, manufactures, statistics, and state of society, of Germany, and parts of Holland and France*. London, 1820.

KAROLINE JAGEMANN, *Erinnerungen*, ed. E. v. Bamberg. Dresden, 1926.

J. H. JUNG(-STILLING), *Lebensgeschichte*. 1777. (Reprint in 'Deutsche Bibliothek'.)

J. KERNER, *Das Bilderbuch aus meiner Knabenzeit* (1849). (Reprint Vienna, 1921.)

J. G. KEYSLER, *Travels*, 2nd English ed. 4 vols. London, 1756–7.

A. v. KNIGGE, *Über den Umgang mit Menschen*. 1788. (3rd ed. 1790, reprinted in 'Deutsche Bibliothek'.)

A. v. KNIGGE, *Der Roman meines Lebens*, 2nd ed. Frankfort-on-Main, 1805.

K. H. v. LANG, *Aus der bösen alten Zeit*. 1842. (Reprint Stuttgart, 1910, 'Memoirenbibliothek'.)

F. C. LAUKHARD, *Leben und Schicksale, von ihm selbst beschrieben*, ed. V. Petersen. Stuttgart, n.d. (? 1908).

J. M. v. LOEN, *Der Adel*. Ulm, 1752.

J. M. v. LOEN, *Freie Gedanken vom Hof*, 3rd ed. Frankfort and Leipzig, 1768.

J. M. v. LOEN, *Der redliche Mann am Hofe*. Ulm, 1771.

K. v. LYNCKER, *Am Weimarischen Hofe unter Amalien und Karl August* (written *c.* 1840). Berlin, 1912.

J. C. v. MANNLICH, *Histoire de ma vie* (written 1813–18, selection printed under title *Rokoko und Revolution*, 3rd ed. Berlin, 1923).

J. MARSHALL, *Travels...in the years* 1768, 1769 *and* 1770, 3 vols. London, 1772.

Lady M. W. MONTAGU, *Letters*. London, 1763–7. (Reprint in Everyman's Library.)

(Dr JOHN MOORE), *A view of society and manners in France, Switzerland and Germany*, 2 vols. London, 1779.

K. P. Moritz, *Anton Reiser, ein autobiographischer Roman*, 4 Teile, 1785–90; 5. Teil, 1794.
J. Möser, *Patriotische Phantasien*. Berlin, 1774. (Partial reprint, Reclam.)
J. J. Moser, *Von der Teutschen Unterthanen Rechten und Pflichten* (*Neues deutsches Staatsrecht* 18). Frankfort and Leipzig, 1774.
J. Nettelbeck, *Lebensbeschreibung von ihm selbst aufgezeichnet*. 1821. (Reprint Munich, 1921.)
F. Nicolai, *Beschreibung einer Reise durch Deutschland und die Schweiz*, 12 vols. Berlin, 1783–97.
J. Owen, *Travels* (in 1791 and 1792), 2 vols. London, 1796.
C. L. Baron de Pöllnitz, *Mémoires*. Nouv. éd. corr. Liège, 1734.
(C. L. Baron de Pöllnitz), *La Saxe galante*. Amsterdam, 1734.
C. L. Baron de Pöllnitz, *Mémoires pour servir à l'histoire des quatre derniers souverains de la maison de Brandebourg*, 2 vols. Berlin, 1791.
Peter Prosch, *Leben und Ereignisse*. Munich, 1789. (Reprint Munich, 1919.)
(A. Rebmann), 'Rabiosus der Jüngere', *Wanderungen und Kreuzzüge durch...Deutschland*. Altona, 1795.
H. A. O. Reichard, *Guide des voyageurs en Europe*, 2 vols. Weimar, 1793. (Many new editions.)
H. A. O. Reichard, *Der Passagier auf der Reise in Deutschland*, 2nd ed. Weimar, 1803.
H. G. Riquetti, comte de Mirabeau, *De la Monarchie prussienne*, 4 vols. 4th ed. London, 1788.
(K. Risbeck), *Briefe eines reisenden Franzosen über Deutschland*, 2 vols. 2nd ed. Zürich, 1784.
Angelika Rosa, *Lebensschicksale einer deutschen Frau im 18. Jh. in eigenhändigen Briefen*. Magdeburg, 1908.
J. Russell, *A Tour in Germany in 1820–22*. Edinburgh, 1828.
J. C. Sachse, *Der deutsche Gil Blas*. Stuttgart, 1822.
A. Schmitthenner, *Das Tagebuch meines Urgrossvaters*. Freiburg, 1922.
Johanna Schopenhauer, *Jugendleben und Wanderbilder*. 1839.
Dr J. S. Semler, *Lebensbeschreibung*, 2 vols. Halle, 1781.
J. G. Seume, *Mein Leben*. 1813.
Mme de Staël, *De l'Allemagne*. (1st ed. Paris, 1810—destroyed. 2nd ed. 1814.)
F. Freiherr v. d. Trenck, *Merkwürdige Lebensgeschichte*. (Written 1786. Printed in Collection Spemann, Stuttgart, n.d.)

ERNESTINE VOSS, *Erinnerungen*. (Reprinted in Kürschners *D.N.L.* vol. 49.)

N. W. WRAXALL, *Memoirs of the Courts of Berlin, Dresden, Warsaw and Vienna in the years* 1777, 1778 *and* 1779, 2 vols. London, 1799.

E. A. W. ZIMMERMANN, *A political survey...of Europe*. London, 1787.

COLLECTIONS OF EXTRACTS

M. BEYER-FRÖHLICH, *Deutsche Selbstzeugnisse*, vols. VII (*Pietismus und Rationalismus*), Leipzig, 1933, and VIII (*Höhe und Krise der Aufklärung*), Leipzig, 1934.

E. BUCHNER, *Das Neueste von Gestern*, vols. II, III (1700–87). Munich, 1912.

E. BUCHNER, *Anno Dazumal*, 2 vols. Berlin, n.d. (1926).

J. BÜHLER, *Deutsche Vergangenheit*, 7 vols. Leipzig, 1923–9.

REICHMANN, SCHNEIDER, HOFSTAETTER, *Ein Jahrtausend deutscher Kultur*, 2nd ed. Leipzig, 1922–4.

B. LATER WRITERS

(i) GENERAL

The Cambridge Modern History, vol. VI. Cambridge, 1909.

Deutscher Kulturatlas, herausgegeben von G. Lüdtke und L. Mackensen. Berlin and Leipzig, 1931– .

Handwörterbuch der Staatswissenschaften, ed. J. Conrad, 3rd ed. Jena, 1909–11.

Propyläen-Weltgeschichte, 6. Band, 'Das Zeitalter des Absolutismus'. Berlin, 1931.

K. BIEDERMANN, *Deutschland im 18. Jahrhundert*. Leipzig, 1854–80.

MAX V. BOEHN, *Die Mode...im 18. Jahrhundert*, 2nd ed. Munich, 1919.

MAX V. BOEHN, *Deutschland im 18. Jahrhundert*, 2 vols. Berlin, 1921.

W. H. DAWSON, *The evolution of modern Germany*. London, 1911.

W. H. DAWSON, *The Germany of the 18th century* (in Harmsworth's Universal History). London, 1929.

W. FRÄNZEL, *Deutschland im Jahrhundert Friedrichs des Grossen*. Gotha, 1921.

G. FREYTAG, *Bilder aus der deutschen Vergangenheit*. Leipzig, 1859–62 (ill. edition Leipzig, n.d. *c.* 1925).

B. GEBHARDT, *Handbuch der deutschen Geschichte*, 2 vols. 7th ed. Stuttgart, 1930–1.

P. KAMPFMEYER, *Geschichte der modernen Gesellschaftsklassen in Deutschland*. Berlin, 1910.

J. KUTZEN-V. STEINECKE, *Das deutsche Land*, 5th ed. Breslau, 1908.

K. LAMPRECHT, *Deutsche Geschichte*. Berlin, 1891–1909 (esp. vols. VII and VIII, i, and for bibliography XII).

H. LICHTENBERGER, *L'Allemagne Moderne, son évolution*. Paris, 1916.

O. HENNE AM RHYN, *Kulturgeschichte des deutschen Volkes*, 2 vols. Berlin, 1886.

W. H. RIEHL, *Naturgeschichte des Volkes*. Stuttgart, 1853.

F. C. SCHLOSSER, *Geschichte des 18ten Jahrhunderts*, 5th ed. Berlin, 1879.

G. STEINHAUSEN, *Geschichte der deutschen Kultur*, 3rd ed. Leipzig, 1929.

G. STEINHAUSEN, *Kulturgeschichte der Deutschen in der Neuzeit*, 2nd ed. Leipzig, 1918.

G. STEINHAUSEN, *Kulturstudien*. Berlin, 1893.

(ii) 'KLEINSTAATEREI' (Part I, Chap. I)

C. T. ATKINSON, *A history of Germany*, 1715–1815. London, 1908.

J. BRYCE, *The Holy Roman Empire*. London, 1864. (Many later editions.)

G. P. GOOCH, *Germany and the French Revolution*. London, 1920.

J. HALLER, *Epochen der deutschen Geschichte*. Stuttgart and Berlin, 1922.

L. HÄUSSER, *Deutsche Geschichte*, I. Berlin, 1854 (and later).

J. A. R. MARRIOTT and C. G. ROBERTSON, *The Evolution of Prussia*. Oxford, 1915.

C. T. PERTHES, *Das deutsche Staatsleben vor der Revolution*. Hamburg and Gotha, 1845.

Sir A. W. WARD, *Germany*, 1815–1890, vol. I. Cambridge, 1916.

W. WENCK, *Deutschland vor hundert Jahren*, 2 vols. Leipzig, 1887–90.

(iii) BENEVOLENT DESPOTISM (Part I, Chap. II)

A. LUSCHIN V. EBENGREUTH, *Die Verfassung und Verwaltung der Germanen und des deutschen Reiches bis zum Jahre* 1806 (Kultur der Gegenwart, Teil II, Abt. II, I). Leipzig and Berlin, 1911.

F. Hartung, *Deutsche Verfassungsgeschichte vom 15. Jahrhundert bis zur Gegenwart*, 2nd ed. Leipzig and Berlin, 1922.
F. Hartung, *Das erste Jahrzehnt der Regierung Karl Augusts* (Jb. d. Goethe-Gesellschaft, ii). 1915.
F. Hartung, *Das Grossherzogtum Sachsen unter der Regierung Karl Augusts*. Weimar, 1923.
R. Koser, *Staat und Gesellschaft zur Höhezeit des Absolutismus* (Kultur der Gegenwart, Teil ii, Abt. v, 1). Berlin and Leipzig, 1908.
F. Kugler, *Geschichte Friedrichs des Grossen* (ill. by A. Menzel), new ed. Leipzig, 1860.
W. Oncken, *Das Zeitalter Friedrichs des Grossen* (Allgemeine Geschichte in Einzeldarstellungen, iii, 8). Berlin, 1880–2.
H. Prutz, *Preussische Geschichte*, 4 vols. Stuttgart, 1901.
L. v. Ranke, *Zwölf Bücher Preussischer Geschichte*, vol. v, 2nd ed. Leipzig, 1879.
G. Schmoller, *Umrisse und Untersuchungen*. Leipzig, 1898.

(iv) The old order of society (Part ii)

H. Brunner, *Grundzüge der Rechtsgeschichte*. Leipzig, 1901.
G. Dehio, *Geschichte der deutschen Kunst*, iii, 2nd ed. Berlin, 1931.
W. Fleming, *Die Oper* (Barockdrama, Band 5). Leipzig, 1933.
A. v. Gleichen-Russwurm, *Das galante Europa*. Stuttgart, 1921.
J. v. Jordan-Rozwadowski, *Die Bauern des 18. Jahrhunderts und ihre Herren* (Conrads Jahrbücher für Nationalökonomie und Statistik, 3. Folge, vol. xx, 1900).
P. Kühn, *Weimar*, 4th ed. Leipzig, 1925.
Chr. Rank, *Kulturgeschichte des deutschen Bauernhauses* (A.N.G. 121), 3rd ed. Leipzig and Berlin, 1921.
K. Spiess, *Die deutschen Volkstrachten* (A.N.G. 342). Leipzig, 1911.
E. Vehse, *Geschichte der deutschen Höfe*. Hamburg, 1851–60.

(v) Economic history—general

A. Beer, *Allgemeine Geschichte des Welthandels*. Vienna, 1860.
J. H. Clapham, *The economic development of France and Germany 1815–1914*. Cambridge, 1921.
W. Cunningham, *An essay on western civilisation in its economic aspects* (medieval and modern times). Cambridge, 1900.
J. Falke, *Geschichte des deutschen Handels*. 1860.
R. Kötzschke, *Grundzüge der deutschen Wirtschaftsgeschichte bis zum siebzehnten Jahrhundert*, 2nd ed. Leipzig and Berlin, 1923.

J. Kulischer, *Allgemeine Wirtschaftsgeschichte*, 2 vols. Munich and Berlin, 1928–9.

W. Langenbeck, *Geschichte des deutschen Handels seit dem Ausgange des Mittelalters* (A.N.G. 237), 2nd ed. Leipzig and Berlin, 1918.

E. Lipson, *The economic history of England*, 3 vols. London, 1915–31.

M. G. Schmidt, *Geschichte des Welthandels* (A.N.G. 118), 4th ed. Leipzig and Berlin, 1922.

G. Schmoller, *The mercantile system*. 1884 (translated Ashley).

H. Sieveking, *Grundzüge der neueren Wirtschaftsgeschichte*, 2nd ed. Leipzig and Berlin, 1915.

H. Sieveking, *Wirtschaftsgeschichte*, II (A.N.G. 577). Leipzig and Berlin, 1921.

W. Sombart, *Der moderne Kapitalismus*, 3rd ed. Munich and Leipzig, 1919.

W. Sombart, *Die deutsche Volkswirtschaft im 19. Jahrhundert*, 5th ed. Berlin, 1921.

W. Sombart, *Der Bourgeois*. Munich and Leipzig, 1913.

R. H. Tawney, *Religion and the Rise of Capitalism*. London, 1926.

G. Unwin, *Studies in Economic History*. London, 1927.

M. Weber, *Wirtschaftsgeschichte*, ed. Hellmann and Palyi. Munich and Leipzig, 1923.

(vi) The German towns (Part III, Chaps. I–III)

G. v. Below, *Das ältere deutsche Städtewesen und Bürgertum*. Bielefeld and Leipzig, 1898.

B. Heil, *Die deutschen Städte und Bürger im Mittelalter* (A.N.G. 43), 4th ed. Leipzig and Berlin, 1921.

G. L. Kriegk, *Deutsches Bürgertum im Mittelalter*. Frankfort, 1868–71.

W. Lotz, *Verkehrsentwicklung in Deutschland seit 1800 bis zur Gegenwart* (A.N.G. 15), 4th ed. Leipzig and Berlin, 1920.

E. Otto, *Das deutsche Handwerk* (A.N.G. 14), 5th ed. Leipzig and Berlin, 1920.

H. Preuss, *Die Entwicklung des deutschen Städtewesens*. Leipzig, 1906.

O. K. Roller, *Die Einwohnerschaft der Stadt Durlach im 18. Jahrhundert*. Karlsruhe, 1907.

P. Sander, *Geschichte des deutschen Städtewesens*. Bonn and Leipzig, 1922.

D. Schäfer, *Die deutsche Hanse*, 3rd ed. Bielefeld and Leipzig, 1925.

G. Schmoller, *Deutsches Städtewesen in älterer Zeit*. Bonn and Leipzig, 1922.

H. Voelker (ed.), *Die Stadt Goethes, Frankfurt-am-Main im 18. Jahrhundert*. Frankfort, 1932.

(vii) Middle-class life (Part III, Chap. IV)

J. W. Appell, *Werther und seine Zeit*, 4th ed. Oldenburg, 1896.

W. Kawerau, *Kulturbilder aus der Zeit der Aufklärung*. Halle, 1886–8.

G. L. Kriegk, *Deutsche Kulturbilder aus dem 18. Jahrhundert*. Frankfort, 1874.

A. Schultz, *Deutsches Leben im 14. und 15. Jahrhundert*. Leipzig, 1892.

A. Schultz, *Das häusliche Leben der europäischen Kulturvölker vom Mittelalter bis zur 2. Hälfte des 18. Jahrhunderts*. Munich, 1903.

(viii) The professional class (Part III, Chap. V)

'Monographien zur deutschen Kulturgeschichte', ed. G. Steinhausen:

E. Reicke, *Der Lehrer*, 1901.

P. Drews, *Der Geistliche*, 1905.

E. Reicke, *Der Gelehrte*, 1900.

H. Peters, *Arzt und Heilkunst*, 1900.

J. Pagel, *Geschichte der Medizin*. Berlin, 1898.

F. Paulsen, *Geschichte des gelehrten Unterrichts*, 2nd ed. 2 vols. Leipzig, 1896–7.

F. Paulsen, *Das deutsche Bildungswesen in seiner geschichtlichen Entwicklung* (A.N.G. 99–100). Leipzig and Berlin, 1920.

Th. Puschmann, *Geschichte des medizinischen Unterrichts*. Leipzig, 1889.

Th. Puschmann, M. Neuburger, J. Pagel, *Handbuch der Geschichte der Medizin*, 3 vols. Jena, 1905.

(ix) The profession of letters (Part IV, Chap. I)

Das Buchgewerbe und die Kultur (A.N.G. 182). Leipzig, 1907.

K. Buchner, *Beiträge zur Geschichte des deutschen Buchhandels*, 2 vols. Giessen, 1873–4.

K. Buchner, *Wieland und G. J. Göschen.* Stuttgart, 1874.
K. Buchner, *Wieland und die Weidmannsche Buchhandlung.* Berlin, 1871.
A. S. Collins, *Authorship in the Days of Johnson.* London, 1927.
A. S. Collins, *The Profession of Letters.* London, 1928.
H. Diez, *Das Zeitungswesen* (A.N.G. 328), 2nd ed. Leipzig and Berlin, 1919.
Joh. Goldfriedrich, *Geschichte des deutschen Buchhandels,* ii, iii. Leipzig, 1908–9.
Viscount Goschen, *Life and times of G. J. Goschen,* 2 vols. London, 1903.
C. Th. Perthes, *Friedrich Perthes' Leben.* 1848–55.
E. Vollert, *Die Weidmannsche Buchhandlung in Berlin,* 1680–1930. Berlin, 1930.

(x) The influence of political, economic and social factors on literature (Part iv, Chap. ii)

In addition to the Histories of German Literature (especially those of Hettner, Nadler, K. Francke) the following are of service:

K. Brombacher, *Der deutsche Bürger im Literaturspiegel von Lessing bis Sternheim.* Munich, 1920.
F. Brüggemann, *Der Kampf um die bürgerliche Welt- und Lebensanschauung in der deutschen Literatur des 18. Jahrhunderts* (Deutsche Vierteljahrsschrift für Literaturwissenschaft und Geistesgeschichte, 3). 1925.
F. Brüggemann, *Die bürgerliche Gemeinschaftskultur der vierziger Jahre* ('Deutsche Literatur', Reihe Aufklärung, vols. v and vi). Leipzig, 1933.
F. Brüggemann, *Lessings Bürgerdramen* (Jahrbuch des Freien Deutschen Hochstifts, 1926).
A. Eloesser, *Das bürgerliche Drama.* Berlin, 1898.
P. Ernst, *Der Zusammenbruch des deutschen Idealismus,* 3rd ed. Munich, 1931.
P. Ernst, *Der Weg zur Form,* 3rd ed. Munich, 1928.
A. Hirsch, *Bürgertum und Barock im deutschen Roman.* Frankfort, 1934.
A. Kleinberg, *Die deutsche Dichtung in ihren sozialen, zeit- und geistesgeschichtlichen Bedingungen.* Berlin, 1927.
H. A. Korff, *Geist der Goethezeit,* 2 vols. Leipzig, 1923–30.
A. Köster, *Die deutsche Literatur der Aufklärungszeit.* Heidelberg, 1925.

M. Martersteig, *Das deutsche Theater im 19. Jahrhundert*, 2nd ed. Leipzig, 1924.

G. Müller, *Höfische Kultur der Barockzeit* (in Naumann-Müller, Höfische Kultur). Halle, 1929.

J. Petersen, *Die Wesensbestimmung der deutschen Romantik*. Leipzig, 1926.

L. E. Schücking, *Die Soziologie der literarischen Geschmacksbildung*. Leipzig and Berlin, 1931.

Mme de Staël, *De la littérature considérée dans ses rapports avec les institutions sociales*. Paris, 1800.

Mme de Staël, *De l'Allemagne*. 1814.

Clara Stockmeyer, *Soziale Probleme im Drama des Sturmes und Dranges*. Frankfort-on-Main, 1922.

F. Strich, *Deutsche Klassik und Romantik*, 3rd ed. Munich, 1928.

F. Strich, *Dichtung und Zivilisation*. Munich, 1928.

H. v. Treitschke, *Deutsche Geschichte*, I and II. Leipzig, 1879–82.

O. Walzel, *Deutsche Dichtung von Gottsched bis zur Gegenwart*, vol. I (Handbuch der Literaturwissenschaft). Wildpark-Potsdam, 1927–9.

W. Wenck, *Deutschland vor hundert Jahren*, vol. I. Leipzig, 1887.

SUPPLEMENTARY BIBLIOGRAPHY, TO JUNE 1971

A. CONTEMPORARY WRITERS

General

Allgemeines Repertorium der Literatur für die Jahre 1785–1790, 3 vols. Jena, 1793–4.

Allgemeines Repertorium der Literatur für die Jahre 1791–1795, 3 vols. Weimar, 1799–1800.

Allgemeines Repertorium der Literatur für der Jahre 1796–1800, 2 vols. Weimar, 1807.

(Very full index to the contents of the *Allgemeine Literatur-Zeitung*, Jena, and other leading periodicals, with classified lists of works on travel, manners, local institutions, secret societies etc. See Paul Raabe, 'Zur Bibliographie der Goethezeit', *Euphorion*, XLVIII (1954), pp. 216–19.)

Individual writers

J. C. Brandes, *Meine Lebensgeschichte*. Neu herausgegeben von W. Francke. München, 1923.

Briefe eines ehrlichen Mannes bey einem wiederholten Aufenthalt in Weimar. Deutschland, 1800. Neu herausgegeben von Paul Stapf. Bern and München, 1962.

Briefe über Jena. Frankfurt am Main and Leipzig, 1793.

Charles Burney's Continental Travels 1770–72. Edited by C. H. Glover. London, 1927.

Karl Gerok, *Jugenderinnerungen*, 6th ed. Bielefeld and Leipzig, 1898.

G. A. G. Guibert, *Journal d'un voyage en Allemagne fait en* 1773. 2 vols. Paris, 1803.

B. F. Hermann, *Reisen durch Oesterreich, Steyermark, Kärnten, Krayn, Italien, Tyrol, Salzburg und Bayern im Jahre* 1780. *In Briefen*. 3 vols. Vienna, 1781–3.

Chr. W. Hufeland, *Selbstbiographie*. Herausgegeben von W. von Brunn. 2nd ed. Stuttgart, 1937.

K. F. v. Klöden, *Jugenderinnerungen*. Herausgegeben von Max Jähns. Leipzig, 1874.

F. Kohlrausch, *Erinnerungen aus meinem Leben*. Hannover, 1863.

T. Nugent, *The Grand Tour, or, a Journey through the Netherlands, Germany, Italy and France*, 2 vols. 2nd ed. London, 1756.

J. Pezzl, *Skizze von Wien unter der Regierung Josephs II.* Vienna, 1789.

Karoline Pichler, *Denkwürdigkeiten aus meinem Leben*, 4 vols. Vienna, 1844.

J. v. Sonnenfels, *Grundsätze der Polizey, Handlung und Finanzwirtschaft*, 3 vols. 5th ed. Vienna, 1787.

B. LATER WRITERS

(i) General

The New Cambridge Modern History, vols. VII–IX, 1957–65.

(In vol. VII, chapter 13, 'The Organisation and Rise of Prussia', and in vol. IX, chapter 13, 'German Constitutional and Social Development, 1795–1830', both by W. H. Bruford.)

Bruno Gebhardt, *Handbuch der deutschen Geschichte*, 8th ed., ed. H. Grundmann, vols. II and III, 1969.

Deutsche Philologie im Umriss, edited by W. Stammler. Berlin and Bielefeld, 1952–9.

W. H. Bruford, *Deutsche Kultur der Goethezeit* (Handbuch der Kulturgeschichte). Konstanz, 1965.

Emil Ermatinger, *Deutsche Kultur im Zeitalter der Aufklärung* (Handbuch der Kulturgeschichte), 2nd ed. Frankfurt am Main, 1969.

Arnold Hauser, *The Social History of Art*, translated in collaboration with the author by S. Godman. 2 vols. London, 1951.

C. A. Macartney, *The Habsburg Empire*, 1790–1918. London, 1969.

F. Schnabel, *Deutsche Geschichte im 19. Jahrhundert*, vol. I, 'Die Grundlagen', 4th ed. Freiburg im Breisgau, 1948.

(ii) 'Kleinstaaterei'

H. Eberhardt, *Goethes Umwelt. Forschungen zur gesellschaftlichen Struktur Thüringens.* Weimar, 1951.

Wolfram Fischer, *Das Fürstentum Hohenlohe im Zeitalter der Aufklärung.* Tübingen, 1958.

(iii) Benevolent despotism

R. Aris, *History of Political Thought in Germany*, 1789–1815. London, 1936.

MAX BELOFF, *The Age of Absolutism*, 1660–1815. London, 1954.
T. C. W. BLANNING, *Joseph II and Enlightened Despotism*. London, 1970.
U. CRAEMER, *Das Zeitalter des Absolutismus*. Leipzig, 1939.
W. L. DORN, 'The Prussian Bureaucracy in the Eighteenth Century', *Political Science Quarterly*, XLVI (1931), pp. 402–23, and XLVII (1932), pp. 75–94 and 259–73.
R. FLENLEY, *Modern German History*. London, 1953.
W. O. HENDERSON, *Studies in the Economic Policy of Frederick the Great*. London, 1963.
OTTO HINTZE, Introduction to vol. VI. i of 'Behördenorganisation und allgemeine Staatsverwaltung im 18. Jahrhundert' in *Acta Borussica*. Berlin, 1901.
OTTO HINTZE, *Die Hohenzollern und ihr Werk*. Berlin, 1916.
OTTO HINTZE, *Geist und Epochen der preussischen Geschichte*, ed. F. Hartung. Leipzig, 1943.
D. B. HORN, *Frederick the Great and the Rise of Prussia*. London, 1964.
P. KLASSEN, *Die Grundlagen des aufgeklärten Absolutismus*. Jena, 1929.
F. MEINECKE, *Weltbürgertum und Nationalstaat*. München and Berlin, 1929.
F. MEINECKE, *Die Idee der Staatsräson in der neueren Geschichte*, 3rd ed. München and Berlin, 1929.
F. MEINECKE, *Die Entstehung des Historismus*. München, 1936.
P. v. MITROFANOV, *Joseph II, seine politische und kulturelle Tätigkeit*. Vienna, 1910.
G. PARRY, 'Enlightened Despotism and its critics in eighteenth-century Germany', *Historical Journal*, VI (1963).
G. RITTER, *Frederick the Great, an historical profile*. London, 1968.
G. SCHMOLLER, Introduction to vol. I of 'Behördenorganisation und allgemeine Staatsverwaltung im 18. Jahrhundert' in *Acta Borussica*. Berlin, 1894.
H. v. SRBIK, *Deutsche Einheit*, vol. I. München, 1935.
F. VALJAVEC, *Der Josefinismus. Zur geistigen Entwicklung Österreichs im 18. Jahrhundert*. München, 1945.
F. WAGNER, *Europa im Zeitalter des Absolutismus*. München, 1948.
F. WAGNER, 'Friedrich Wilhelm I' in *Historische Zeitschrift*, 181 (1956).
R. WITTRAM, *Formen und Wandlungen des europäischen Absolutismus*. Giessen, 1948.

(iv) The old order of society

Max Braubach, *Kurköln. Gestalten und Ereignisse aus zwei Jahrhunderten rheinischer Geschichte.* Münster, 1949.

Otto Brunner, *Adeliges Landleben und europäischer Geist. Leben und Werk Helmhards von Hohberg* (1612–1688). Salzburg, 1949.

Dr Karl Siegmar, Baron v. Galéra, *Vom Reich zum Rheinbund. Weltgeschichte des 18. Jahrhunderts in einer kleinen Residenz.* Neustadt an der Aisch, 1961. (About the Riedesel family, in the series *Familiengeschichtliche Arbeiten*, vol. 29.)

A. Goodwin (editor), *The European Nobility in the eighteenth century.* London, 1953.

W. E. Mead, *The Grand Tour in the eighteenth century.* Boston and New York, 1914.

(v) Economic history—general

The Cambridge Economic History of Europe, vols. IV–VI (1967–).

H. Bechtel, *Wirtschaftsgeschichte Deutschlands*, vol. II (1500–1800). München, 1952. (The relevant period in great detail, with full bibliography.)

N. Hausherr, *Wirtschaftsgeschichte der Neuzeit vom Ende des 14. bis zum Ende des 18. Jahrhunderts*, 3rd ed. Weimar, 1958.

E. F. Heckscher, *Mercantilism.* Translated by M. Shapiro. Revised ed. 2 vols. London, 1955.

J. J. van Klaveren, 'Das Zeitalter des Merkantilismus', *Vierteljahrsschrift für Sozial- und Wirtschaftsgeschichte*, 50 (1963).

R. Krzymovski, *Geschichte der deutschen Landwirtschaft*, 3rd ed. Stuttgart, 1961.

F. Lütge, *Deutsche Sozial- und Wirtschaftsgeschichte, ein Überblick*, 3rd ed. Berlin, 1966.

F. Lütge (editor), *Die wirtschaftliche Situation in Deutschland und Österreich um die Wende vom 18. zum 19. Jahrhundert.* Stuttgart, 1964.

W. Treue, *Wirtschaftsgeschichte der Neuzeit.* Stuttgart, 1962 (Kröners Taschenausgabe).

(vi) The german towns

P. Dollinger, *The German Hansa*, translated by D. S. Ault and S. H. Steinberg. London, 1970.

Wolfram Fischer, *Handwerksrecht und Handwerkswirtschaft.* Berlin, 1955.

(vii) Middle-class life

Geneviève Bianquis, *La vie quotidienne en Allemagne à l'époque romantique* (1795–1830). Paris, 1958.

Hans Friederici, *Das deutsche bürgerliche Lustspiel der Frühaufklärung* (1736–50) *unter besonderer Berücksichtigung seiner Anschauungen von der Gesellschaft.* Halle, 1957.

Curt Gebauer, 'Studien zur Geschichte der bürgerlichen Sittenreform im 18. Jahrhundert', in *Archiv für Kulturgeschichte*, 15 (1923) and 20 (1930).

Curt Gebauer, *Geistige Strömungen und Sittlichkeit im 18. Jahrhundert. Beiträge zur deutschen Moralgeschichte.* Berlin, 1931.

A. W. Holzmann, *Family Relationships in the dramas of A. v. Kotzebue.* Princeton, 1935.

Hans Hubrig, *Die patriotischen Gesellschaften des 18. Jahrhunderts.* Weinheim, 1957.

P. Kluckhohn, *Die Auffassung der Liebe in der Literatur des 18. Jahrhunderts und der deutschen Romantik.* 2nd ed. Halle, 1931.

Wolfgang Martens, *Die Botschaft der Tugend. Die Aufklärung im Spiegel der deutschen Moralischen Wochenschriften.* Stuttgart, 1968.

G. M. Ott, *Das Bürgertum der geistlichen Residenzstadt Passau in der Zeit des Barock und der Aufklärung.* Passau, 1961.

Helmut Paustian, *Die Lyrik der Aufklärung als Ausdruck der seelischen Entwicklung von* 1710–1770. Berlin, 1933.

Wolfdietrich Rasch, *Freundschaftskult und Freundschaftsdichtung in dem deutschen Schrifttum des 18. Jahrhunderts vom Ausgang des Barock bis zu Klopstock.* Halle, 1936.

Wolfgang Schaer, *Die Gesellschaft im deutschen bürgerlichen Drama des 18. Jahrhunderts.* Bonn, 1963.

P. E. Schramm, *Hamburg, Deutschland und die Welt.* 2nd ed. Hamburg, 1952.

P. E. Schramm, *Neun Generationen. Dreihundert Jahre deutscher Kulturgeschichte im Lichte der Schicksale einer Hamburger Bürgerfamilie* (1648–1948). 2 vols. Göttingen, 1963–4.

Rudolf Stadelmann and Wolfram Fischer, *Die Bildungswelt des deutschen Handwerkers um 1800. Studien zur Soziologie des Kleinbürgers im Zeitalter Goethes.* Berlin, 1955.

Barbara Zaehle, *Knigges Umgang mit Menschen und seine Vorläufer, ein Beitrag zur Geschichte der Gesellschaftsethik.* Heidelberg, 1933.

(viii) THE PROFESSIONAL CLASS

WILHELM RÖSSLER, *Die Entstehung des modernen Erziehungswesens in Deutschland.* Stuttgart, 1961.

(ix) THE PROFESSION OF LETTERS

RUDOLF JENTSCH, *Der deutsch-lateinische Büchermarkt nach den Leipziger Ostermesskatalogen von* 1740, 1770 *und* 1800 *in seiner Gliederung und Wandlung.* Leipzig, 1912.

WALTER KRIEG, *Materialien zu einer Entwicklungsgeschichte der Bücherpreise und des Autorenhonorars vom* 15. *bis zum* 20. *Jahrhundert.* Wien–Bad Bocklet–Zürich, 1953.

WERNER MAHRHOLZ, *Deutsche Selbstbekenntnisse, ein Beitrag zur Geschichte der Selbstbiographie von der Mystik bis zum Pietismus.* Berlin, 1919.

H. SCHÖFFLER, *Protestantismus und Literatur.* Leipzig, 1922.

H. SCHÖFFLER, *Das literarische Zürich* 1700–1750. Frauenfeld and Leipzig, 1925.

G. WITKOWSKI, *Geschichte des literarischen Lebens in Leipzig.* Leipzig and Berlin, 1909.

(x) INFLUENCE ON LITERATURE

ILSE-MARIE BARTH, *Literarisches Weimar. Kultur, Literatur, Sozialstruktur im* 16.–20. *Jahrhundert.* Stuttgart, 1971.

W. H. BRUFORD, *Theatre, Drama and Audience in Goethe's Germany.* London, 1950.

W. H. BRUFORD, *Culture and Society in Classical Weimar,* 1775–1806. Cambridge, 1962.

H. BRUNSCHWIG, *La crise de l'état prussien à la fin du* 18*e siècle et la genèse de la mentalité romantique.* Paris, 1947.

E. DOSENHEIMER, *Das deutsche soziale Drama von Lessing bis Sternheim.* Konstanz, 1949.

E. CASSIRER, *The Philosophy of the Enlightenment.* Princeton, 1951.

NORMAN HAMPSON, *The Enlightenment.* Penguin Books, 1964.

PAUL HAZARD, *European Thought in the eighteenth century.* Penguin Books, 1965.

F. HERZ, *The Development of the German Public Mind,* vol. II, *The Age of Enlightenment.* London, 1962.

GERHART KAISER, *Pietismus und Patriotismus im literarischen Deutschland*. Wiesbaden, 1961.

LEONHARD KRIEGER, *The German Idea of Freedom. History of a political Tradition*. Boston, 1957.

F. J. SCHNEIDER, *Die Freimaurerei und ihr Einfluss auf die geistige Kultur in Deutschland am Ende des 18. Jahrhunderts*. Prag, 1909.

INDEX